I GOT BY

HARRY MARLIN

I GOT BY

The Best of Harry Marlin Volume 2

A Collection of Short Stories told in a way that only a man like
Harry Marlin could tell.

Trafford rev. 08/16/2012

 www.trafford.com

North America & international
toll-free: 1 888 232 4444 (USA & Canada)
phone: 250 383 6864 ♦ fax: 812 355 4082

Contents

ABOUT THE AUTHOR..1

ACKNOWLEDGMENTS 3

FOREWORD..5

A TRIP DOWN A LONG MEMORY LANE
THAT HASN'T ENDED 7

WITH KNOWLEDGE COMES ARTHRITIS 9

A COLD SPELL MAY BE COMING AND
FREEZE OUR TEXAS LANGUAGE 11

A HANDICAPPED PARKING PLACE IS
GETTING IS HARD TO FIND 13

A JUMP-START FROM A GOOD CAR
BATTERY MIGHT DO ME SOME GOOD.......................15

REACHING THE AGE OF ASSISTED LIVING 17

WE HAD NO MIRACLE DRUGS BUT
WE HAD COAL OIL 19

A LITTLE HISTORY OF THE WAY IT
WAS AND STILL IS 21

A LITTLE MIXED-UP HISTORY OF
HOW BLANKET GOT ITS NAME 23

A BOTTLE OF WINE, A LOAF OF
BREAD AND A PLUSH PLOW...25

A LITTLE STIMULUS FOR THE OIL
COMPANIES MIGHT BALANCE THINGS OUT............27

A LITTLE TOO MUCH SHAKING GOING ON 29

OUR NICE, QUIET LITTLE TOWN IS
GOING THE WAY OF THE HORNED TOAD 31

A SHORT INTERVIEW WITH A GOOD OLD BOY 33

A TIME TO HOLD AND A TIME TO
FOLD WHEN THE SHERIFF COMES CALLING 36

A TRIBUTE TO A GREAT AIRPLANE
AND THE MEN WHO FLEW IT 38

A WATCHED POT NEVER BOILS AND
OTHER USELESS INFORMATION 40

TAKE YOUR MEDS BUT DON'T
DRINK THE WATER 42

SOME WWII MEMORIES THAT
STICK IN MY MIND 44

GOOD BOOKS, GOOD WRITERS AND
ESCAPE FROM A COTTON PATCH 46

LIVING IN A HOUSE AT THE END OF A LANE 48

MISSING A BIG NIGHT OUT AND A
FREE GOURMET DINNER 50

SPEAK SOFTLY BUT CARRY A BIG STICK 52

AN ENCOUNTER WITH A MOUNTAIN
LION AND A WILD RIDE IN A PORSCHE 54

A RUSTY PLYMOUTH AND FIVE
GALLONS OF CHEAP GAS 56

HUNGRY AS A HOUND DOG AND
DOOMED BY SOUL FOOD 58

BACK IN THE THIRTIES, WE HAD NO
MODERN DISEASES AND LITTLE ELSE 60

WATCHING OUT FOR ALLIGATORS
AND MISSING OUT ON BACKPACKS 62

BARKING DOGS IN NEW JERSEY AND
STEALING IN TEXAS 64

BE CAREFUL WHAT YOU DO. BIG
BROTHER HAS A CELL PHONE 66

BEAUTY IS IN THE EYE OF THE
BEHOLDER WHO SOMETIMES HAS
POOR EYESIGHT 68

BIG FOOT, IVORY-BILLED
WOODPECKERS AND UFO'S 70

MY BISCUITS GO A LONG WAY BUT
NOT FAR ENOUGH... 73

BOMBING OUT ON USED CAR DEALS 75

BUILDING 700 MILES OF FENCE TO
STOP THE CHICKEN PLUCKERS.................................... 77

CELL PHONES, TREE THAT SPOUTS
WATER AND GREEN CHUNKS FROM THE SKY 80

CREDIT CARDS, MORTGAGES AND
COTTON PATCHES 83

COAL OIL, CHEAP WHISKEY, GRAVEL
AND BEDBUGS.. 85

COME FLY WITH ME, OR WITHOUT
ME, OR WHATEVER... 87

COME WITH ME INTO THE CASBAH
OR WHATEVER.. 89

COOKING CABBAGE ALL DAY AND
LIVING IN THE GOOD OLD DAYS.................................. 91

COOKING, DOORKNOBS, CHICKEN
SNAKES AND CHINESE AILMENT 94

ASK YOUR DOCTOR ABOUT THAT
SOAP IN MOTEL BATHROOMS....................................... 96

WE LAUGHED AS WE LIVED IN FAME
OR WENT DOWN IN FLAMES 98

CORN TORTILLAS, CORNBREAD,
ETHANOL AND GLOBAL WARMING 100

MY WASTED YOUTH AND A CORNCOB PIPE 102

A GOOD PLACE TO LIVE BUT YOU
WOULDN'T WANT TO VISIT THERE 104

CRIME DIDN'T PAY AND NOTHING
ELSE DID EITHER.. 106

PULLING THE TAB ON CULTURE IN TEXAS.............. 108

SOLVING MURDERS ON TV AND
DANCING WITH THE STARS 110

A CHICKEN-FRIED STEAK AND
SOMEBODY TO CALL ME DARLIN' 112

OUR JAILS WERE EMPTY AND CRIME
WAS AGAINST THE LAW 114

SELLING THE SAME OLD BALONEY
BUT A NEW WINE IS ON THE MARKET 116

THE DUCHESS OF YORK AND
SOUTHERN COOKING 118

ON THE ROAD AGAIN LOOKING FOR
A GOOD MOTEL.. 120

DON'T PLAY THAT SONG AGAIN,
SAM—I CAN'T STAND IT 122

ERUPTING VOLCANOES ARE BEST
SEEN FROM A DISTANCE 124

ESCAPING TORNADOES, HIGH
WINDS, HAIL AND TV WEATHERMEN....................... 126

BEER BOTTLES, CHICKEN WIRE AND
40 YEARS OF COUNTRY MUSIC 128

FIGHTING A WAR FROM THE
BOTTOM OF A BOMBER.. 130

FISHING FOR MEMORIES AND
CRAWFISH IN COGGIN PARK...132

I MIGHT HAVE FLOWN ON UNSAFE
PLANES IN WWII 134

A FEW MEMORIES OF FT. SAM
HOUSTON WHEN THEY PAID THEIR
ELECTRIC BILL 136

GOOD LUCK, BAD LUCK, DUMB LUCK
OR NO LUCK AT ALL ON FRIDAY THE 13TH 139

FRIENDLY FOLKS AND BUTCHERING HOGS 142

GETTING A CLOSE-UP LOOK AT OUR PAST 144

BOXCARS: CORNCOBS AND GETTING
AN EDUCATION THE HARD WAY.................................146

GOING SIDEWAYS AND LEARING
ABOUT WINE AND OTHER STUFF..............................148

GOOD DOGS, BEER JOINTS AND
COUNTRY MUSIC 151

HAPPY TRAILS TO US AND YOU AND
THEM—WHEREVER THEY ARE 153

HEAD 'EM UP AND MOVE 'EM OUT,
BUT DON'T COME HERE 155

HEMINGWAY NEVER PICKED
COTTON OR DANCED IN A HONKEY-TONK 158

GENEALOGY OR MYTH 160

HOG KILLING DAY AND GETTING A
GOOD SCALD ON LIFE 163

THE HOME BREW THAT
NEVER FOUND A HOME 165

ASHES TO HOMINY AND LYE TO SOAP......................167

HOT TAMALES, CORN SHUCKS AND
NOISY MATTRESSES 169

BE IT EVER SO HUMBLE, HOME IS
WHERE THE HOUSE IS 171

HUNTING FOR THE JUMPING OFF PLACE 173

THE ILL WINDS OF TEXAS MAY BLOW
US NO GOOD 175

TRAIN ROBBERS, BANK ROBBERS AND HERMITS... 178

ACROSS THE RIVER AND INTO THE FENCE 180

I MIGHT BUY IT IF I KNEW WHAT
THEY WERE SELLING 182

I MISSED BEING NAMED HARRY
POTTER BUT NOT MUCH ELSE 184

I NEVER WROTE A BEST SELLER OR
LEARNED TO JUGGLE CATS 186

WATCH OUT FOR THE SIDE-EFFECTS
OF SIDE-EFFECTS 188

MOST ACCIDENTS HAPPEN AT HOME
BUT SOME DON'T 191

ICED-TEA ON SUNDAY WHERE THE
WHEELS STAY ON YOUR BUGGY 193

IF I'M CALLED BACK IN SERVICE, I
HAVE A NEW SET OF RULES 195

IN TOUGH SITUATIONS, ALWAYS TRY
TO SAVE YOUR BRASS 197

OLD MEMORIES, OLD INDIAN
FIGHTERS AND DOUBLE-DIP
ICE CREAM CONES 199

IT IS BETTER TO PROTEST IN AN
ELECTION BOOTH THAN A DITCH AT
CRAWFORD 202

IT COULD BE DANGEROUS TO
BELIEVE EVERYTHING PEOPLE TELL YOU 205

IT'S FINE TO FILL GRANDPA'S SHOES
BUT DON'T WEAR HIS PANTS.....................................207

WHEN YOU GET OLD, NOTHING
WORKS AND YOUR SHOES WON'T FIT 209

FROM OKLAHOMA DUST TO
CALIFORNIA WINE 211

THIEVES, METH LABS AND A MISSING HOUSE.......213

TRYING TO KEEP UP WITH A WORLD
THAT MOVES TOO FAST 216

KICKING THE SANDS OF TIME....................................218

ARMING BEARS, PLAYING DIXIE AND
BUTCHERING SONGS 220

LAUGHING OUR WAY THROUGH
THE GREAT DEPRESSION 222

NEVER RUN WITH THE SCISSORS IF
YOU CAN'T RUN..224

LEARNING ABOUT GIRLS AND THE
FICKLE FINGER OF FATE..226

LEARNING NEW WORDS AND
GETTING SCAMMED AT ANY AGE.............................228

ROMANS, COUNTRYMEN, ROCK
CONCERTS AND LEFT-OVER RABBIT 230

HANGING AROUND A FILLING
STATION MIGHT CAUSE A LIGHT STROKE 232

THEY ATE Béchamel SAUCE AND
THOUGHT IT WAS GRAVY 235

LOOKING BACK TO THE PAST AND
PONDERING THE FUTURE..237

THE GOOD OLD DAYS ARE GONE BUT
HAVE A LOT TO BE THANKFUL FOR 239

SEEKING A ROAD LESS TRAVELED...............................242

DON'T WORRY ABOUT OLD AGE
UNLESS IT MOVES IN WITH YOU 244

A LITTLE TOO MUCH EXPOSURE AND
TOO LITTLE DISCIPLINE 246

LOOSE SKIN, SHATTERED
WINDSHIELDS AND EXTREME MAKEOVERS 248

LUBBOCK, TEXAS THROUGH MY WINDSHIELD 250

STRANGE HAPPENINGS IN A STRANGE WORLD 252

LYING MIGHT CAUSE A HOLE IN YOUR BOOT 254

TAKE A LEFT TURN TO THE ALAMO MOTEL 256

THE NIGHT THE SOLDIER AND
SAILORS MEMORIAL HALL BURNED 258

THE GOOD AND THE BAD OF LIVING
IN THE FIFTIES 261

HOOKED ON CABLE WITH THE WRONG NAME 263

A FEW MEDALS, A FEW MEMORIES
AND A LOT OF BRAVE MEN 265

NEURONS, MORONS, SCIENTISTS
AND SHAMPOOING RATS 267

NEVER CARRY A BLUNT OBJECT INTO
A HOSPITAL 269

NEVER KICK A DRY COW PATTIE
ON A HOT DAY 271

DON'T WEAR A CHICKEN SUIT TO
ROB A GROCERY AFTER MIDNIGHT 273

NO APPOINTMENT NEEDED TO GET
YOUR CHRYSLER THUMPED 275

NO SUVS OR BEER AVAILABLE BUT WE
TRIED IT ALL ANYHOW 277

NO BRUSH CUTTING, BICYCLE
RIDING OR PROTESTING AT MY PLACE 279

AWARD WINNING MOVIES, GOOD
BOOKS AND HOW I LEARNED TO READ...................281

WHEN THE SUN GOES DOWN, IT
GETS DARK IN MARFA.......................................283

NOTHING IN A BIND BUT US.......................................286

OBSERVATIONS WHILE WAITING TO
SEE THE DOCTOR...289

WATCHING CHEF EMERIL ON TV AND
TRYING TO LEARN TO COOK.......................................291

OLD ACTORS, OLD BUILDINGS AND
OLD MEMORIES...293

OLD BILL BORROWED EVERYTHING
BUT TIME, WHAT HE NEEDED MOST.......................295

OLD CEDAR CHOPPERS AND
HEAVENLY BISCUITS.......................................297

OLD FIDDLERS, OLD DRUMMERS
AND THE DECLINE OF MUSIC.......................................299

OLD GALS, JOHNSON GRASS AND
PROWLING AROUND WITH GEORGE.......................301

ONE DAY IN THE LIFE OF A BALL
TURRET GUNNER...303

BUTTERFLIES AND BUTTERCUPS
AND PEOPLE WERE ALL FREE.......................................305

PHASE OUT THE LIGHTS, THE PARTY'S OVER.........307

PINTO BEANS MAY HAVE WON THE WEST...............309

POLITICS, RELIGION AND THE LAST
PARKING SPOT AT WAL-MART.......................................311

TEXAS WRITER PUTS TOO MUCH
SALT IN THE GRAVY.......................................313

GETTING BY WITHOUT SMOKING
IN AN IMPERFECT WORLD.......................................315

RAW OYSTERS, PARKING METERS AND
TECHNOLOGY WE LOST 317

THE LORD GAVE US THE LARD AND
GOD GAVE US A LOOPHOLE 319

ONE MORE RIVER TO CROSS MAY BE
ONE TOO MANY 321

ROBBING BANKS IN A '34 FORD AND
BOILING EGGS IN A SACK 323

LIGHT BREAD ROLLS AND ROSEBUD SALVE 325

ROYAL ALLEGATIONS IN THE BRITISH EMPIRE 327

RUNNING BOARDS, HUDSON
TERRAPLANES AND DRIVING MRS. BROWN 329

SAUCERED AND BLOWED AT
TWO-BITS A POUND 331

BRIGHT AND EARLY COFFEE 333

SAVE YOUR KNEES AND HIPS FOR
WANDERING IN THE DESERT 335

CONFUSED ABOUT TAXES AND A LOT
OF OTHER STUFF 337

SITTING ON A BENCH SOMEWHERE
WAITING FOR EVERYBODY ELSE 339

FEELING GOOD ABOUT A NEW
PORCH AND THE KIDS WHO BUILT IT 341

SLEEP TIGHT BUT DON'T LET THE
BEDBUGS BITE—THEY'RE BACK 343

SMOKE IF YOU'VE GOTTEM 345

ALL IS WELL THAT ENDS WELL 347

SOME SIDE EFFECTS OF GETTING OLD 349

COUNTRY CORRESPONDENTS AND
BIG CITY COLUMNISTS 351

SOMEWHERE IN THE WEST, WHERE
THE HAWKS BUILD NESTS.................................353

SPRING IS ON THE WAY
AND THE LIVING IS EASY...............................356

STORMS NEVER LAST, THEY SAY BUT I
HOPE WE DO 358

SUN-DRIED POSSUM, BLACK
DRAUGHT AND BABY PERCY 360

TAKE A CRUISE TO NOWHERE OR
CATCH A RIDE ON A TEST TRACK...............362

TAKE MY ADVICE GRANNY—STAY IN OAK CLIFF ...364

TALKING MULES AND BORROWING
WHAT I CAN TO WRITE A COLUMN 366

TEXAS IS FAMOUS FOR MANY THINGS
BUT WE MISSED OUT ON THIS 368

THE BIG BUGGY WRECK OF 1930 370

THE BIG DANCE OF 1944 AND
TAINTED TURKEY FOR EVEYBODY 372

THE CAR DAD NEVER BOUGHT
BECAUSE OF A GUITAR PLAYING WOMAN 374

WHEN THE RABBITS WERE DRIVEN
AND THE COWS WERE SHOT 376

THE GOOD OLD DAYS ARE GONE
FOR GOOD, OR WORSE...................................378

THE GOOD TIMES, THE BAD TIMES
AND THE MEMORIES OF BOTH 381

WE HAVE MET THE GREATEST
GENERATION AND IT IS US............................383

THE KEY TO SUCCESS IS GETTING
A GOOD START..385

THE LACK OF ONIONS COULD CAUSE
A RECESSION 387

THE LITTLE BROWN MULE
THAT WENT ASTRAY...389

THE NIGHT ELVIS LOST HIS COAT...............................391

THE ONIONS ARE PLANTED AND THE
CHIPS ARE DOWN...393

THE REVOLTING DEVELOPERS MAY
GET US ALL YET..395

THE RICH HAD ICE IN THE SUMMER
AND THE POOR HAD IT IN THE WINTER 397

THE SEVEN DEADLY SINS THAT
DOESN'T INCLUDE IRON SKILLETS............................399

THE UFOS ARE BACK BUT MAYBE
THEY NEVER LEFT...401

POKE SALET GREENS, SCRAMBLED
EGGS AND ROSE BUSHES..403

DON'T GET UP A LOAD UNTIL YOU
READ MY COLUMN 406

THINGS THAT GO BOOM, WHISTLE
AND BAWL IN THE NIGHT 408

TIME MARCHES ON AND SOMETIMES, IT JOGS 410

TO CATCH AN IVORY-BILLED
WOODPECKER, TAKE A COAL OIL
LANTERN AND A TOW SACK...412

MY WISH IS TO GATHER AGAIN FOR
SOME ORGANIC FOOD AND A POT OF STEW 414

TOMATO PLANTS, SNOWSTORMS
AND BOMBERS 416

TOO SLOW ON THE DRAW TO BE A
GUNSLINGER AND TOO HONEST TO
RUSTLE COWS 418

TRAFFIC CONTROL, SELF-CONTROL
AND THE WORST DRIVERS ON EARTH 420

TRAILER PARKS, USED CARS AND THE
STUDY OF BUGS 422

WHEN OLD PETE PLAYED THE TRUMPET 424

TWELVE CENT GAS, NICKEL BREAD
AND OUTRAGED LAWMAKERS 426

WAITING FOR A TRAIN OR A
SALESMAN TO LIVEN UP OUR LIVES 428

SOME MEMORIES OF WALKING
DOWN DIRT ROADS 431

I WOULD HAVE WASHED MY HANDS
IN THE BAYOU TECHE 433

STICKING AROUND TO WATCH THE BUZZARDS ... 435

ROADRUNNERS, VARMINTS AND A
JUDGE WITH A HEART 438

WATERMELONS, SWEET POTATOES,
AND FREEDOM 440

WE HAD MOSTLY NOTHING WHEN I
WAS A KID, BUT WE GOT 100% OF IT 442

WEAVING A WEB WE CAN'T GET OUT OF 444

IT TAKES A LOT OF SPACE TO BE A
GENUINE TEXAN 446

WHEN MODEL T. FORDS BOUNCED
AT FIVE DOLLARS A DAY 448

WHEN THE LAW WORE A COLT .45
AND THE CRIMINALS HAD NO RIGHTS 450

WHO KNOWS? CHICKEN LITTLE MAY
HAVE BEEN RIGHT 454

GREASING THE WINDMILL AND
USING UP THE WIND..456

WHEN THE COTTON BLOOMS,
WORRY ABOUT THE PEACHES 459

WRITING A COLUMN AND MILKING
COWS ON THE OVERPASS...461

SEPARATED RIBS AND WRITING ONE
SENTENCE PARAGRAPHS...463

YOU AND ME AND US AND THEM
AND BOBBY MCGEE..465

THERE ARE 700 NEW LAWS ON THE
BOOKS NOW, SO WATCH YOUR STEP 467

HARRY MARLIN DISCONTINUES
COLUMN—AUG 5th, 2008...469

HARRY DECIDES TO HANG'EM UP—
AUG 5th, 2008..471

THE END OF AN AMAZING JOURNEY 474

FAREWELL HARRY: 'PRAIRIE
PHILOSOPHER,' CHARACTER, PATRIOT 478

MARLIN LAID TO REST IN THE
COUNTRYSIDE HE LOVED 481

'FRIEND' GIVES LITTLE GIFTS OF
TIME AND PLACE..484

ABOUT THE AUTHOR

Harry Marlin met everything including life head on. He spent his childhood in tiny depression-ridden Blanket, Texas, and matured during 50 combat missions over Germany. His thinking and personality were forever colored by both experiences. Opinionated, blunt and uncompromisingly candid, he was talented beyond belief. He was a Steel guitar musician, photographer, Police Officer, Columnist and Book Author. Harry could be humorous, hauntingly profound and compassionate, all in the one paragraph. He was one of a kind and we can all be thankful for that.

Referenced as the "Will Rogers of Central Texas", Harry Marlin wrote a weekly column for the Brownwood Bulletin over a period of 11 years. This book is a compilation of his best stories which take a humorous look back at growing up and facing life's challenges through every generation.

ACKNOWLEDGMENTS

Many thanks to the nice folks at the Brownwood Bulletin for printing my columns since 1997.

To Laura and Jimmy, my two oldest offspring who laugh at my columns and to Ken, my youngest who happens to be a computer engineer who built my computers and cures them when they get sick.

To my faithful readers who read my columns and buy my books while overlooking my frequent, outright murder of the English language. As my friend Charles Stewart said, I try to "Put the fodder where the calf can get it."

To Bernell and Carla who always help me when I need help as I often do.

"With age comes knowledge" somebody once said. If I'm allowed to stick around a little longer, I may find out what in hell I'm doing.

Anyway, I'm still wondering whatever happened to Randolph Scott.

To all the good old boys and the good old girls I met along the way, and to the good people of Blanket, Texas, who during my formative years during the Depression, taught me honesty and integrity, and to my parents, Jesse and Myrtle Marlin who taught me love and compassion and that no mountain was too high to climb, or no river too deep to cross.

To my teachers in the Blanket School System, who did the best they could with what they had.

Harry Marlin

To the Good Lord, who lacking enough talent to go around, gave me what he could.

To the staff at the Brownwood Bulletin who printed my columns and to the late Shelton Prince who hired me. To columnist Mary Ficklen, my most severe critic who helped me over the humps.

To the great Texas writers who influenced me to take up writing years before I started. Writers Larry L. King, formerly of Putnam and Scranton, Texas, and now of Washington D.C., Bud Shrake of Austin, Texas, John Graves of Glenrose, Texas, Elmer Kelton of San Angelo, Texas, and Larry McMurtry of Archer City, Texas.

My thanks to Charles Chupp of the Messenger magazine at DeLeon, Texas, and Bud Lindsey of The Old Sorehead Gazette at Stanton, Texas, both of whom printed my stuff when probably nobody else would. To Dr, Charles A. Stewart of Taos, New Mexico, who helped me keep the faith.

To the Good Lord, who lacking enough talent to go around, gave me what he could.

Harry Marlin—2004

FOREWORD

This book, volume 2 in the series, consists of selected columns published by the Brownwood Bulletin between 2003 and 2008, and maybe some more stuff. Harry wrote the following in one of his earlier books and we wanted to include it here just as he wrote it:

I may have written some of these stories before which could be, if repeated over twice in one day, a sign of something called Senile Dementia. If you get it, don't worry. It has its good points. You are able to watch reruns on TV, read the same books over and over and hide your own Easter eggs. Auto mechanics call it "transmission trouble" or "slipping clutch."

This is my last book even though it is hard to find a quitting place; I have a good reason to quit. It seems that due to circumstances beyond my control, I suddenly got old. Worse still, I may get older, or I may not.

I really think I should stop now and spend more time with my dog. She likes me.

Besides that, not being John Grisham, I have to sell the things to pay the printer. I really appreciate the nice folks who have bought my other books in the past and I hope you enjoyed them as much as I did writing them. I had several requests to assemble a book of my columns. I can think of at least two.

Anyway, don't worry about me. As I wrote in one of my other books, I plan on being the last to leave so I can eat all of those good steaks and drink all that good stuff left behind by those who left.

I think I can handle that.

Harry Marlin

A TRIP DOWN A LONG MEMORY LANE THAT HASN'T ENDED

One of my readers who resides up near the Red River in Montague County recently wrote by e-mail, "Your columns take me down memory lane." I'm sure she knows just how long that lane is. It was sometimes a joyous lane and sometimes a sad lane. I remember both.

I remember the difficulty in cranking a Model T Ford on a cold morning when it became necessary to jack up a rear wheel to get enough momentum to turn the engine fast enough to start.

Often, when the thing finally started and the jack was let down, it would pin whoever was cranking to the nearest building. The Ford had no "Park" and its planetary transmission had no neutral on cold mornings. All anybody could do about it was to holler "Whoa." Unfortunately, Henry's machine didn't understand horse language or any other kind, including profane. Profanity was used a lot on Model T's, with little or no results.

My memory lane even goes further back than that when on Saturday, the whole family piled into a wagon for the usual trip to Blanket. Back then, nobody ever went to town and bought what they needed and went home. They stayed until the sun went down. It was a social event where gossip was exchanged and crops discussed.

Sometimes when a little money was left after buying groceries, we were treated with big hunks of cheese and baloney which we ate on the way home. The grocer would usually throw in a big onion free. To us, it was pure gourmet stuff and a temporary respite from our usual supper of warmed over beans.

The word "lane" in those days meant a small road leading from the county road to wherever we happened to be living at the time. To look down that lane and see somebody coming was a welcome event in our lives. We had little company.

Most of the time, the visitor turned out to be the Raleigh Man, selling his wares or a magazine salesman selling the "Progressive Farmer." We always read it in hopes that we might sometime become progressive enough to get away from that farm. The best part of the deal was that the salesman would take a couple of our non-laying hens for a year's subscription. He didn't seem to be progressing much either.

I still remember a lot of sad times on my memory lane that I can't forget. One that sticks in my mind was when I watched a family pass by the road in their wagon having just buried their 12 year old daughter in the Blanket cemetery and were going home to a lonely house where at the supper table that night would be one empty chair.

There were good times on that memory lane too and we were poor but free from a lot of things we have today. Crime was almost nonexistent and we were a people united. I saw no activists beating drums and raising hell about one thing or another.

We attended Chapel in school every Monday morning and it started and ended with a prayer. Nobody complained. Then, war came and the whole country responded. Nobody ran off to Canada. We were fighting what seemed to me like half the world but we won.

My memory lane is long but it hasn't ended yet. When it does, to paraphrase Martha Stewart, I think I can truthfully say, "It was a good thing."

WITH KNOWLEDGE COMES ARTHRITIS

There are a couple of things a man is sure to acquire as he grows older, a little knowledge and a lot of arthritis. The knowledge is sure to come in handy at one time or another. If a fellow knocks on your door early some morning offering to sell you the Brooklyn Bridge, it's a wise move to call City Hall in New York and find out the latest quote. On the other hand, if he's selling a cure for arthritis, buy it.

Even old cats accumulate knowledge. They won't jump on a hot stove but once, and from then on, they won't jump on a cold one either. We should be so smart. I have no idea who made that statement about the cats. If I did, I'd sure give proper credit. For years, I thought plagiarism was a disease caused by not eating enough fruits and vegetables. Then, along with the arthritis came knowledge and I learned better.

Ben Franklin made a lot of profound statements along those lines, so maybe he did. He gained a lot of knowledge too, by flying kites during thunderstorms, mostly to refrain from doing it. He bought kites by saving the pennies he earned, though it was his ambition to buy the Brooklyn Bridge. Unfortunately, it hadn't yet been built.

I knew a fellow who claimed he knew Fred Gipson personally. Whether he did or not, I don't know. Fred, an old Mason, Texas boy, wrote the classic, "Old Yeller." I had a lot of respect for Fred's writing. I had never met Fred, and probably never would, but I was interested.

"What sort of fellow is Fred?" I asked.

"Oh," he said, "just a damned old drunk."

I was somewhat shocked by his reply. How could a "damned old drunk" write words that carried us to places we had a deep feeling for and make us feel the joy and the pain of his characters as he did?

I was aware that the man who had this opinion of Fred Gipson didn't drink, and seemed to have no use for anybody who did, but talent is to be respected, whether the man who has it drinks or not, or how much, or when.

Were Faulkner, Hemingway and Steinbeck, to name a few, all "damned old drunks? All had a fondness for tipping a bottle now and then, some more often than others, but like an expression my mama used, none, as far as I know "got down in the yard."

They were the pioneers of our modern writing, and what they gave us, today's writers are still striving to duplicate, and can't. Maybe a good shot of Bourbon could help, or if that doesn't work, a good shot of living, something they had a vast knowledge of.

A COLD SPELL MAY BE COMING AND FREEZE OUR TEXAS LANGUAGE

Folks in Texas have always built "fars," had flats on our "tars," ate dinner around noon and supper before dark. For years, we have been "fixin'" to do something whether we ever did it or not. We all know where "yonder" is, having been going there for years and we always went to a cellar, when everybody had one, to escape "cyclones."

I hear that the more affluent folks keep wine in a cellar with no thought of a "cyclone" hitting it. I wonder if they keep a coal oil lantern down there too.

We never had "tornados" in Texas until somebody brought in trailer houses, sometimes called "Mobile Homes" even though they are not mobile until hit by a tornado.

We all bundle up when we get hit by a "blue norther" which has nothing to do with blue Yankees. They are all are sent to us by the folks somewhere north of Amarillo and cause us to have what is known as a "cold spell."

We still buy a loaf of "light bread" in the grocery and "iced tea" still comes in boxes. Even though we may attend Harvard or Yale, nuclear still comes out "nuclar." We even go to the "liberry" to check out a book. We know that a "fur piece" is a good ways down the road.

We went to school in a "schoolhouse" but didn't learn much. To us, cold beer is one word. We still keep our food in the "icebox" and the beer in a "cooler", usually kept in the back of our pickups. A truck is one of those 18 wheelers that drive in the left lane of our highways and a "pickup" is what we drive to work with our dog watching the cooler.

We are all familiar with Moon Pies and peanut patties and we learned long ago not to kick a dry cow pattie on a hot day. We know that a "stern wheel" is what we hold our pickups between the bar ditches with.

We still go to the "picture show" instead of the movies and some of us still think that John Wayne was at the Alamo and a "bar stool" was what Davy Crockett stepped in.

We accuse people who are "not from around here" and television of bastardizing our language. They say it was bastardized before they got here. They may be right but I have no trouble understanding it.

The actors on TV speak a different language than ours. My lady-friend tells me almost on a daily basis, "Harry," "You need a hearing aid." I deny it emphatically. I can hear every word they say. I just don't know what they're saying. Kids, these days, are obviously speaking Farsi. Are they teaching that in school now?

The English language, they say, is one of the hardest to learn. Too many of our words mean the same thing. We have simplified that problem in Texas but nobody will accept it. We say it like it ought to be said but we may be losing the battle of our unique way of saying things.

I hate to see that happen in my lifetime, or any other time. Where are we going to buy a new "icebox" when our old one quits, or a loaf of "light bread" or a "box of iced tea", or a new set of "tars."?

I think we ought to build a "far" under somebody and leave the way we talk alone.

A HANDICAPPED PARKING PLACE IS GETTING IS HARD TO FIND

I have decided that the best way for any store or place of business to increase their trade is to install handicapped parking in front of the place. It is rare that I ever see an unoccupied handicapped parking spot. It is a known fact that some folks will drive 25 miles on a cold day to park in a handicapped parking place.

Some are handicapped and some are not. The ones who aren't are not in the least deterred by a threat of a $250 fine. Obviously, they are financially well off, or optically impaired. These are the same people who take 106 items through the 15 item checkout line at the supermarket.

Back in the summer after a session at the VA clinic in Temple, I saw a sweet young thing with a pair of shorts on that struck her somewhere around Waco park in the only handicapped spot left in front of Appleby's where I meant to park.

My handicaps got better from watching her walk from her car and I decided a little walk wouldn't hurt me. If there was anything wrong with that gal, I couldn't see it and most of her was visible. Maybe her eyesight was bad and she couldn't read the sign.

I am board-certified handicapped myself and have one of those placards which I hang the mirror. Part of my disability is mental and is known as "Columnist's Syndrome." The symptoms can sometime be severe and mostly consist of lying awake at night trying to think of something to write.

I have other handicaps too and there are a lot of things I can't do. I can't rob a convenience store as the police would arrive before I could get out of the store. I would probably trip on my cane and shoot myself in the foot. Anyway, any handicapped parking they might have would be occupied by a girl in shorts and I'd get distracted and forget the whole idea.

Burglary is out too. I'd trip on tricycles, bicycles, roller skates and beer cans causing a lot of racket. Anyway, I don't see too well at night. If I had a key to the place, I couldn't get it in the lock. I have that trouble at home.

I have been warned against heading maize, picking cotton, baling hay and gathering corn unless there is a handicapped parking spot at the field. I already know there would be a sweet young thing parked there. Probably wearing shorts too.

I may be stuck with lying awake all night and writing columns. The pay is good but not much of it. At least, it's not hazardous. I haven't been threatened in almost 9 years doing that. On my previous job, I was threatened daily by somebody and my picture wasn't in the paper.

One fellow chased me with a pool cue and another with a hammer. Thanks to my military training, I knew when to retreat, or as they say, when to hold and when to fold. I folded a lot. Mama said, "If you can't whip them, try to outrun them." I did.

Remember folks. Always respect those handicapped parking places unless you're disabled and have something to prove it. You just might run across some old boy whose only disability is hip trouble caused from wearing a .45 semi-automatic on it.

They do, you know.

A JUMP-START FROM A GOOD CAR BATTERY MIGHT DO ME SOME GOOD

There has been a lot of publicity recently about the danger of lead poisoning. It seems that cheap jewelry, some of which contains lead, has been made available from vending machines and appeals mostly to children.

Children and dogs learn about stuff mostly by tasting, so they are prone to put the jewelry in their mouths. We have all done this, and still do, tasting everything we cook. Lead poisoning, they say can cause learning disabilities, behavioral problems, retarded growth and hearing impairment.

I have had all of the above and there may be a good reason for it. Back when I was a kid, we had no toys to play with and my brother and I did the best we could with what we had. We discovered some old car batteries in a dump ground and immediately took them home.

We took a hammer to the cases and took the lead out. We beat it with a hammer, tasted it, and even tried to make money out of it by laying a nickel on a piece of it and pounding with a hammer. The result was our very own nickel which we then trimmed down to size with a knife. I assume this could be regarded as a behavioral problem.

As to learning disabilities, I never was good with algebra or geometry in school. In fact, it was a total wipeout for me. I was never able to figure the height of a flagpole by measuring its shadow. I couldn't see any reason for doing it anyhow. I didn't really care how high it was.

My memory of geometry has something to do with "Pi being square" We all knew that pie was round and cornbread was square. We were not that retarded, lead or no lead.

I had other behavioral problems too. I was always getting into some kind of trouble in school with the Superintendent. He was a rather narrow minded sort. I doubt he ever had any real fun in his entire life. I also didn't play well with our milk cow.

During WWII, I was once booted off the Isle of Capri. Some sort of behavioral problem, they said, like putting the Provost Marshall's jeep on a porch 16 steps above the street.

All of this may have been caused by playing with and tasting that lead out of those old car batteries. I remember back when I was taking basic training in the military. We would be doing close-order drill and the sergeant would single me out and holler, "Hey, you," "Get the lead out." How did he know?

Actually, growing up back in the thirties, I think we were immune to nearly everything. We had to be. We tasted everything we found growing in the woods and ate everything that didn't eat us first. We were always a little hungry.

As for retarded growth, I was tall enough to see over the corn in our corn field. To me, that was tall enough as long as I could see our house at supper time. As for hearing impairment, I think the lead finally caught up with me after all of these years.

The good thing is that I've heard nearly everything anyhow.

REACHING THE AGE
OF ASSISTED LIVING

Recently, I turned the ignition key in my pickup and nothing happened. No friendly roar of 8 gas-guzzling cylinders. In fact—not even the friendly click of the starter relay. I knew immediately that I was in trouble. Thirty years ago, one phone call to a friend would have solved my problem. He would have been there in 5 minutes with jumper cables in hand. If he wasn't at home, somebody else would have been.

Today, however, it seems that I have reached the age of "assisted living." All of my friends are either deceased or have reached the same age as I have. I can no longer do anything that requires any stamina without assistance, a bad situation that I had been warned about a long time ago. An old man once told me, "Son" He said "Getting old is no damn good." He was right.

I quickly diagnosed the problem as a bad battery but on that particular day, I was waiting to enter the hospital in 3 days for hernia surgery, my second this year. I was told to do no lifting or bad things could happen but no mention was made that the battery on my pickup would die.

I did the only thing I could do. I called my lady-friend for a little assisted living. One big problem is that she often needs it as much as I do. I needed a new battery but first the old one had to be removed. She couldn't lift it and I was given strict orders not to. Nothing is ever simple when we get old.

Finally, we solved the problem after much thought and discussion. She managed to raise the battery up a bit and I hooked my cane under it and with it braced on the air conditioner blower, we flipped that sucker out. Getting the new one in place was mostly a matter of dropping it over the edge of the bracket. About all I could do I was say a short prayer that the thing wouldn't break in a hundred pieces, leaving me with $86 worth of something I might sell to China if I was lucky. They do use a lot of lead in paint over there.

I could hardly wait to start my trusty pickup. But—when I did, the engine had only one speed—wide open. Since I had been confined in the hospital and at home for about 3 months for another ailment, I assumed that dirt daubers had built nests in wherever dirt daubers build nests. It wasn't safe to drive.

I had my assisted living lady-friend drive me to a mechanic. We discussed possible causes, wrecker fees and what I might add to a doctor's bill, hospital charges and how long I might have to declare bankruptcy. The mechanic was not familiar with that as no mechanic has ever been known to declare bankruptcy.

The day arrived for my surgery. I was wheeled into the operating room on a gurney and found the surgeon sharpening his scalpel on a large whet-rock and before I knew it, my hernia was fixed.

As soon as I could, I got the pickup to the mechanic and left it. He called me later with good news. "I can't find anything wrong with the pickup." He reported. "The only explanation," He said, "Is that the new battery you installed had to get acquainted with your engine and now works fine." That sounded reasonable to me and there was no charge for his service.

In fact, I wasn't even charged for new fluid in the turn signals and that's unusual.

WE HAD NO MIRACLE DRUGS
BUT WE HAD COAL OIL

A friend of mine out in West Texas sent me an e-mail informing me that he and his wife had seen a gallon of kerosene in a Home Depot store in Midland for only $8.00. He was shocked about that price. I guess there is not much demand for the stuff these days. I wonder how many pesos it would take to buy a gallon.

I just read that a pizza place in Dallas is selling pizzas for pesos. I'm not even sure how many pesos it takes to buy a pizza. I have no desire to find out.

Kerosene is somewhat like the coal oil we used when I was a kid except coal oil was made from coal and kerosene is a petroleum product. If coal oil had been $8.00 a gallon, I wouldn't even be here. It cured nearly everything and cost a dime a gallon.

A kid could step on a rusty nail, put his foot in a wash pan full of coal oil and come out with no infection and nearly an instant cure. I know that for sure because it happened to me more than once.

It was used in our lamps, our lanterns and in a pinch, would even make a Model T Ford run. A coal oil soaked cloth tied around your neck would cure a sore throat. We said it did to get rid of it.

I heard a story once about a cowhand on a remote ranch who called the doctor and said, "Doc, I just got bit by a rattlesnake. What do I do?"

"Hitch up the wagon, put your foot in a pan of coal oil and get to town as fast as you can," the doctor said.

About an hour later, the cowhand came roaring into town with his foot in a pan of coal oil and the doctor quickly found that he had been bitten on his hand. He survived anyhow, proving the power of coal oil.

The best part about it was that it had no side-effects. Anybody could use it and safely operate machinery including wheel barrows and Model T Fords.

Can you imagine one of those hundreds of ads on TV we see every day that might say, "Ask your doctor about coal oil."

Actually, my doctor asks me all the questions. "Do you still smoke?" How much do you drink?" "Do your feet ever tingle?" "Do you have headaches or double vision?" "Is there any history of insanity in your family?" "Have you ever put your foot in a pan of coal oil?" "What are you writing about next week?"

Doctors are a lot like lawyers. They hardly ever ask a question they don't already know the answer to. They just want to find out if you're still lying. Some of us do, you know.

Other than the coal oil, when I was a kid, we could engage the services of any one of our three doctors. No appointment was necessary. They could usually be found sitting on a bench in front of Ernest Allen's drug store. Their entire diagnosis was usually done with a stethoscope and a good thumping. They had no modern diagnostic gadgets and what you saw was what you got.

They were dedicated and did a good job in spite of their limited resources and the absence of any miracle drugs. We were fortunate to have had them and we should appreciate the ones we have today.

We even manage to get by without coal oil.

A LITTLE HISTORY OF THE
WAY IT WAS AND STILL IS

I was born on a farm about 5 miles northwest of Blanket, Texas, the youngest son of Jesse and Myrtle Marlin. I entered military service in March of 1943 and completed basic training at Sheppard Air Force Base at Wichita Falls, Texas. After attending radio school at Sioux Falls, South Dakota for a brief period, I attended aerial gunnery school at Las Vegas Army Air Base, Las Vegas, Nevada.

Following completion of gunnery school, I was assigned to Buckingham Field in Florida as an instructor in fifty caliber machineguns. From there, I was then assigned to a bomber crew as a ball-turret gunner and trained with this crew for 3 months at Drew Field at Tampa.

Then, we picked up a new B-17 bomber at Savannah, Georgia and flew it to southern Italy by way of Gander, Newfoundland, the Azores, then to North Africa, ending up about 12 miles south of Foggia, Italy which was our assignment until we either completed 50 missions, or became a victim of the German aerial gunners or fighter pilots, neither of which occurred.

We lived in old world War One tents in the middle of an olive orchard. We were assigned to the 414th squadron of the 97th Bomb Group, 15th Air Force, a B-17 group, until we completed our missions and were sent home.

As far as I know, I never reached hero status, at least in the eyes of my other crew members. We did what we had to do by dropping bombs on military targets in Germany and the Balkan countries. The German gunners did what they were supposed to do and tried their damndest to shoot us down.

I was awarded the Air Medal with three oak leaf clusters, the European theater ribbon with 8 battle stars and maybe one or two others I don't remember. Somehow, I even got the Good Conduct Medal which could be compared to Al Gore being awarded the Nobel Prize for discovering global warming.

I suppose I could have been awarded some type of prize for finding out how cold 65 degrees below zero was in that ball turret, hanging out from the belly of that B-17 at 30,000 feet, but I didn't.

I also, for whatever reason I don't recall, joined the Army Reserve and in 1951, I think it was, they asked for my help again and Lord help us, they sent me to Arkansas.

Anyway, I survived and I couldn't ask for more.

Harry Marlin—July, 2008

A LITTLE MIXED-UP HISTORY OF HOW BLANKET GOT ITS NAME

I recently received an e-mail from a nice lady who lives in Oregon, asking how the town of Blanket got its name. Since I wasn't there at the time, I don't really know. All I could do was to tell her the story I have heard all of my life, which may, or may be true. History, as we all know, has a way of getting mixed up with pure myth. Sometimes, it's hard to separate the myth from the facts.

The story I heard was that a group in covered wagons came upon Blanket creek, which following several days of rain, was in flood stage and they couldn't cross. Obviously, they were on their way to somewhere else as the town of Blanket wasn't there then.

According to the story, a group of Indians were also stuck at the creek, waiting to cross. Having been in the downpour, they were rather damp and were drying their blankets by hanging them on trees near the creek. Somebody, later on, then named the town Blanket.

What makes me wonder about this story is where the Indians acquired their blankets. Wal-Mart stores didn't exist back then, or any other stores. The Indians who frequented our area back then were Comanche.

The Comanche tribe was not known to be blanket weavers. They lived in teepees and slept under buffalo robes and their principal tool of trade was the tomahawk which they used to remove scalps from the settlers at every opportunity.

How the folks from the wagon train escaped losing their hair is not a part of the story I heard. Maybe the buffalo robes hadn't dried when the wagon train pulled out for parts unknown. As I have indicated, this story, as far as I know, was never confirmed.

When my Dad came to Blanket from Palestine at the age of 2, the town of Blanket was about 3 miles further west from where the Indians supposedly hung their blankets up to dry and nearly a half-mile from Blanket Creek. He lived in Blanket until he died at age 93. The Comanche tribe never bothered him.

Sometime before I was born, the town was moved to its present location. No blankets were hanging on trees when I was born, or when I left. The fact is, during my entire childhood, we never owned a blanket or a buffalo robe either.

We kept warm in the winter under quilts Mama made and cool in the summer with cardboard fans furnished by the local funeral homes. How the Comanche tribe made out, I don't know.

I heard that they moved on up in the Panhandle to a place called Adobe Walls where they got into a fight with some buffalo hunters and came out on the little end of the stick.

Or—they may have gone to Oklahoma and opened a Casino.

Anyhow, should anybody be interested in writing a history of Blanket or Brown County, it might be best not to ask me about it. I was much too busy living through the Great Depression and trying to get enough to eat to worry about history.

I still am.

A BOTTLE OF WINE, A LOAF OF BREAD AND A PLUSH PLOW

It was recently revealed that the apes and monkeys in the Budapest, Hungary zoo drink 55 liters of red wine a year to build their red blood cells. That is a lot of wine. The anthropoids, the animals in the same group as humans, drink most of it. That's not surprising.

Some humans, since the beginning of time have been drinking anything they can get their hands on.

The monkeys and apes in this zoo only get a small amount daily in their tea. Wine in tea? That should be enough to put them on the wagon for good, but I can't speak from experience about that. I've never had any. I don't plan on it.

Back when I was a kid growing up on a farm near Blanket, Mama would send my brother and me to gather wild grapes on the creeks. We usually got several tow sacks full. Mama would then make grape jelly. If she had any grapes left, she made her own version of wine.

I don't know her formula but the stuff, when fully fermented would stop a freight train. She hid it in the cellar so Dad, who was a staunch prohibitionist, wouldn't know about it. We were allowed about a half snuff glass of the stuff when we had a cold, or pretended to have one.

It was far better than coal oil and sugar or Vick's salve, our usual cure-alls.

At that time in history, there was only one winery in Texas, the Val Verde Winery in Del Rio. That winery, the oldest in Texas, is still in operation. In addition to it, there are now 113 others, scattered from North Texas, to the high plains and one in the desert near Fort Stockton. They are all doing quite well.

The apes and monkeys on both sides of the Atlantic are not likely to run out of red blood builder.

I once visited the Val Verde winery in Del Rio, arriving about eight in the morning. They were friendly folks and gave liberal samples of their product, unlike the Fredericksburg wineries that pass out about a thimble full.

I don't recommend visiting this winery at eight in the morning unless you plan on spending the rest of the day under the International Bridge. They don't furnish bed and breakfast.

Several years ago when Dad was in his eighties, living alone and doing his own cooking, he lost his appetite. A doctor in Brownwood recommended drinking a little red wine to whet his appetite and maybe build up his red blood cells.

Still being the prohibitionist that he always was, he refused to buy it. He called me to get it for him. I bought him a bottle of good red wine and took it to him. I guess it went down pretty good. About 3 weeks later, he told me one day, "Harry, can you get me another bottle of that appetizer?"

I guess it done him a lot of good as one day I saw him breaking up his garden with a push plow. He also lived to the ripe old age of 92.

Wine in Texas is now big business and is generally accepted as a social drink or to drink with meals. No longer, when wine is mentioned, do people get a vision of a derelict lying on a sidewalk drinking Sweet Lucy from a bottle in a paper sack.

Progress, in some cases, has its good points.

A LITTLE STIMULUS FOR THE OIL COMPANIES MIGHT BALANCE THINGS OUT

I just received a notice from the IRS that I would receive my stimulus check on June 6. I'm wondering if this is a coincidence that they started mailing out the checks around the time gasoline started getting higher than a cat's back. Surely the check is not to help the oil companies. Anyhow, a lot of people will be forced to spend a major part of the money for gas to get to work.

I assumed that with the price of gasoline headed for $4 a gallon, the traffic in Brownwood would be noticeably less. It hasn't happened that I can tell. I live on the busiest street in town and traffic is still about the same. Back in the seventies when gasoline got scarce, driving 55 miles an hour was recommended to save gas. I can report that folks are doing that but the speed limit is still 35 in front of my house.

One day this week, I was at the Veterans Administration Clinic getting my blood tested when a fellow stopped me on the parking lot and asked me to give him $15 for gasoline to get home. I assume he didn't live far. I don't know yet how my blood tested, or if the fellow ever got home. Apparently, I had more blood than he did gasoline. I kept all of my money and most of my blood.

Anyway, the fellow didn't look like he was "from around here." I can assure you that I'm from around here and have been for a long, long time. I was here when gasoline was 12 cents a gallon and nobody had any money to buy it. I was here long before TV was invented and radio didn't amount to much but I'm not hanging around parking lots trying to beg money for gas.

I just read on the National News that folks all over the country are running out of gas on the road. Obviously, they're trying to stretch 10 gallons of gas into 12. It doesn't work.

I was running out of gas on the road before these drivers even learned to drive, if they ever did.

The last time I put a smidgen of gas in my second tank on the pickup to keep the fuel pump cool, the lady filling up in front of me was taking a long time. When she finally took the hose out and left, the figure on the pump showed she had put $100 worth of gas in her Suburban.

The high price of gas is not my only problem. About 6 or 8 years ago, I started losing my balance. I'm subject to falling at any time. I have noticed that it is not always the fall that gets me—it's what I fall into. The last time, one day this week, a doorknob got me, cutting a gash in my head. I showed it to my lady friend in hopes she might put something on it and she said, "Blunt object, huh?" "Nope," I said, "Round object."

I once consulted a neurologist who ran my head through a MRI. "It appears," He said, "that the part of your brain that controls your balance is partly deteriorated." He told me there was nothing I could do but it wouldn't get any worse. It did, so I consulted another neurologist. His diagnosis was much simpler. "You drank too much beer during WWII" He said.

I just settled for that and gave up.

A LITTLE TOO MUCH SHAKING GOING ON

State representative A.L. Edwards, a Democrat from Houston, has filed a bill to stop what he refers to as "bumping" and "grinding" being done by High School Cheerleaders. If his bill passes, the only thing they will be able to shake is their pom-poms. Any violation could result in the school losing a part of their state funding.

It might also change Friday night football forever. Of course, I'm sure that hardly any of the fans ever pay much attention to the cheerleaders, their attention totally absorbed in the game. Mr. Edwards, being a Democrat, apparently took notice of it.

When I was a student in the Blanket High School, I don't remember us ever having cheerleaders. Maybe we didn't have much to cheer about. Larry L. King, a noted Texas writer who now lives in Washington D.C. and played football with Scranton tells me that their team once beat Blanket eighty to nothing.

I do remember that we played Scranton but I don't remember any team ever beating us that bad. Larry, however, unlike some writers, is not known to stretch the truth any more than necessary. Maybe the reason for the big loss was our lack of cheerleaders.

Our football field was a section of a rocky hillside, without benefit of any grass or artificial turf. The bumping and grinding was all done by the players falling on the rocks. Our quarterback was never "sacked" but was "rocked." Any of our surviving team members were never known to order any drink in a bar "on the rocks."

I remember one occasion when our team was scheduled to play a team from a town about a hundred miles southwest of Blanket. They were a tough bunch and known to regularly use illegal players on their team. Our coach was aware of it and decided to give them a dose of their own medicine.

He went downtown and picked up all the hefty loafers he found sitting on the benches, took them all to school and suited them out. One fellow weighed about 250 pounds, was about 6-4 and known locally as "Mule."

There was some difficulty finding a suit large enough to fit him. Unfortunately, "Mule" was almost killed in the melee, suffering from various bumps, grinds, and rock bruises. He limped around town for a week or two. The best I remember, we lost the game anyhow.

Anyway, it is not whether you win or lose but how much you remember about the game 65 years later. I was not a member of the football team, my interests being more in the literary field, like reading books. So far, I have never got bruised up reading a book.

I most likely would have shown some interest in the cheerleaders however, if we had been fortunate enough to have had some. Bumping and grinding in their case wouldn't have bothered me a bit.

I know of only one of the original football team who is still around and even 65 years later, he is still a bit stove up. Our football coach, a man I admired in spite of the fact that he regularly warmed up his yardstick on my rear nearly every morning in science class, has gone to where all the football fields have Astroturf and cheerleaders.

Both Larry L. King, the Scranton football player and I are still here. He writes books and Broadway Plays and I write columns and neither of us have bruises.

OUR NICE, QUIET LITTLE TOWN IS GOING THE WAY OF THE HORNED TOAD

As everybody probably knows by now, I was born and raised at Blanket and I managed to stay there until 1943. Then, one day somebody from the Army Air Corp came by and dragged me off the front porch and sent me to Sheppard Field at Wichita Falls. I've still got splinters under my fingernails.

Their purpose in sending me to Sheppard Field was to make me mad enough to fight in a war. The Air Corp taught me how to take a .50 caliber machine gun apart and put it back together blindfolded and how to operate a ball turret on a B-17 bomber at 30,000 feet and 65 degrees below zero.

Then, they sent me to Italy where I assisted in winning WWII with the 15th Air Force. Then, I came back to Brownwood where I've been ever since except for a year in the army during the Korean fracas where I didn't do much of anything because my military occupation specialty didn't fit anything they had. They didn't need any ball turret gunners, they said.

They did need a supply sergeant bad, or a bad supply sergeant. I was assigned to the job and they got one.

In Brownwood, they needed a police officer and I was given the job. I stayed until my waist size got the same caliber as my gun and got a job that paid more.

In those days, Brownwood was a nice, quiet town where nearly everybody knew everybody else. I could go in the Coggin

Avenue Drug to get a sandwich or buy a magazine and it was rare that I didn't know everybody in there, including the nice lady that made the sandwiches and George, the clerk and Al the pharmacist.

Now, the store is gone and the people are gone. Brownwood is no longer a nice quiet town and in reading the police report, it seems to be full of thieves and dope peddlers. If you find one in a town, you find the other.

Just last week, there was another shoot-out at the O.K. Corral. The County jail is almost full to capacity and still it happens. The State raised the speed limit to 80 on Interstate 10 and 20 but our Brownwood drivers think it also applies to Austin Avenue and Main Street. Traffic laws are ignored as if they didn't exist. The police officers do check to see if you're wearing your seat belt. They know you may need it.

I have no idea where all the thieves came from. Surely, they are not home grown right among us. I'm sure our law officers are doing the best they can but they're outnumbered. By now, at least, they know where all the thieves and dope peddlers live.

Thousands of illegal aliens are pouring across our borders and the government is sending the National Guard down there, unarmed, to build fences. Nobody ever stopped an invasion with posthole diggers. A fence can be compared to trying to stop Niagara Falls with a minnow seine. Congress is doing little or nothing and they won't. Where would they get their campaign money? President Bush says, "We can't move 12 million people to another country". Jay Leno says, "Mexico did."

I don't know what the military occupational specialty number is for building fences but I know what mine is.

Maybe a few good ball turret gunners could straighten the whole mess out.

I still know how.

A SHORT INTERVIEW WITH
A GOOD OLD BOY

Back when I was gainfully employed as an investigator for insurance companies, I was sent by a West Coast insurance company to interview a well-known movie actor. I was looking forward to the assignment as I had seen most of his movies and I thought he was a "good old boy."

I was wrong. I was really wrong.

This "good old boy" had applied for a large life insurance policy and the underwriter was in need of a lot of information before he could approve of the policy. Apparently, the underwriter had no idea who he was.

Underwriters, as a general rule, spend a lifetime in a little cubicle somewhere and their only interest lies in health history, occupation, habits, finances and mortality tables. Since the applicant lived in Texas on a ranch near a small town and had the usual Texas double first name, there was a lot he needed to know.

It was my job to find out what he did need to know, and I had no idea I was about to run into a brick wall.

I drove down a dirt county road and turned off on his ranch road. I noted signs about every hundred feet that proclaimed "Speed Limit 20." This should have been a tip-off. I ignored both the tip-off and the signs.

I arrived at the ranch to find nobody at home. Since I had driven quite a distance, I found a Hollywood director's chair on the large front porch and made myself comfortable. I didn't have to wait long.

The subject of my investigation came roaring up in a Porsche 911, obviously ignoring his own speed signs. He was dressed in jeans stuffed into the tops of boots that came to his knees. He was wearing a big hat and had a red bandanna around his neck. He appeared to be disturbed about something and stayed that way the whole time I was there.

He headed straight for the front porch and me. "What in the HAIL," he said, "Do you think YOU are doing?" (Texans say hail a lot). I quickly presented my ID and explained the purpose of my visit. "That," he said, "Is none of your blankety-blank business, or the insurance company's either." I assured him that it was.

Our short interview went downhill from there. We went in the ranch house so he could call his insurance broker and he proceeded to give him what I got. There was nothing in the room but two saddles, a telephone and two cane bottom chairs. I was not invited to sit.

I could hear both sides of the conversation due to the fact that both were shouting. The insurance broker informed him that I was indeed legitimate and to tell me what I wanted to know.

I told him again what I wanted to know.

He told me again that it was "none of my blankety-blank business." Having 30 years experience in interviewing people reluctant to give information, I had learned to ask them about their hobbies, their jobs or anything to get them talking.

"Do you have any new movies coming up?" I asked. "Are you a director or do you want to invest in a new picture? He asked. I admitted I wasn't a director and that I was about half broke.

"Well," he said, "That's none of your blankety-blank business either".

At this point, I got in my car and left, driving 40 miles an hour past his blankety-blank 20 miles an hour signs. I have no idea if he got the insurance and I don't care. Obviously, he needed it.

I have not mentioned this "good old boy's" name for a good reason. I blankety-blank well don't want to see him again now, or ever.

Updated: This actor was famous for his roles in Men in Black and the Fugitive.

A TIME TO HOLD AND A TIME TO FOLD WHEN THE SHERIFF COMES CALLING

Steve Nash gave me another boost to my ego when he found another fan for me. I think that's the second one he has found, or least written about in his column. I need all the help I can get. In fact, I need help to get up from a couch.

As for fans, I'm like the little boy catching moles. An elderly man who noticed what he was doing asked, "How many have you caught, son?"

The kid replied, "If I catch this'n I'm after and two more, it'll be three."

Anyway, the new fan I didn't know about is deputy sheriff' Lt. Ellis Johnson who remarked that he thought my recent roadrunner story was funny. I don't personally know any deputy sheriffs. I do, however know the sheriff.

As far back as I can remember it has always been important for everybody in the county to know the sheriff. Nobody knows when they might need him, or not need him. As the old saying goes, there is a time to hold and a time to fold.

When I was a kid growing up in Blanket, we all knew the sheriff. At least once a month, the sheriff would come out and drive up and down the street. We all scattered like a covey of quail. We couldn't think of any particular thing we might have done but we were almost sure, the way he looked at us, that we had done something.

We folded.

Actually, what the sheriff was looking for was votes. A sheriff who was never seen didn't get reelected.

The occasion Nash wrote about took place at the City firing range at the top of Round Mountain where firearms qualification was being held for two new jailors. He was there to take pictures for the Bulletin.

They even allowed him to shoot, I assume after the entire crew took cover behind the mountain. He was allowed to shoot what he calls a "Smith." I assume it was a six shot .38 revolver made by Smith & Wesson. It is a safe gun. All six bullets are visible by rotating the cylinder. In the event only 5 are showing, it is possible to take a quick look down the barrel to see if it is in the chamber. This is not highly recommended by firearms instructors.

When I was a cop back in the fifties, the Smith & Wesson was the standard firearm used. Today, officers carry semi-automatics with enough bullets in the clip to wipe out Iran's Revolutionary army.

It is my thinking that if you can't bring a man down with six .38 caliber bullets, it might be best to throw the gun at him and as we used to say, "Light a shuck" to somewhere else.

My expertise, if I have any left, is with .50 caliber machine guns. With the two of them I had in my ball turret on the B-17 bomber in Italy, I think I could bring down the old Brownwood Hotel in short order. In the interest of neighborhood improvement, I think that would be a good idea.

Of course, law officers can't wear one for several reasons. There is an old Country song, by Marty Robbins, I think, about a man who wore "a big iron on his hip."

Now that would be a big iron.

A TRIBUTE TO A GREAT AIRPLANE
AND THE MEN WHO FLEW IT

During WWII, the Boeing Company of Seattle, Washington built some 12,000 B-17 bombers. Few are left today. They were flown by 12,000 pilots. Few of those are left either. Following the war, many of the bombers were scrapped but a few were bought and preserved by the Commemorative Air Force along with other WWII planes.

Many of the bombers were inadvertently dropped on Germany, France and whatever territory Germany occupied at the time. Being a ball turret gunner on one of these great planes, I saw a lot of this happening. All were victims of the German Air Force or the accuracy of the German anti-aircraft guns. It was a great ride and I am proud to have been a part of it. Ball turret gunners are scarce too. A.I. Sutton of Brownwood is the only one I know.

As for the living pilots, I have no idea how many are left. My pilot, Bob Boudreaux is living and well within rock-throwing distance of the Mississippi in Gramercy, Louisiana. My co-pilot, Ned Hawkins, lives in Chico, California. Bob, they say, is a good golfer if somebody points out the ball to him.

There are four members of my crew left. These members consist of the pilot, the co-pilot, the radio operator and me. We all are, no doubt, living on the edge. None of us are bothered. We got used to it in the 15th Air Force in Italy in 1944 and 1945.

Yes, the crew members of these bombers who flew the frigid skies of Germany are getting scarce. In Brownwood, there are two former B-17 pilots, Joe Harper and Grady Thompson. In Trickham, Felton Martin, and living on a farm west of Deleon is Joe Morgan. In Stephenville, Bob Henningsen is also a survivor. If you see one of these men, thank them for what they did.

At Mesa, Arizona, the CAF owns a B-17 in perfect condition. They fly it all over the country in the summer months, giving folks a chance to see it, go through it and ride in it if you happen to have $350 for a 30 minute flight. If I had been paid that when I was flying, I'd never pick another boll of cotton.

If you choose to take a ride, do not worry about an 86 year old pilot flying it. Their pilots are young, most being Southwestern Airlines pilots who take time off from their jobs for the opportunity to fly this great airplane.

Sometime back, I took my youngest son Ken through the B-17 at Mesa. He was puzzled as to how I ever got into the ball turret. I told him it was easy. "There was a big man with a 20 foot blacksnake whip standing by the plane before each mission. When he said get in it, I got in it." He thinks I lie a lot.

Alan Williamson, the former Commander of the CAF unit at Mesa recently gave me a 20x24 picture of the plane which hangs on my wall. I look at it every day and wonder how, and why, I'm still here. Sometimes I get a lump in my throat and I don't know why.

If I could be considered as any kind of hero, then there are 20 million others who fought for freedom in WWII and are still doing it today.

Somebody said that when stuff hits the fan, it is never evenly distributed. It wasn't then, and it isn't now.

Everybody gets some of it.

A WATCHED POT NEVER BOILS AND OTHER USELESS INFORMATION

Thirty years ago, due to circumstances beyond my control, I had to learn to cook. After all of these years, I'm still not good at it. Out of pure necessity, I do, as Mama used to say, "Take a stab at it."

I'm not good at cooking anything that takes over 5 minutes to cook. I have better things to do than stand around and watch a pot all day. Beans, however, I do have to cook about once a week. Beans, when soaked overnight will cook in about 3 hours. They, along with chili, require some attention.

Recently, I had a doctor's appointment. I forgot the beans and left them merrily simmering on the stove. At the very moment, I was up next, I remembered the beans. I told the nurse, along with an office full of people my problem.

"Harry," She said, "You go on home and see about the beans. I'll move you back a notch" I drove like a teen-ager to my house, about 3 miles away and arrived just as the pot was going dry.

On my return, everybody in the waiting room yelled, "How were the beans?"

Most of my cooking utensils were given to me by somebody. Some of them look like the wreck of the Hesper. The Teflon coating has long ago been consumed by somebody. I also have a unique set of silverware, all of which have made at least one trip through the garbage disposal. I did that myself.

Due to the mutilation, I have some spoons that can only be used left-handed and some right-handed. I have become used to them and it no longer bothers me. When I eat at a restaurant, I do have trouble though. Their forks all have more than one tine.

I have watched those chefs on TV take something in a skillet, do a nice flip with it and turn the contents over. I tried that once with a skillet full of okra. Mine all went on the floor. The reason may possibly lie in the fact that I don't possess one of those $8,000 stoves where they turn the flame up just short of the ceiling and cook everything in two minutes.

I go by the philosophy that if it's brown, it's cooking. If it's black, it's done. Well—except beans. It doesn't work with beans. I have already tried that.

Recently, due to the increase in price of bread, I took out my bread maker, and following the directions carefully for French bread, I turned the machine on. After something over three hours, the machine surrendered, along with the bread.

It never did rise and weighed at least 15 pounds and a large bull could have been knocked down with it at 50 feet. I'm now looking for a recipe for "South Bread." I have been informed by numerous sources that it will rise again.

The one dish that I do watch carefully is chili. With the high cost of good meat and spices, necessary to make good chili, I never wander far from the pot. The results of waiting, stirring and watching are cause to lock all the doors and disconnect the phone. Distant kin may drop by I haven't seen in years.

I get out my right-handed spoon and try to eat it all. Sometimes, I do. I'd be a fool not to.

TAKE YOUR MEDS BUT
DON'T DRINK THE WATER

According to a news article I read by the Associated Press, we are taking too many pills. In fact, in a test of water supplies for 62 major metropolitan cities, 24 showed a level of drugs including antibiotics, hormones and mood stabilizers. They report only "minuscule" amounts were found. A "minuscule" here and a minuscule" there and before you know it, you have a good dose of something you didn't take, or need.

The drugs get in the water supply of various cities through the sewage treatment plants which dump the water in rivers and lakes where the cities get their water. People's bodies don't absorb all the medication they take which is flushed down the toilet. This is known as "toilet water." Water treatment plants do not remove the drugs from the toilet water.

Since I don't drink water, I'm only getting the drugs I take. I can't stand the taste of water. The only water I can remember that I liked was from an old vinegar jug wrapped in wet burlap and left under a tree at the end of a row in the cotton patch where I labored when I was a kid.

Like everybody else over the age of 70 and who regularly see a doctor, I take drugs too. I take a blood thinner 7 days a week. For whatever reason I don't know, my blood is thicker on Mondays and Wednesdays and I take a whole pill. The rest of the week, it gets thinner and I take a half pill. None of the pills go in my water that I know of.

Judging from the number of ads I see on TV for drugs, there must be thousands on the market. One of several drugs which are advertised several times a night is apparently used for snake bites as they frequently mention getting "reptile dysfunction." At least, that's what it sounds like to me but my hearing is slightly impaired. Whatever it is, I don't want it.

Another drug frequently advertised for lowering cholesterol is something called Lipitor. ABC News recently reported that a number of patients taking Lipitor and related drugs reported memory loss. Now the ad agencies can say, "Ask your doctor if you're taking Lipitor."

When I was a kid, back in the dark ages, we had to get by without pills with the exception of one called "Carter's Little Liver Pills." Finally, the FDA made the drug company change the name to "Carter's Pills" as they had no effect on anybody's liver and an investigation revealed that nearly everybody had big livers anyhow.

There was no way that Carter's pills could get in our water which came from windmills on 200 foot deep wells. Anyhow, there wasn't a thing on the place that would flush.

Since the amount of drugs going into drinking water is not under any control, medical experts are worried that the amount of antibiotics and other stuff may lead to overexposure and an inability to fight infection or the ability to cure snakebites. That worries me. A man never knows when he might get a snake bite.

Wildlife too may be affected, get hooked and start breaking into drug stores at night. Already, it has been reported that male fish are taking on female characteristics, causing reproductive problems due to the hormones in the water. Wait until you see an alligator on steroids.

I really don't know what we can do about this situation and I have plenty of other things to worry about.

Like reptile dysfunction.

SOME WWII MEMORIES THAT STICK IN MY MIND

The last time I flew on a B-17 bomber was sometime in April of 1945. I had finished my required 50 missions and was packed up and ready to leave Italy and go to that magic place called home, some 4000 miles away.

Along with about 15 other veterans, all, to borrow an old expression, as nervous as a long-tailed cat in a room full of rocking chairs, were loaded into an old B-17 for the 90 mile flight to Naples where we would catch a boat to Boston, and then home.

The first thing we noticed was that our two "hot-rock" pilots who were flying the plane both had what we called a "fifty mission crush" in their caps. We all knew then we might be in trouble.

We made an unusually low approach to the Naples airport, barely missing some buildings. Then, our pilot put the plane into a steep bank and side-slipped it in, landing about half-way down the runway.

The first thing any good pilot learns is that the runway behind the plane is no longer usable. He did the only thing he could do under the circumstances. He put his full strength on the brakes causing a tire to blow, and the B-17 to start making short circles on the grass by the runway at about a hundred miles an hour. The German Air Force would have been proud of him. He almost killed us and they couldn't.

It took some restraint on our part to walk away without first impaling the pilot on the propeller of the number four engine, or any of the other three. There is an old saying that any landing you can walk away from is a good landing. Forget old sayings. That was a bad one.

We were then transported to a replacement depot operated by the infantry to await our trip home. The reception we got was about as bad as the landing. The infantry hated the Air Corp. They claimed we slept in warm beds every night, ate gourmet food and were entertained by dancing girls between missions.

We were immediately put on guard duty or KP even though our rank should have exempted us. They showed no mercy. I was given a rifle and a specified area I was to guard. Just what I was guarding, I was not sure about.

Shortly after reaching my post, the officer of the day, an infantry major came by. According to military protocol, I was to "present arms" when he approached. I had no idea how. Being friendly, I said, "How're you doing?" All he said was "Damned Air Corp" and stomped off.

I was placed in a tent with a black fellow. This was long before the military desegregated. I was not bothered and we quickly became friends. I had never in my entire life mastered tying a tie. He taught me how in about two minutes. I have never forgotten when, and how I learned, or who taught me.

Finally, we were put on a floating crap game called the USS Mariposa and after going through the Straits of Gibraltar, we sailed to Boston and from there to Texas, our Promised Land. As we passed the Rock of Gibraltar, I remembered hearing that it was occupied by the British, a colony of large apes and the Prudential insurance company.

I didn't see any of those things.

GOOD BOOKS, GOOD WRITERS AND ESCAPE FROM A COTTON PATCH

Whitney Peeling, publicity director for Public Affairs Publishing Company in New York recently informed me that Larry L. King's new book, In Search of Willie Morris, was released on March 1. Better yet, being informed by Larry King that I wrote a column, he sent me a copy of the book.

I am somewhat familiar with the writing of Willie Morris, having read North Toward Home some thirty years ago. He was the editor of Harper's magazine at age 32, taking it from near bankruptcy to be the top magazine in the country.

Like other writers of that period, he had some problems. Often talent and various excesses go hand in hand, getting him fired from Harper's. Larry King, in the book, covers it thoroughly, warts and all. Larry, having worked with him on Harper's and being a long-time friend, knew him probably better than anybody.

I have known Larry for several years, thanks to my friend Bud Lindsey of Midland who introduced us. We both of us grew up in similar circumstances during what folks called "hard times." He grew up on a farm near Putnam, Texas and I grew up on a farm near Blanket. Willie Morris, in Yazoo City, Mississippi, was not far behind us.

At an early age, we all had "seen the elephant and heard the owl." Willie and Larry both achieved literary fame and I escaped from a cotton patch but never got far away from one.

In Search of Willie Morris is a good book, written about a good writer by another good writer. To use an old Texas expression, Larry "puts the fodder where the calf can get it." In Texas, we don't settle for less.

I have been reading everything I could get my hands on since I first learned to read. I read every book in the Blanket school library by the time I was twelve. They gave me gold stars until they ran out.

When I was a kid, we lived in various old farm houses, always looking for a better place. The old houses were built as cheap as they could be, using one by twelve boards with cracks in between. No double walls back then.

To keep out the cold northers, Mama, lacking the money to buy wall paper, used old newspapers. I read them all, over and over. When we had guests for dinner, which was rare, conversation was at a standstill while everybody read the walls.

She tried to change papers about every three months so we wouldn't get behind on world affairs if there were any back then. The best I remember, nobody was protesting anything and we had more oil than we needed.

I am sure that my reading over the years furthered my education, helping me to obtain a good job and put the cotton patches behind and live in a house that was not papered with newspapers.

I know that there are a few cotton patches where I spent my childhood still out there. Sometime back, I was returning from Midland and somewhere near Sweetwater, I observed prisoners in white coveralls from a State Jail Facility in a field picking cotton.

I don't know what they were serving time for but whatever it was, their punishment probably fit the crime.

I know because I've been there.

LIVING IN A HOUSE AT THE END OF A LANE

When I was a kid growing up, or trying to, in the middle of what was called "The Great Depression," we always lived in a remote area at the end of a lane. The lane was usually a rough wagon road and not well suited for cars. Not many people owned cars anyway and we seldom saw one.

Sometimes the Raleigh man would make it, trying to sell his wares. About once a year, the banker from Blanket drove his old 1928 Chevy out to check on his crops and livestock, all mortgaged to the bank. He was always interested in any new calves we had on the place as the mortgage always included cows and "increase."

If the mortgage was not paid, or renewed at the end of the year, the bank owned everything but us. Of course, Dad always managed to either pay or renew the mortgage but there were times when I wondered how.

I also wondered why we couldn't live on a road at sometime in our lives where we could see somebody now and then.

It got awful lonesome living at the end of that lane. Sometimes late in the evening we might hear the distant sound of a car passing on the county road at the other end of the lane. I would run out and look down the lane but hardly anybody ever came.

About once a year, usually in the fall, Mama's brother and his brood would show up and stay a week or so. He had an old Dodge flatbed truck equipped with sideboards on which they hauled all the kids and mattresses to sleep on. They lived at a place called Quitaque, somewhere on the plains. One of his kids told me the place was named by the Indians and meant "Buffalo Chips."

His boys told me a lot of things I didn't need to know and tried to teach me things I shouldn't know. There were two or three boys in the bunch who dipped snuff and could spit in a horned toad's eyes from 20 feet.

I'm sure all of the horned toads on our place left when they heard the truck coming.

Our old Mule, Pete, could open any gate on the place and he left too, shortly after the horned toads. Dad usually took his hounds and left with Old Pete and the horned toads. He was never fond of Mama's kinfolks.

Since they lived on the plains, the kids were not familiar with trees and they climbed every tree on the place, leaving a trail of broken limbs in their wake.

I knew a fellow several years ago who built mobile homes which were sold all over Texas. They were delivered using a special short-bed truck which pulled the trailers. He had a hard time keeping drivers and he had one driver who as they say here in Texas "drank" a lot.

One day, he told me, he got a phone call from a sheriff somewhere up on the plains. "We've got your driver in jail up here." "What did he do this time?" The fellow asked. "Well," The sheriff said, "Besides being drunker than Cooter Brown, he drove his truck, trailer house and all into the only damn tree in the county."

Finally, when the gravy started getting thin and the biscuits getting flatter, they loaded up the old Dodge truck and either went back to the plains or on down the road to visit more kinfolks. Old Pete came home, the horned toads returned and the trees put on new limbs.

It was still lonesome living at the end of that lane.

MISSING A BIG NIGHT OUT
AND A FREE GOURMET DINNER

Just last week, I received an invitation in the mail to attend a complimentary gourmet dinner at Anton's Restaurant, established in 1960. Of course, along with the complimentary gourmet dinner, I was to listen to a lecture by a fellow who was going to make me independently wealthy. I guess he was paying for the gourmet dinner.

It sounded interesting to me, considering the fact that a big night out for me is when I get to wear my shoes to a Dairy Queen.

I wondered how my name and address was obtained. Had someone stolen my identity? Stealing my identity would be comparable to burglarizing a trailer house in Study Butte, Texas.

There was one hurdle I would someway have to overcome to attend this big event. Anton's Restaurant is located at 1628 Battleground Avenue in Greensboro, North Carolina. Are they reading my columns in Greensboro?

I figured that by the time I bought gas for my pickup and even with bedding down in Motel 3, it would cost me five or six hundred dollars to attend. If I stayed in Motel 6, it would cost even more. By the time I got there, any money I had to invest would be gone.

I was asked to be sure to call within 24 hours as seating was going fast. The literature did look good though with those senior citizens eating big steaks and drinking fine wine. I was really sorry I couldn't make it.

I must have missed out on a lot of gourmet meals in my lifetime and didn't have to drive 900 miles to do it. When I was a kid, we never ate out at all. In fact, we didn't have a gourmet dinner when we ate in, which was all the time.

There was one small restaurant in Blanket and it specialized in chili and stew at fifteen cents a bowl. A steak could be had for around a dollar. Even at those prices, it was beyond our financial means. We were all on the famous Hoover diet, beans and cornbread for dinner and swell up for supper.

By the time I was a teen-ager, there was a café down on highway 67 where a good hamburger could be had for a quarter. I had a paper route then and I could afford it. They also had a juke box and a small dance floor. A pretty girl from Oklahoma taught me how to dance to the music of the Ink Spot's "Java Jive" and Bob Will's "San Antonio Rose."

I'll always have a warm spot in my heart for the Ink Spots and Bob Wills, sort of like a hot bowl of cornmeal mush on a cold morning.

I guess, like we say in Texas, the Ink Spots, along with Bob Wills, have "passed away." I still wonder what happened to her. Maybe she too was invited to the gourmet meal in North Carolina and I missed it.

Anyway, like Sam Goldwin, a famous Hollywood movie mogul who was also famous for his anomalies said, "We have passed a lot of water since then."

With a little luck, we'll all pass some more.

SPEAK SOFTLY BUT
CARRY A BIG STICK

It seems that nearly every county in Texas has one of those state operated prisons. Some are run by private companies. Most stay filled to capacity. The purpose of these prisons is to relieve the overcrowding in the State Penitentiaries and county jails.

Being somewhat older than rope, I remember when county jails served the purpose of keeping crime down. Most were rather old structures and not built for comfort. They had none of the amenities found in county jails today. There was no TV, no weight rooms and no law libraries.

Also, most of the time, they had few occupants. Nobody wanted to be there.

I knew a fellow here who was either bad about drinking or good about bad drinking. Anyway, he was arrested for DWI and placed in the old Brown County jail. He told me about the only two other occupants he described as "just plain mean."

"I didn't sleep a wink at night, afraid they would kill me. I don't know what they were in for, or how long but they seemed to have been there long enough to have tenure as they practically ran the place."

"One of them weighed about 300 pounds and carried a big club which appeared to have been made from an ax handle. He threatened me with it the whole time I was in there." He said.

The fellow told me that when he finally got out, he "totally and absolutely quit drinking."

The last time I saw him, about 15 years ago, he was still sober as a judge.

Comfort, as our modern jails prove, doesn't stop crime. Neither does TV and weight lifting. Neither does lengthy confinement. Most prisoners when released go back to their old ways, using new techniques they learned while being confined, or possibly while watching TV. Felony Convictions don't help on job interviews.

Back in the thirties, the State Penitentiaries were a lot tougher than they are today. Larry L. King wrote about a letter his Dad received from an uncle who was confined in one. The uncle wrote, "Dear Clyde, I wisht you'd try to get me out as I'm not-a-tall satisfied down here."

I don't think anybody else was then. Nobody wanted a confinement in what they called "Uncle Bud's Farm." They worked long hours doing farm labor and picking cotton. No TV, no weight rooms or law libraries.

I heard a story one time about a prisoner who failed to pick his daily quota of cotton and received a dose of a blacksnake whip. After about the fifth whipping, he told the guard, "I'll tell you one thing. If that cotton is out there tomorrow, I'll get it."

That big club the fellow had in the Brown County jail seemed to work well too but due to various do-gooder organizations we have today, it wouldn't be permitted. I assume that nobody ever burglarized their offices or shot one of their employees.

Crime today is more prevalent than it ever was. I still remember when the Brown County sheriff had only two deputies. The county had one constable, one Justice of the Peace and one prosecuting attorney. No more were needed.

Most of the crime can be blamed on drugs and the people who use them. It seems to be a never ending battle to get rid of it. As long as there is a market for it, somebody will sell it.

Teddy Roosevelt said, "Speak softly and carry a big stick." It might work.

AN ENCOUNTER WITH A MOUNTAIN LION AND A WILD RIDE IN A PORSCHE

Leon Hale who writes a column for the Houston Chronicle says that it is his ambition to see a mountain lion. He has plans to drive to the Big Bend National Park in the summer in hopes of finding one. Leon has been writing since Roosevelt was President and being no spring chicken, should know better.

Several years ago when I was still young and reasonably good-looking, A.L Lindsey gave me one of his famous wildlife calls, which when blown with some practice would call up anything wild but women.

I was camped out in the Big Bend National Park and I decided to try it and take movies of whatever I called up.

I drove to the Grapevine Hills, a rather remote place with boulders bigger than my house. I walked up a canyon, set up my tripod and 16mm movie camera and gave the thing a good blow, imitating the cry of a wounded rabbit as Mr. Lindsey had taught me.

Shortly after the first blow, a mountain lion appeared looking over a boulder about 25 feet from me. I picked up my tripod and camera, quickly making a decision to go somewhere else.

The lion, however, wanted that rabbit, so he followed me. The bad part was that I didn't have a rabbit. I wanted one worse than the lion did so I could drop it and get far, far away while he ate it.

I finally reached my car but the lion; I guess realizing that he had been snookered, gave up the chase about 50 feet from my car and went back in the rocks. It took me 10 minutes to get my key in the door lock

On another occasion, I was camped out at Rio Grande Village in the park next to a young couple from New York driving a Porsche. We got acquainted while I admired the Porsche. I had always wanted one but my chances of having one were slim and none.

They informed me that they had never seen a coyote. Having one of my trusty Lindsey wildlife calls in my pocket, I informed them that I could fix that. That night, we got in the Porsche and were doing 60 before we left the campground and was still in second gear.

I had them drive about 6 miles down the River Road, a rough desert road that ended 40 miles away at Castalon. We both had a new experience that night. They had never seen a coyote and I had never ridden 90 miles an hour on a jeep trail in a Porsche.

We stopped, turned off the lights and I got out with my famous lion caller. I blew it several times. "Now, turn on your lights," I said. The road was full of coyotes.

I guess they went back to New York, happy at seeing coyotes and I was happy to still be alive after the wild desert ride.

A.L. Lindsey and I spent many happy hours back in the sixties calling up coyotes in Brown and San Saba Counties. He did the calling and I operated the camera. He used the films to promote his wildlife callers all over Texas.

One thing I learned; it is the little things that make life worth living.

Well, except a mountain lion looking for a rabbit.

A RUSTY PLYMOUTH AND FIVE GALLONS OF CHEAP GAS

An unusual event recently took place in Tulsa, Oklahoma, according to the Associated Press. I am always interested in unusual events so I took special note of this one.

In 1957, to celebrate Oklahoma's 50 years of statehood, a 1957 Plymouth Belvedere was buried on the courthouse lawn. Actually, it was wrapped with several layers of plastic and placed in a concrete vault. None of this, they found out 50 years later when they dug it up last week, helped to preserve it one bit.

It was, to put it mildly, one big piece of rust and mud. In the trunk, they had placed a 5 gallon can of gas which in 1957 was selling for 24 cents a gallon and some Schlitz beer, also rusted. The best I remember, beer was selling for $2.40 a case, un-rusted.

The day the Plymouth was buried, folks were asked to guess at the population of Tulsa in 2007 and their names were put on a spool of microfilm which they haven't located. The correct guess would win the car.

There was a good crowd on hand when they buried the car, as you might imagine. Folks back in 1957 might stop what they were doing to watch somebody change a tire. I think folks had more fun back then but things did get a little dull at times.

The digging up attracted a number of people too, some of whom probably had no idea what they were digging up but wanted to be there to find out. With cars today, being far more expensive than they were in 1957, there is some question as to the kind they would bury today, should they desire to do so.

Maybe a PT Cruiser? That would cause a lot of confusion 50 years from now. That car confuses me already.

I don't know what is planned for the car. I'm almost sure that if I lived in Tulsa, somebody would try to sell it to me. I might even buy it. Believe me; I have bought some real doozies in my time. I had a knack for falling under the spell of used car dealers.

I can hear their spiel now on this Belvedere. "Son," He says. This car has received the best possible care for the past 50 years, protected from the weather and not driven at all."

As for the rust, He might say, "A little WD 40 will take care of that." I'm sure I would be given the used car dealer's best guarantee, 30 days or 30 minutes, whichever comes first.

I have bought a number of lemons in my lifetime but I don't recall ever buying a Plymouth. My specialty was worn out Fords and Chevrolets. I have bought several that should have been buried in Tulsa.

Back in the fifties, I knew a young preacher with a wife and two kids who barely subsisted by preaching at several small rural churches. His only means of transportation was an old Plymouth with more miles on it than a used space shuttle.

One Sunday, he was returning from preaching somewhere south of Brownwood. Just as he topped a hill, a loud clatter came from under the hood. He was trying to assess the damage when a Mexican family in an old beat-up pickup stopped to help.

The man said, "You have troubles Senor, perhaps I can help". He walked over, looked at the large hole in the engine block and said, "My apology, Senor. Many people I can help, but for you, I can do nothing."

Could this be the Plymouth they dug up in Tulsa? I sure don't know.

HUNGRY AS A HOUND DOG
AND DOOMED BY SOUL FOOD

Anybody who plants a garden will agree that January was not the best month for it. It was cold and it was dry. In addition to that, I was struck with something called ill health which was maybe worse than shotgun pellets. I had much rather been quail hunting with the Vice-President.

Thanks to my kids and a nice lady, who in spite of my sometimes bad demeanor, manages to put up with me, and with the help of them all, I now have an onion patch. I mostly supervised but did manage to plant a row myself.

I love green onions and have as long as I can remember. Somewhere out there, somebody in my age group will remember coming home from school, grabbing a piece of leftover cornbread, pulling up 5 or 6 green onions from the garden and having a nice snack before supper.

I also have memories of raw turnips. Dad always planted a turnip patch in the fall, somewhere in the field, usually a different location every year. My brother, sister and I would get off the school bus on a cold wintry day and find one of Dad's turnip patches.

We would pull up those delicious turnips, shake the dirt off and eat them on the way home. Believe it; they would make a freight train take a dirt road.

I recently read where dieticians are trying to get people in the South to give up eating "soul food." They are saying that collard greens, fried chicken, chicken-fried steaks, cream gravy, fried potatoes and beans cooked with salt pork will all lead us straight to an early grave.

I guess I was raised on soul food and wasn't even aware of it. What else is there? What do these dieticians have in mind?

I grew up in an era when nobody had much but we had that, and plenty of it.

I remember sitting down to dinner with most of that stuff on the table, along with corn-on-the cob, tubs of country butter and plenty of fresh black-eyed peas and fried okra and somebody always remarked, "I wonder what the pore folks are having."

Television hadn't been invented at the time so we had no knowledge of cholesterol. Maybe it's a good thing. Nobody had money to buy the pills used to control it. If there had been, the government wouldn't have paid for them.

When I was a kid, the government didn't pay for anything. What we had was up to us to work and get it or raise it ourselves. A hard day's work in the fields cut down on cholesterol considerably, if there was any.

Mama could wring a chicken's neck and have it in a skillet of lard before it knew what happened to it. The dieticians would frown on lard today. Back then, it was pretty hard on chickens but nobody else noticed anything.

There are still a lot of old soul food eaters around and we sometimes antagonize the young folks by driving 30 in a 40 mile an hour zone but we're in no hurry.

Thanks to what the dieticians tell us about eating that soul food, we have been warned about our imminent demise.

BACK IN THE THIRTIES, WE HAD NO MODERN DISEASES AND LITTLE ELSE

According to what I read in the papers and on the internet, there have been large numbers of E-coli cases around the country. This can be a serious disease if not diagnosed and treated properly. In severe cases, it may even cause kidney failure.

Nobody, as far as I know, has any desire for kidney failure, with the possible exception of a few folks over the age of 80 who might welcome it on a temporary basis. At least long enough to get the dishes washed and the dog's bowl filled. A good night's sleep wouldn't hurt anything either. An uninterrupted trip to the grocery store would be nice.

The first outbreak occurred in California and was finally isolated to spinach, grown in a field which apparently was too close to a cow pasture. Cows, they say, carry E-coli in their stomachs. Up to now, I've never seen one in a restaurant and they don't get it. They are, however, known to spread stuff around a little.

The next outbreak occurred in New Jersey, Pennsylvania and a few other places where folks had been dining at Taco Bell restaurants. This outbreak was no fault of Taco Bell and the culprit thought to be green onions or maybe lettuce. It's like picking up a porcupine. You don't know for sure which spine got you.

Getting any disease from green onions is hard for me to believe. I usually plant at least 500 green onions every year but

I don't have a cow on the place. I have never had E-coli either which might prove something.

Back in the thirties when I was growing up, I'm amazed that we didn't have terminal cases of both E-coli and Salmonella. We violated every health rule in the book. There was not a lot we could do about it.

We had no refrigerator and it was a long time before we ever had an icebox which required putting a big chunk of ice in it every week. The icebox brought the temperature down to about 60 degrees, an ideal temperature for growing bacteria. We did the best we could with what we had.

Today, we are told that left-over food should be kept at a certain temperature before eating. That, we couldn't do unless it was put in the oven of our old wood burning stove. The thing might burn a cord of wood before supper. Nobody delivered the stuff—we had to go out and cut it.

What Mama did was spread a tablecloth over what we had left from dinner and we had it for supper. The purpose of the tablecloth was not to keep the food warm but to keep the flies off. Screen doors hadn't been invented then. If they had, we wouldn't have had any.

Screen doors are mostly to attract flies anyway. Put one up and flies come from everywhere. We never worried about where they were at the time but where they had been before they got there.

I guess we must have been immune to nearly everything back then. Other than the usual colds in the winter, we were never sick. We had no insurance and no Medicare. We couldn't get sick.

My brother-in law once came down with Typhoid fever. After the doctor told him what he had and the reason he had it was drinking from a stock tank, he told the doctor; "That can't be right doc, there ain't a cow on my place with Typhoid fever."

Probably none with E-coli either.

WATCHING OUT FOR ALLIGATORS AND MISSING OUT ON BACKPACKS

My friend who lives in Johnson City is known to sit on the front porch and whittle a lot. When he whittles, he gets to thinking about stuff. Last week he said he sees a lot of kids on their way to school, either with a backpack firmly attached to their backs, or dragging one on the sidewalk behind them. He was wondering about those backpacks, like when they originated and what's in them.

I don't whittle myself but he got me to thinking about the things too. I guess I might whittle but my neighbor who used to sharpen my knife "passed away" as we say in Texas, leaving me with a knife that won't cut hot butter, neither of which was his fault.

I know nothing at all about the backpacks used by kids. I always thought they were carried by folks who were foolish enough to climb Mount Everest and freeze their buns off. Then too, the military forces soldiers to use them, one way they have to make them fighting mad. When I was going to school, we had no need for a backpack. We never carried over a couple of books home at a time and in most cases, never opened them.

We did have a tried and proven method for carrying them though. We simply took our belts off and put them around the books. This provided us with a good weapon that we could swing and hit anything in a three foot circle in case we were attacked by lions or tigers. With my geography book, I could hit them with Oklahoma, Missouri or Nebraska. If they were mean enough, I could use California.

From the time I was in the first grade through the third, we lived in a rather remote area of Brown County, bordering on Comanche County. We were not sure what wild animals might occupy that county. Brown County was bad enough.

Every fall before school started, Dad had to take an ax and hack out a trail through the brush to where we caught the school bus. It was about a three mile walk through some rather wild territory.

I always felt sure that rattlesnakes were coiled to strike all along this trail and I could hear all sorts of wild animals rustling in the brush, waiting to attack. This included armadillos, gone mad from being confined in those armored shells, which prevented them from swimming across creeks and crossing the Brazos at Waco.

Our trail took us across a roaring stream called Waterfall Branch. Actually, it only roared in the spring after heavy rains and was supposed to be free of alligators. Still, they might have been there and I didn't know it. We don't know everything. Only recently, a fellow in Houston was given a jail sentence for beating his girlfriend with a three foot alligator which he kept in the bathtub.

I have no idea when the kids started dragging backpacks to school, or what they carry in them. Maybe they carry an extra pair of jeans in case the size 40s they wear fall off and they lose them.

Anyway, I'm too old to worry about minor things like that. I stay busy checking my bathtub for alligators.

I know they're out there somewhere.

BARKING DOGS IN NEW JERSEY AND STEALING IN TEXAS

I just read a story from the Associated Press about a town in New Jersey that is expected to pass an ordinance setting a limit on how long dogs can bark. They will not be allowed to bark more than thirty minutes on two consecutive days.

I can't help but wonder if the dogs are aware of this. If they are not, how and who is going to break the news to them. Dogs, even in New Jersey, as far as I know, can't read.

I admit, what little I know about New Jersey is what I have read, and it might not be right. Isn't New Jersey that State where folks buy their pre-needs from concrete companies?

I once went across a part of New Jersey on a troop train and it looked pretty nice to me. They even had trees growing everywhere and like dogs, I'm fond of trees too.

When I was growing up on a farm near Blanket, we always had a dog or two. They never barked unless they had a good reason to but we had no limit set on how much they could bark if they wanted to.

Dad always had several hounds he kept for recreational purposes; chasing wolves from Salt Mountain to Sidney. When the wolves finally disappeared from our area, he switched to fox chasing, which also required hounds.

I never heard a hound bark. They bayed. They didn't bay unless they were on the trail of something. The rest of the time, they just stayed under the porch and didn't bother anybody. A man who didn't have a few hounds under the porch wasn't well thought of.

We never lived anywhere near a public road so if the dogs barked, it usually meant somebody was coming to visit or the Raleigh man was coming by. Either one was always welcome. It would have been rather unhandy if, like the town in New Jersey, we'd had some kind of law limiting when the dogs could bark.

Company could have slipped up on us and we wouldn't even know they were there. Even in the country, nobody wants that to happen. Depending on who the company was, a man might want to put on a pair of clean overalls.

Back in the thirties when times were regarded as being hard, folks visited a lot. One of the reasons for visiting being that like today, misery loved company. Folks wanted to see if their neighbors had about the same stuff to eat as they did. If they had anything different, they'd borrow some of it.

Unlike New Jersey, there was no limit on visiting or barking or borrowing. Back then, stealing was practically unheard of. If a neighbor had something that another neighbor needed, he just borrowed it.

Of course, if something was borrowed, it was to be returned. I knew one fellow who had a reputation for borrowing stuff and never returning it. It finally got so bad that folks wouldn't loan him anything but a tom cat and it would come home on its own.

Anyway, with every dog on the place being allowed unlimited barking, it was pretty hard to steal something. Hardly anybody had anything worth stealing anyhow.

It seems to me that today folks have more dogs in town than we had in the country. They do bark a lot but it does little good. Maybe we should just let the dogs bark and limit the hours the thieves can steal.

It might even work in New Jersey.

BE CAREFUL WHAT YOU DO.
BIG BROTHER HAS A CELL PHONE

I have to admit, I get a big kick out of reading the police reports in the Bulletin each week. I can't help but wonder where all of these weird people came from and I sympathize with the policemen who have to answer these calls. Some of this stuff is unbelievable.

Having been a member of the police force back in the fifties, I'm relieved that all those folks lived somewhere else then. Our biggest problem working the night shift was boredom. It was difficult to stay awake. There were no bars then, nobody was using dope and cell phones hadn't been invented.

Of course, we had the usual domestic disturbances known as "Maggie and Jiggs" calls. Maggie would hit Jiggs with a skillet and Jiggs would call the police. We reached the point where we all knew them both well.

With all the cell phones around it is hard for a man to get by with anything these days.

A good old boy, driving on one of our endless Texas highways where traffic is visible for 20 miles in both directions decides to violate the open container law and pop the cap on a cold beer. He takes one last look front and back and sees nothing coming.

But—he didn't look right or left. A farmer plowing his field reaches for his trusty cell phone and blows the whistle on him. He wonders where that State Trooper came from. There is hardly any place in a car or pickup to hide a half can of beer.

The State Legislature passed over 600 new laws last year but not one against cell phones. I have to admit, I have one myself and in the 2 years I have had it, I think I have used it 3 times. All 3 times, I woke up some little old lady from her afternoon nap. The numbers on the thing are just not big enough for me to hit.

During my tenure with the Police Department on the night shift, I think my partner and I had only one big arrest. Somebody reported seeing a thief steal a car from a car lot on North Main. My partner, who was about half psychic and possibly a little psycho to boot drove out the Bangs highway at a high speed and we caught the car thief before he ever got in high gear.

He was duly arrested, handcuffed and placed in the lockup. In court, we both testified and pointed the thief out to the jury. He was sitting with his defense attorney and I noticed that both had a smirk on their faces.

We had to sit there and listen to the judge turn our one big arrest loose. We had charged him with stealing the wrong model car. Well—it was a little dark out that night and a 1950 and a 1951 Pontiac do look a lot alike in the dark. They do in the daylight too, for that matter.

Just this week, I read that a woman was charged with driving 80 miles an hour on Austin Avenue in a 35 mile an hour zone. Since I live on Austin Avenue, I thought that was about the average speed folks are driving there. About six each day, I get to see some really good races that compare to any NASCAR race. I don't even have to leave home to do it. The fact is, I have trouble leaving home at all.

I can't get out of my driveway.

BEAUTY IS IN THE EYE OF THE BEHOLDER WHO SOMETIMES HAS POOR EYESIGHT

I never have believed in "arranged" marriages. The couples involved often have no idea of what they're fixin' to get. Yet, in several different cultures around the world, this is still happening.

I just read about one case where a fellow was convinced that he should marry the cousin of the arranging couple who lived in a country I won't mention. I'm not going to get into that.

The fellow they were trying to marry off, a former resident of that country, now lives in this country and besides being good-looking, also speaks perfect English. He was assured that the cousin in question was also "Attractive and spoke good English." The picture he received was rather blurry, and appears to have been taken against a background of junked cars in a wrecking yard.

None of what he was told was true. The fellow was out a fortune on phone calls and even paid the cost of a passport which, these days is not cheap.

Finally, he flew to the country in question to finalize the marriage. More expense was involved, including the airline ticket and other expenses like hotel rooms and food.

It turned out that his prospective bride, to use an old country expression, "Was so ugly she had to slip up on the water bucket to get a drink." She not only had protruding bad teeth and a bad complexion but didn't speak a word of English.

She had one good point though. She could eat watermelon through a picket fence.

The old boy is suing for $200,000 to try to get some of his money back and for "emotional distress." It seems to me that he has a good case. At least he learned one important lesson. Women everywhere are not all pretty.

Beauty, they say, is in the eye of the beholder. All beholders don't have good eyesight.

My Hill Country correspondent recently told me that they held a beauty contest in the county where he lives and nobody won. The contestants were all too ugly. I'm not going to reveal the name of that county either.

There are advantages, however, to having an ugly wife. She is not likely to find some old boy to run off with, leaving you with a mortgage and two small kids.

She is not likely to hang out at bars while you're at work, get car-jacked or kidnapped. It is perfectly safe for her to take long walks through a rough part of town and not get molested. She can even walk through Central Park in New York at night or ride the subways and be perfectly safe.

Still, it is just human nature to want perfection. Nobody ever goes into a florist shop and asks for a dozen ugly roses. We buy the best looking pork chops and steaks in the meat market. A farmer who goes to market buys the prettiest pig in the pen.

We have been programmed for most of our lives by Hollywood, TV and magazines that beauty is what counts. That is not necessarily true. We are not all movie star material. Mama always told me, "Son, there is a lid for every pot somewhere."

Even Hugh Hefner, the fellow who brought us Playboy Magazine and is now older than rope still keeps a bevy of pretty girls at his mansion. All it takes is money.

One fact we have to accept—we can't all do it.

BIG FOOT, IVORY-BILLED WOODPECKERS AND UFO'S

A prominent ornithologist is of the opinion that the ivory-billed woodpecker observed last year in Arkansas, believed to be extinct since 1920, was just a common pileated variety. I don't know and I have no intention of wading in a snake-infested swamp to look for one.

Besides, don't they call them peckerwoods in Arkansas? I heard that somewhere.

I see a lot of woodpeckers around here. I think our variety is the "stainless-steel-billed" kind. I saw one pecking on a concrete utility pole once. Maybe he was just as confused as I am about these things.

Over in East Texas and Louisiana folks have recently been seeing what is being called "Big Foot." This unidentified "thing" is described as being from 6 to 8 feet tall, covered with hair, walks upright like a farmer crossing a plowed field and sometimes screams like a woman who finds a grey hair. They are also called Sasquatch for some reason. Maybe the Indians called them that.

Folks in Washington and Oregon have been seeing them for years. In fact, the first UFOs were observed in Washington State in 1947. That started the UFO sightings.

Up to now, no remains or bones of the Big Foot have ever been found. Since they have been seen worldwide for a hundred years, they obviously have a long lifespan.

A fellow I know who resides down in the Texas Hill Country and whose veracity has never been fully explored told me he once saw two of these Sasquatch, a male and a female, one night on a country road near Luckenbach. "The female," He said, "was holding up the rear of a pickup while the male changed a tire. She was screaming at him to hurry up as her back was hurting."

I have, over the years, seen some strange sights at Luckenbach myself but nothing like that.

In 1986, I had been camping in the Big Bend National Park and on the way home; I decided to cut through from north of Study Butte on a ranch road which came out at Persimmon Gap just inside the park. I found the road to be in bad condition and it was dark when I got through it.

I decided to spend the night in a roadside park between Marathon and Fort Stockton. The park was in a remote area, located off the highway in a grove of pinyon trees.

I made the bed down in my VW camper and my Chihuahua dog and I went to bed. About 2:30, I was awakened by a bright light. The entire area was lit up like daylight. I pulled the curtain aside and looked through the rear window.

A large silver-colored conveyance was parked directly behind my camper. I was in the process of putting on my pants and boots to investigate when the light went out and the thing left, as silently as it came. My dog never became excited at all. We went back to sleep.

The next morning, I checked the ground behind my camper without finding any sign that anything had been there. The only thing that I noticed was a lot of filmy substance on the pinyon trees which resembled spider webs. This quickly dissipated in the morning sun. I didn't tell anybody about what I saw for two years.

What it was, I still don't know, but it was there and I saw it—up close.

Maybe those folks are really seeing Big Foot and Ivory-billed woodpeckers.

Who knows?

MY BISCUITS GO A LONG WAY
BUT NOT FAR ENOUGH

I'm fond of biscuits and gravy. Since I live alone, if I have any, it's strictly up to me to make it. I do reasonably well with gravy but my biscuits are a total flop. I have tried various recipes folks have sent me but have had no success yet.

My biscuits would be perfect for serving in jails. They might even contribute to the inmates swearing off crime for good. Anyway, the jailer wouldn't even have to open the jail door. My biscuits would slide right under it.

Mama made the best biscuits I ever had. She mixed them in a wooden bowl and kept flour in it at all times. When she made biscuits, she would add buttermilk and the other ingredients needed which I don't remember. I wish I did. I guess I thought that Mama would live forever.

Her biscuits didn't fall apart like biscuits do today. A kid could stick his finger in one, pour it full of syrup or honey and have a good snack.

Sometimes, a few were left over from breakfast and they were good for about two days. On the third day, a bull could be knocked down at fifty feet with one. They were also handy to keep in the car in case of a flat tire. One under each wheel kept the car from rolling off the jack.

I remember Guich Koock telling about an old cedar chopper's wife who revealed to him her secret for making her famous biscuits. "Don't ever," She said, "Use more than a mouthful of buttermilk" I don't remember Mama ever doing that. Up to now, I haven't tried it either.

I don't know if the success of her biscuits was caused by using the wooden mixing bowl or by the flour she used. Dad bought our flour in 50 pound sacks to save several trips to town to get more. Also, a flour sack that size would make two pairs of underwear with "Bewley's Best" across the seat instead of "Fruit of the Loom."

Nearly everybody owned a pair but we all wore pants back then that fit and they didn't show. Today, you're likely to see more underwear on the streets than on the shelves in J.C. Penney. Mama wouldn't have approved of that.

Sometime in the eighties, I bought a pedal steel guitar. It was a complicated musical instrument which used pedals and knee levers to change chords and get special effects. It was much different from the guitar I had been playing.

I really didn't know what to do with it so I went to school in Nashville to be taught by a professional.

The first thing I discovered about Nashville was that it was a biscuits and gravy town. Every restaurant in town had a sign outside advertising this specialty. We were all housed at the school and had a kitchen to cook in if we so desired. Directly across the highway from the school was one of those biscuits and gravy restaurants. What more would anybody want?

One kid from Amarillo ate biscuits and gravy three times a day. He thought he was in heaven. I would assume that anybody from Amarillo would think the Gobi desert was heaven, with or without biscuits and gravy.

I managed to learn a little about playing my pedal steel but nothing at all about what I really wanted to learn.

How to make those good biscuits like Mama made.

BOMBING OUT ON
USED CAR DEALS

When I finished flying my allocated 50 missions as a ball turret gunner on a B-17 bomber in Italy, I had dreams of returning home, buying a nice new car from my savings and driving the thing day and night.

Prior to my military service, I had never owned a car. I meant to make up for a lot of lost time. I figured I needed a car bad. What I wound up with was a bad car. I was not aware that few new cars were being manufactured during the war.

The few cars that the dealers got were already on hold for the folks who were forced to stay on the home front making money while I fought the war for less than $200 a month.

It didn't seem fair to me. Besides getting shot at by the Germans on a regular basis, I had helped entertain half the girls in Italy and assisted the grape growers in selling their product.

I was forced to make my choice from what the used car dealers had on hand, known as "junkers." In those days, to use an old Biblical quotation," A used car dealer could no more go through the eye of a needle than a camel could go to heaven." Or something like that.

I finally located an older model Ford for only $450.00. The dealer told me it had been driven by an elderly woman who only used it to take her canary bird to the mountains in the summer. Obviously, she had made a lot of trips and had a canary bird older than I was.

The Ford did have the necessary essentials I was looking for—a seat, a steering wheel, a clutch, brake and accelerator. I assumed it had an engine though I didn't raise the hood and look. I was anxious to hit the road. I found out quickly that it was equipped with a 60 horsepower engine. Both Ford and I had made a mistake.

It would do 40 miles an hour on the road with everything hanging out. I once got in a race with a man on a bulldozer and was doing fine until he raised the blade and left me in the dust. Bugs accumulated on the back window, trying to pass.

It had another problem that I didn't know about. It used a quart of oil every 25 miles. I thought about all of those oil refineries I had bombed in Germany and the Balkan countries and hoped they had been repaired. The good part was that with all the smoke the car put out, mosquitoes in Blanket were nonexistent.

All this transpired in 1945 and the war with Japan was not yet over and employment was easy to come by. I obtained a good job with the Santa Fe railroad for $4.75 an hour and bought a later model used car, trading the junker in on it. I laughed all the way home knowing that I was getting even with one used car dealer.

A short time later I learned that I had been taken to the cleaners again. The dealer had put sawdust in the rear end to muffle the sound of the worn out gears that howled like a chainsaw hitting a knothole.

Finally, I bought my first new car—a Volkswagen, made by the very people I had spent part of 1944 and 1945 dropping bombs on. There must be a lesson there somewhere. I was happy if they were.

BUILDING 700 MILES OF FENCE
TO STOP THE CHICKEN PLUCKERS

The Congress has voted to build a 700 mile fence on the border between the United States and Mexico. It seems that there may be a couple of problems. They haven't appropriated enough money to build it with and as far as I know, they don't know who is going to build it.

Labor is scarce along the border. A fellow in South Texas has 500 acres of onions ready to harvest and is unable to find anybody to harvest them. Bo Pilgrim in Pittsburg, Texas, one of the largest chicken processor in the country, is concerned that he may have to scald and pluck his own chickens.

He has scads of money and although it may, or may not buy happiness, it won't buy chicken pluckers. The chicken pluckers are all doing construction in Dallas and Houston. Construction work has always paid more than plucking chickens or pulling up onions.

According to a story from the Christian Science Monitor, written by Patrik Jonsson, on Labor Day, agents from the Homeland Security raided the small town of Stillmore, Georgia where a plant processed chickens among other things and arrested 120 chicken Pluckers and 300 more escaped to Kentucky, or the tall timbers, turning the town into what one resident termed a "ghost town."

As dark approached, few lights were burning in the windows of the town, the story indicated. I assume that front yards were empty of cars all over town. Bo Pilgrim, it seems, will not be alone in his quest for chicken Pluckers.

I still remember back during the Depression if anybody wanted to earn a little Christmas money for their family, they plucked turkeys at the Southwest Poultry Association located east of the Courthouse. Nobody wanted to do that either, but they did. Nobody was constructing anything.

As for fence building, I have dug a few post holes and stretched some wire myself. It is not easy work It would be even harder along the border where the ground is hard as a rock. Actually, I think it is rock.

President Fox of Mexico is against building the fence. Most of us, I think, would be against supermarkets building a fence between us and the Blue Bell ice cream. It amounts to about the same thing.

The illegal immigrants in our country send billions of dollars back to Mexico boosting the economy there and President Fox likes that. Mexico is not a poor country by far. They just don't distribute the wealth among the poor. They send them north to pluck chickens and pull onions.

My correspondent in the Hill Country tells me that his family was so "pore" they couldn't even afford screens to attract flies. My family fit that category too but we never even thought of going to Mexico. I guess we didn't know where Mexico was.

A few folks who had any kind of transportation other than a wagon and team did go to California to pick grapes. I guess California had no chickens to pluck. Anyway, it's easier to pluck grapes than chickens.

There is some question as to whether the fence will ever be built. Cost is estimated to be in the billions and it might not be effective. After all, ladders can be built in Mexico a lot cheaper than fences here.

It may turn out that in order to get the fence built, we may have to hire the very people to build it that we are trying to keep out.

Now that would be a revolting development.

CELL PHONES, TREE THAT SPOUTS WATER AND GREEN CHUNKS FROM THE SKY

I read all sorts of strange happenings in the news on the internet. Some of is even stranger than the events we have happening here. Actually, I thought we held the record.

According to an Associated Press story, a lady in San Antonio has a Red Oak tree in her yard that has suddenly started running water from the trunk. Nobody, including sources from the Texas Forestry Service and the Edwards Aquifer Authority can solve the mystery.

The lady's son is collecting the water and putting it the refrigerator to drink. He says it tastes better than the water out of the faucet. It has been my experience that nearly anything tastes better than water out of a faucet unless you have developed a taste for chlorine.

The woman in whose yard the tree is growing thinks the water has curative powers. She says her insurance man put some on a spider bite and the welt immediately disappeared. She rubbed some on her aching ankles and found immediate relief.

It might be best if she keeps quiet about that. She may find hordes of folks tearing down her fence to get to that water.

This reminds me of something I read about a number of years ago when a farmer in the Midwest found a large chunk of frozen green material in his field.

Being somewhat mystified and not having any idea what it was, he took it to the local feed store where all the experts hang out. They chipped off pieces and everybody tasted it trying to determine just what the mystery item might be. It seemed to have a slight taste of alcohol.

Finally, with the help of an outside source, it was determined that it was a large piece of frozen material that had somehow fallen from the toilet holding tank of a high flying commercial airliner.

There was a decided jump in the sale of mouthwash products all over town.

I too, have a large Red Oak growing in my back yard. If it suddenly started spouting water from the trunk, I would be tickled pink, considering the size of my water bill.

However, I would not consider drinking the stuff until I found out how far my tree is from the sewer line.

Another story I read from the Associated Press told of three fellows from Dallas who was in Caro, Michigan, visiting Wal-Mart stores in the early morning hours buying those prepaid cell phones, all they could get. As far as I'm concerned, even one is too many.

Since this appeared to a rather suspicious act, the checker called the police. A check of the van they were driving revealed that they had 1,000 cell phones. These phones enable one to make calls that are untraceable and are used by terrorists.

The three are currently cooling their heels in jail while the FBI makes an investigation which includes their being involved in terrorism. Not one of the three is allowed to have one of their 1,000 cell phones in their cell.

Their relatives are accusing the law officers of "ethnic profiling."

If that is what it takes to catch terrorists, I'm all for it. At least, maybe that will be 1,000 cell phones that won't be stuck in somebody's ear while I'm trying to check out at the grocery.

I always think they're talking to me.

CREDIT CARDS, MORTGAGES AND COTTON PATCHES

My lady-friend often tells me that I'm "tighter than the bark on a tree." I fully admit to it but I do take her out to eat every Thursday night. I tell her she can have anything she wants, within reason. Of course, I caution her to forget those baby back ribs. The restaurants think a lot of those. Besides, there's not a whole lot of meat on them anyhow.

She reminds me rather often that she worked for a funeral home for thirty years and never once saw a hearse with a trailer hitch. She says that if I plan to take it with me, I must know a way she hasn't heard of.

"You need to buy a new pickup" She says. "You've had that one now for years."

"That pickup is fine, I tell her. It hasn't missed a lick in 15 years and it takes me to the grocery, the library and the doctor's office. I don't go anywhere else except to your house."

"Well, at least," She said, "you ought to consider me when you park that thing in front of my house." "What do the neighbors think?"

There is a reason for my frugality. I still remember when a dollar and a half meant a full day chopping cotton in somebody else's field or dragging a cotton sack at a dollar a hundred pounds. Few people today have any idea how much cotton it takes to fill a cotton sack, or how hot it was in that cotton patch.

My short-term memory may be getting bad but I still remember not very long ago when a chicken-fried steak was $2.95, not $8.95. It is the same steak and the same gravy. No doubt, the waitress is still paid the same.

My lady-friend says, "You need to give the waitress a tip." "I did give her a tip" I say. "I told her not to play with matches and stay out of cotton patches and corn fields."

Sometimes I think I don't belong anywhere. I grew up in one era and lived so long I'm in another. I have lived in both the twentieth and twenty-first Centuries. I'm not sure which one is the worst.

Back during the Depression, we had to scratch for everything we had and we didn't have much but what we had wasn't mortgaged to the hilt. It is still hard, even today, to mortgage nothing. You can, however, mortgage your soul.

I see those ads on TV where a friendly man wants to pay off your first mortgage, your second mortgage, your credit card debts and probably your gambling debts, if you have any, and save you "hundreds of dollars every month." All he wants is your soul and your house.

If you already have a first mortgage, a second mortgage and a big credit card debt, you may have already lost your soul. Obviously, you never picked cotton.

If you have a pocket full of credit cards along with a new SUV and have a fondness for baby-back ribs and Angus steaks, it doesn't take long to get between a rock and a hard place.

With the "hundreds of dollars" you save by dealing with that friendly man, you can buy a little place in the country and raise cotton.

Then, if you're careful, you might live as long as I have.

COAL OIL, CHEAP WHISKEY, GRAVEL AND BEDBUGS

Along with terrorists, bridge rail damage and crime, we now have something else to worry about. According to the Associated Press, the large news service that keeps up with such stuff, we now have an infestation of bedbugs in 35 states and spreading. They are even found in Iowa, apparently carried there during the Democratic caucuses.

Most folks today are not familiar with bedbugs, a small pest having the appearance of an apple seed which crawls into your bed and feasts on your blood during the night. The US, being free of these pests for years has now been invaded again.

Since our borders being mostly open to any pest that walks, flies, drives, or swims, we can expect nothing less.

Back in the late twenties and thirties, bedbugs were more common. The only recourse was to wipe everything down with coal oil. Bedbugs hated coal oil. Kids in those days hated coal oil too. It was often used to cure the croup by tying a coal oil soaked rag around the neck of the affected kid. Wearing this thing to school was no fun at all.

In those days, coal oil was a cure for most everything including rattlesnake bites along with bedbugs. Also in those days, everybody had bed springs in addition to bedbugs. Wiping a set of bed springs down with coal oil was an unbelievable chore, but that's where the bedbugs spent their days. Only the nights were spent on their hosts.

Bedbugs, they say, carry no diseases, but then and now may bring about a serious case of the vapors in women.

Back in the thirties when bedbugs were more common, another cure other than coal oil was discovered by the drinking class. Pouring whiskey mixed with small gravel around the house would do the trick too. The bugs got drunk and stoned each other to death. Of course, whiskey was more expensive than coal oil which sold for a dime a gallon. Still, a man had to do what a man had to do and still does.

These days, we have a problem. Whiskey is much more expensive than it was back then, being heavily taxed and a gallon of coal oil is impossible to find. Kerosene or diesel fuel might work but is still untried.

According to the Associated Press, we still have at least 15 states that are bedbug free. Of the 35 states infected, they only mentioned Iowa and Florida. California may remain bedbug free. They have about all the trouble they need.

Texas too might have a chance. We already have chiggers, ticks, fire ants and an abundant supply of stray cats. We don't deserve bedbugs this time around. We already had them once. Believe me, once is enough even if we don't use bed springs now.

Still, it might be a good idea to lay in a supply of cheap whiskey and order a pile of gravel in case they do eventually get here.

If it doesn't work, we can always drink the whiskey and stay up all night.

COME FLY WITH ME, OR WITHOUT ME, OR WHATEVER

I recently read where two people were suing Southwest Airlines for causing "embarrassment and humiliation" for making them pay for two seats because they didn't fit into one. One person, best I remember, was a California resident and the other from Oregon.

Southwest Airlines has had this "obesity" rule in place for some time and is strictly for the comfort of other passengers who are slim and trim and fit. By "fit" I mean they fit in the seat. I see nothing wrong with that. There are folks, maybe through no fault of their own who don't.

What little flying I do is always done with Southwest. The flight attendants are nice and on occasions, they sing and tell jokes. The flights are always on time and the price is right. I like that. Furthermore, nobody is likely to get obese on their planes as all they serve is a small packet of peanuts.

So far, I have never had to fly with anybody who overflowed into my seat. One time, I did sit next to a couple who were wet to their knees and were devouring a big sack of fried chicken. I suspected they might have just recently waded across the Rio Grande. They ate fried chicken all the way from Austin to Phoenix.

I was nice to them though and even tried to help them open the window to throw out the bones. We never did get it open.

On one occasion, my son booked a flight for me from the internet on a different airline. We spent more time at the terminal and on the tarmac than we did in the air.

At Phoenix, after the passengers were all loaded, we sat there for 30 minutes.

Finally, the pilot came on the intercom and said, "You folks scrunch down as much as you can back there so I can see. I've got to back this big sucker out of here."

Finally, we got in the air. Then, our pilot once again got on the intercom with further instructions. "All you obese folks move up toward the front and you skinny ones get in the back. I'm having a little trouble trimming this big sucker out."

Then, about thirty minutes into the flight, the pilot came on again. "If you folks on the left side of the plane will look out the window, you may either see the Grand Canyon or Lake Tahoe, which seems to be dry as a bone. If you see either one, we're lost."

I knew from experience that the crew on Southwest frequently joked a lot but this one, I wasn't sure about. Apparently they did. I did notice a lot of the passengers making frequent trips to the restrooms. I didn't go myself, being glued to my seat. At least, I hoped it was glue.

We finally arrived in Austin, safe and sound. I noticed the flight attendants were still with us. I was worried. I hadn't seen them since we left Phoenix. Were they flying the plane?

It was obvious that whoever was flying was thoughtful enough to lower the landing gear as it was not necessary to turn on the afterburners to taxi to the terminal. That sometimes happens you know.

There are times, strictly for entertainment purposes; I may take certain liberties with the truth. I learned this from the national news media and various politicians.

It works for them, so why not me?

COME WITH ME INTO THE CASBAH OR WHATEVER

I hope that somebody at the Brownwood Bulletin doesn't give me a Performance Review like the City Council gave the City Manager. Like him, I'm afraid I would be "in the wind," a term used by cops when they have a perpetrator they can't find. No severance pay either.

I'm sure that a performance review would reveal the fact that I have been passing myself off as a writer for several years, and I'm not. Actually, I never claimed to be. I have no degrees in anything and my only college experience was attending Daniel Baker for two or three semesters following WWII.

Everybody seemed to be a lot younger than me and I felt like an illegitimate son at a family reunion. After all, I was already a world traveler and had been shot at in a bomber over several foreign countries. I had knowledge about things the young students would never have. I do admit that none of it would contribute to my ability to earn a living.

I had explored the Casbahs, both in Marrakesh and Tunis in North Africa at great risk to life and limb after having been warned not to go there. Never tell a 19 year old not to go anywhere.

I guess what contributed the most to my leaving college was they wanted me to stand guard on the bell tower all night to keep the Howard Payne students from getting the bell.

Somebody eventually did steal the bell and I may be blamed because I was no longer there and didn't guard it. It didn't matter anyway because Daniel Baker ended up being a part of Howard Payne, bell and all.

Another student and I occasionally walked to a cafe on Austin Avenue. We passed by some fellows digging a ditch. The other student told me, "If we don't finish this school, that's what we'll be doing."

We both quit and he was half right. He wound up digging ditches for a local plumber but due to my vast knowledge of the Casbahs in Marrakesh and Tunis, I didn't.

The reason I went there was that I still remembered a movie I had seen where Charles Boyer told Hedy Lamar. "Come with me into the Casbah." I wanted to see if they were still there. I was always fond of Hedy but if they were, I never found them.

What I did find was a bunch of Arabs who seemed to be dead-set on doing me some bodily harm. I couldn't understand a word they were saying but I don't think they wanted me to guard their bell tower.

Somebody said, "It is good to know what the enemy is doing but better to know what he can do." I had a pretty good idea of that. Taking the advice Mama gave me, I outran the whole bunch.

She said, "Son, if you can't whip somebody, try to outrun them."

I never got much advice from Dad. He thought I was smart enough to know what to do in a difficult situation. During his entire life, he always managed to do exactly what he wanted to do. He thought I should too. However, he wasn't familiar with the Casbahs in North Africa.

My advice to anybody in college is to stay there. Guard the bell tower if you have to. You might actually get my job one day. A performance review might send me packing.

I won't last forever anyhow.

COOKING CABBAGE ALL DAY AND LIVING IN THE GOOD OLD DAYS

I cooked some cabbage and ham the other day. I like cabbage. I remember when I was a kid, Mama would put a pot of cabbage on the old wood burning cook stove, stoke it up good with wood and when we could smell it all the way to the cotton patch, we knew that supper was ready. All we needed was a pan of cornbread.

I didn't cook my cabbage quite that way for a couple of reasons. I have no cotton patch or wood stove and I was happy being without either.

I frequently have people my age tell me, "Them was the good old days." Maybe they were in some respects but they and I all know different.

I'm glad I grew up in that era. We all learned a lot of good things, like respect for our elders, honesty and the difference between good and bad and right and wrong. We also found out that hard work never killed anybody.

Our only medications were Vicks salve, aspirin, Black Draught and coal oil. It didn't kill us but I was convinced the Black Draught would.

There were a lot of things we have today that we didn't have then. Nobody was hooked on drugs and thieves were few and far between. Actually, few people had anything worth stealing. We had never heard of carjacking. Can you even imagine somebody carjacking a Model T. Ford?

The Brown County jail hardly ever had over two occupants and they were regulars, recovering from a Saturday night binge. Today, all of our jails are full.

The sheriff would frequently drive through Blanket, mostly for political purposes. The closer it got to the election, the more often he appeared. It was also his duty to buy every kid hanging around the drug store a double-dip ice cream cone. I guess that's where lobbying first started. It worked, and didn't cost much.

I still remember when a fellow came out from Brownwood looking for some easy money and broke into Ernest Allen' drug store. All he got was fifteen cents that Ernest, who couldn't see well, left in the cash register. While he was there, he made himself a vanilla milk shake and left his fingerprints on the glass. I heard the judge gave him 5 years.

Then, our country went to war for good reason with Germany and Japan, Camp Bowie was being built and the hard times slowly got better. Thousands of young men, me included, went off to war. We won the war in Europe with thousands of ground troops and hundreds of bombers like the B-17s and B-24s.

Strangely enough, the war with Japan was eventually won with only one bomber, a B-29 named the Enola Gay and a whopper of a bomb that nobody had ever heard of, built in secret at Los Alamos, New Mexico.

President Truman who gave the order to drop it always took the blame for what he did and said, "The buck stops here." Today, it would stop in the Senate.

We still have wars in progress, in Iraq, in Afghanistan and one in Washington between the Democrats and Republicans. Two of them we may eventually win but I'm not sure about the one in Washington.

We still have one B-29 left in flying condition which belongs to the Commemorative Air Force at Midland and a lot of those whopper bombs but I guess we'll have to win that war at the ballot boxes.

Think about it and do the best you can for us all.

COOKING, DOORKNOBS, CHICKEN SNAKES AND CHINESE AILMENT

After living alone for the past 30 years, I have discovered that it is much better being called to dinner than having to cook it myself. Dinner to me is not one of those candlelight and wine things that some folks might have in mind that happens in homes featured in Good Housekeeping. At my house, if it happens at all, it would be somewhere around noon or maybe as late as two. I'm not good at good housekeeping either.

On the other hand, there are times when I don't have anything to cook or don't have an urge to. There is never a surprise involved when I do cook as I know what I have and exactly what I paid for it. I go to the grocery stores regularly and hunt diligently for something to cook that I'm experienced in cooking. That doesn't leave me much of a choice.

I can cook chili, meatloaf, pinto beans, collard greens and fried potatoes. I also cook Chicken Fettuccini with Alfredo Sauce, my low cholesterol dish.

I still spend a lot of my time in stores looking for something edible. I once found something called "Country-fried steak." I bought it since it was already cooked and required only a short time in the oven. I'm still trying to figure out what it was and the country of origin.

It is pretty easy for an old country boy like me to find stuff in stores that nobody would eat. Up to now, I think I have tried all of it. I gave up on frozen foods a long time ago. I have never found anything that was frozen that has any taste when it is unfrozen.

A week or so ago, one of my readers brought me a large sack of poke salat greens which he said he remembered me writing about. I was glad to get them, not having a good mess of poke salat in a long time. There is some controversy over just what a "mess" of anything consists of. When I cook it, there is no doubt.

After washing the greens, I placed them in a pan with some chopped red onion and bacon grease and simmered for about twenty minutes. They brought back a lot of memories and the taste was like I remembered.

My readers are always sending me stuff but not all of what they send is good to eat. I once wrote about taking all the door knobs off our doors to put in the hen's nest to kill the chicken snakes. We had used up all the artificial eggs designed for this purpose.

The snake would normally swallow an egg whole, and then crush it. The artificial eggs or the doorknobs wouldn't crush. This caused a problem the Chinese have a name for. They call it "Hung Chow." It was fatal to chicken snakes.

Shortly after I wrote about this, a lady sent me two white doorknobs and I don't have a chicken on the place. I wish I did.

Another time, I wrote about a medication Mama insisted I take when I was a kid called "Baby Percy." This stuff would, no doubt, cure the Chinese disease. The firm that has been making this medication for a hundred years sent me 6 bottles. It is now called "Percy Medicine." I guess they changed the name to expand the market. Babies worldwide should be celebrating.

I have always appreciated the stuff my readers occasionally send me and the many suggestions I get about what to write.

I could have used a little help today.

ASK YOUR DOCTOR ABOUT THAT SOAP IN MOTEL BATHROOMS

Scientists and medical biologists, those folks who wear white coats and do weird experiments in hopes of finding a new cure for something or other, have just discovered that Gila Monster spit will control blood sugar of diabetics. I just read that on the internet so it must be true. I almost never doubt that stuff.

Neither does anybody else apparently. Somebody started the rumor on the internet just recently that the Texas Legislature had passed a law against cell phones in automobiles. Cell phone users statewide were about to go on the warpath. Unfortunately, it was not so.

Anyway, to get back to the Gila Monster spit; getting one to spit may be a problem. They hardly ever spit. They all live in Arizona where it is so hot and dry that the residents don't spit either. It takes awhile out there to work up a good spit even when they want to. Snuff sales out there go way down in the summer as the users are forced to swallow the juice, if they manage to work up a little.

I have wondered for years why these scientists don't do a study of buzzard's stomachs and find out why they don't get a classic case of E.Coli after every meal. After all, they don't eat anything but rotten meat and the riper it is the better. They are known to throw up a lot, so maybe they do get it. A buzzard can smell a dead cow from 10 miles away.

Most people have the same ability except politicians who can't smell anything but money.

I remember one time several years ago when a truck, hauling a load of dead animals, accidentally dropped a load of choice cuts from the intersection of highway 183 to the Bayou bridge. Drivers slipped and slid through that smelly stuff for hours until the company was notified and came out and cleaned it up. Car washes did a booming business for days.

Somebody said they rendered the stuff down and made those small bars of soap found in motel bathrooms. Like the "no cell phone law" in cars, this may have been just a rumor. I sure hope so.

We can thank those scientists and biologists however, because over the years they have come up with hundreds of new medications with numerous side effects which the ads on TV say, "Ask your doctor." This is one reason for the long wait to see a doctor these days. There are bunches of people in his office asking him about these medications.

Maybe there are some folks in there asking him why buzzards don't get E.Coli. Good question.

When I go to a doctor, I always let him ask the questions. After all, he is the expert—not me. So far, not one doctor has ever asked me about buzzards or Gila Monsters. I guess it's a good thing too. I just plain don't know.

I know the answer to a lot of questions and it is irritating that nobody ever asks me those.

Maybe one day they will.

WE LAUGHED AS WE LIVED IN FAME OR WENT DOWN IN FLAMES

Back in 1943 when I was taking basic training in the Army Air Corp at Sheppard Field near Wichita Falls, it seemed they played the Air Force song constantly. I was impressed by it. I liked the part about "Living in Fame, or Going Down in Flames." Being 18 years old, going down in flames didn't bother me. I was convinced that only old people died anyway. I knew nothing at all about war.

When I arrived at the 97th Bomb Group near Foggia, Italy in August of 1944 and flew my first mission as a ball turret gunner on a B-17, I got a quick lesson in war. I was no longer enthusiastic about "going down in flames." I no longer cared about fame either. What I wanted to do most was to go back to Blanket, Texas.

War, I found out, was a serious thing. However, we were all stuck with it until we flew 50 missions, win, lose, or draw. We decided there was no use in being morose about it so we found humor where we could and laughed at ourselves and each other.

On one mission, our pilot got hit in the ear flap on his steel helmet by a large piece of flak which flattened it as we say in Texas, "flat as a fritter." We all laughed about that, with the exception of the pilot, who didn't.

On another mission where the temperature hovered around 65 degrees below zero in the unpressurized and unheated plane, our bombardier was stricken with a bad case of diarrhea. Unlike the TV commercial where a fellow in a hot tub with two gorgeous women gets it, the poor bombardier had no place to run and no place to hide. He had no Imodium either.

He finally found an empty K-ration box, but the really bad part was that he had to remove his heavy flying suit and the heated suit under it before the box was of any use. He was taking a chance on a bad case of hypothermia, not to mention frostbite in tender places. Somehow, he managed to survive that part but it was months before he survived the laughter.

Since he and the navigator were the only ones in the nose of the plane, there was only one witness. Naturally, the minute we returned from the mission the navigator spread it all over the squadron. (No pun intended.)

There were numerous instances that happened on missions providing us with something to laugh about. There were other times when we watched our comrades blown out of the sky where there was nothing to laugh about.

On one mission, I watched a B-17 hit by flak going down fast. I saw the crew bail out. One sight I'll never forget was one kid who came within 50 feet of my turret in the middle of heavy flak and waved as he went by. That boy had more guts than a slaughterhouse. I hope he made it.

We all found out that war wasn't funny but a little humor made it a little easier. Maybe we were heroes and maybe we were not. If we were, there were two million of us.

We were not escorted home in an army convoy or met by brass bands or CNN. We bought our own tickets on Greyhound busses. Maybe we had the last laugh after all.

We won that war.

CORN TORTILLAS, CORNBREAD, ETHANOL AND GLOBAL WARMING

I read in the news that 75,000 Mexicans marched in protest of the high price of corn tortillas. It seems that the price of corn tortillas has gone up as much as 45 percent which is ten percent higher than they were.

The cause of this big increase is the use of corn in the United States to make ethanol. This stuff is supposed to make gasoline burn cleaner, cutting down on global warming. I have seen none on the market here. Maybe they are using it to make margaritas, while the Mexicans march. After a month of miserable cold weather here, I'm ready for some global warming.

The new president elect of Mexico, Felipe Calderon, is getting the blame for it. It's all part of the job. I'm amazed that our president Bush is not getting the blame for it. He usually does.

Half the people in Mexico live on $5.00 a day, or less, and corn tortillas are a basic part of their diet. Since, due to the bad weather, my gas and electric bills have soared, I thought I would give the corn tortillas a try and get my eating cost down to $5.00 a day.

I have news for the folks in Mexico. They're not giving corn tortillas away here either.

Anyway, it didn't work. The Mexicans must know something I don't. Flour tortillas, I understand. I can heat one, wrap nearly anything in it and eat it. Corn tortillas don't wrap too well. They are a little dry too. I have never cared much for tacos which use corn tortillas. When I try to eat one, everything in it falls out in my lap.

I guess I was about half-grown before I ever saw a tortilla of any kind. The stores in Blanket didn't sell them. Maybe there was no demand for them back then. We were stuck with cornbread and biscuits and we consumed a lot of both. We were lucky they didn't make ethanol back then or we would have been in the same fix the Mexicans are today.

I wonder why cornbread never caught on in Mexico. It is reasonably easy to make and goes well with nearly anything. Maybe it has too many ingredients to make it on $5.00 a day. Best I remember, we had even less than that to live on but we had cornbread.

Beans without cornbread would have been like sunset without dark. Or dawn without sunrise. Like corn tortillas in Mexico, we had to have it.

About 40 years ago, I used to spend my week-ends exploring the small villages along the Rio Grande west of Presideo. This was in the area of Capote Peak, visible for many miles into Mexico. A Border Patrol friend told me the illegal immigrants used the peak as a reference point of where to cross the river. In the summer, the river was usually totally dry here.

On one trip, I was walking up a creek on my way to Capote Falls, a beautiful 80 foot waterfall about 12 miles from Candelaria on a privately owned ranch. I noticed footprints going into a side canyon, but none coming out.

I walked into the canyon and found the campsite of 6 Mexican Nationals who were cooking tortillas on an old iron stove lid on a small campfire. Obviously, they had walked a long distance with nothing to eat but tortillas. They carried flour, lard, salt and the stove lid to cook on.

Not a word was said and I left without a tortilla.

MY WASTED YOUTH AND
A CORNCOB PIPE

Every kid in Blanket who ever ran headlong down a long string of boxcars on the railroad siding, and jumped the space between each one as if there was no tomorrow, had a corncob pipe. This was long before General Douglas McArthur, wading ashore on some Pacific island, after the marines had safely secured it, made these pipes famous.

Unlike McArthur, we made our own. It was a simple process. Cut off about two inches of a corncob, leave the inside in on one end, and find a piece of wild grapevine. The piece of grapevine was necessary to make the stem. This involved another process. We heated a piece of baling wire over the stove until it was red hot, ran it through the grapevine to remove the stuff that was in there, and we had ourselves a pipestem.

Our next step was to find something to smoke in it. This presented no problem. Tobacco products were sold in every grocery store, to anybody, regardless of age, who had the money to buy them. We had a choice of Prince Albert, Bull Durham, Dukes Mixture, Golden Grain, or something called RJR which we called "Run Johnny Run."

We usually chose Dukes Mixture, or Golden Grain, the mildest of the bunch, mostly because they cost a nickel a sack. Among the bunch of us, we could usually raise a nickel. After some experimenting, we found that the "Run Johnny Run" gave us the ability to walk on water and speak in tongues. We stayed away from it from then on.

About the only product we were prohibited from buying were birth control items labeled "For the prevention of disease only." These items were kept under the counter. Sometimes, a package of these things, obtained from an older brother, was carried in the belief that it would keep us healthy. Today, such items are prominently displayed everywhere, and tobacco products are kept behind the counter. What, I wonder, is the message we are sending to our youth? Could it be that morals are unimportant, but don't smoke?

We would puff on our corncob pipes, while observing our part of the world sitting atop the boxcars in the railroad yards of Blanket, and perhaps think about our futures, if we had any, which at that time looked doubtful. We worried little about it though. We were young., and at the time, we were sitting on top of the world on that boxcar, or at least, as close as we could get to it.

Recently, I was struck with nostalgia, as elderly people are prone to do, and was obsessed with the idea that it would be nice, once again, to smoke a corncob pipe. I searched for a week and finally finding one, paid enough for it to have bought our entire corn crop in 1936. I found that I couldn't keep it lit, blistered my tongue, and burned a hole in one of my good shirts. I guess we can't recapture our youth, or smoke a corncob pipe, at least without climbing to the top of a boxcar. I have doubts that I can do that.

A GOOD PLACE TO LIVE
BUT YOU WOULDN'T WANT
TO VISIT THERE

If you've always had a desire to visit Crawford, the small town where President Bush's ranch is located but didn't want to get involved with the protestors, now is your chance.

According to a story in the Star-Telegram by Angela Brown of the Associated Press, there's hardly anybody there these days.

You won't find Cindy Sheehan camped in a bar ditch, surrounded by ardent admirers, but you can take a look at the house she is reported to have bought there that she will never live in. The gift shops and trinket shops are disappearing like puddles of water in West Texas after a rainstorm.

The apparent reason that folks are staying away in droves is the unpopularity of the president over the war in Iraq and his fewer visits to the ranch recently. Of course, the protestors go where he goes and when he is in Washington, they are there.

A lot of tourists visited Crawford hoping to see the president, or get a look at his ranch. They didn't get to do either. State troopers and Secret Service agents stopped traffic on the ranch road long before reaching the ranch gate.

These days there are no TV satellite trucks parked in Crawford so your chances of appearing on CNN are slim and none. Crawford still has one restaurant, two gas stations and a bank but not many tourists. I suppose President could ride his bicycle to the post office to get the mail and not be bothered.

It is my personal opinion that it is how it should be. He puts his pants on one leg at a time like I do.

I remember that when Lyndon Johnson was president and anybody who wanted to get a look at his ranch only had to drive to Stonewall to do it. His ranch was on one side of the Pedernales River and Ranch Road 1 was on the other side with a good view of the ranch.

Tourists could park on Ranch road 1 under the nice shade trees and look all they wanted. Well—except during deer season. Deer hunters would park their pickups and look at the ranch through their rifle scopes, hoping, no doubt, to see Lyndon sitting on the front porch having a bourbon and water.

Such action, as you might imagine, unnerved the Secret Service no end and they had the road closed during deer season. It probably wouldn't have bothered Lyndon at all.

Back when he was president, I was the official photographer for the Brownwood Mafia, a group that, among other things, showed an interest in politics. I took so many pictures of President Johnson, he somehow thought he knew me but couldn't figure out when or how.

Anyway, I guess that if President Bush lived where President Johnson did, Ranch Road 1 would have been closed the year round due to the anti-war protestors headed by Cindy Sheehan.

President Johnson is gone now but Stonewall and the ranch are still there. Tourists still come. In January of next year, President Bush will leave office but Crawford and the ranch, along with some Secret Service agents will still be there. I'm sure President Bush will be there, at least part of the time. The tourists will still come but the protestors won't.

The George W. Bush library may be built there. Some board members of Southern Methodist University, the proposed site, don't want it.

It would help business in Crawford and they need it. SMU doesn't.

CRIME DIDN'T PAY AND NOTHING ELSE DID EITHER

I'm a firm believer in reading newspapers, especially the local paper. It's not what's in it that interests me as what's not in it. Right away, I learn what my status is. If I'm not listed in the obituaries, I know I didn't die.

If my name is not in the lists of arrests, I know I wasn't busted for selling, smoking or manufacturing some illegal substance. I'm not in the county jail which means I can still feed my dog and fill up the bird baths.

It's not that I worry about doing all of these things but during the night, somebody might have stolen my identity. They do that, you know

I know that my house didn't burn down during the night because I'm still in it and its cold as a Greenland morning.

I don't have Central Heat. I have never cared for it. I managed to live most of my life without it. Besides, I like something I can back up to and warm my backside. Anyway, it reminds me of a bad smell in an elevator full of people. You know it's there but you can't tell where it's coming from.

Back when I was a kid, Mama laid down some pretty stringent rules. We were never to steal, although at the time, there was nothing in the entire county worth stealing. "Crime doesn't pay" She said. Nothing else did either, or at least not much.

We could hoe cotton for a dollar and a half a day, or pick the stuff for a dollar for a hundred pounds. That took all day.

Crime, we thought, if it paid more than that, it must be a better occupation to get into. Mama, however, wouldn't have allowed it.

The only crime I knew anything about was when an old boy from Brownwood broke into Ernest Allen' drug store one night proving that crime didn't pay. Ernest could hardly see well enough to tell daylight from dark and he left fifteen cents in the cash register.

That's all the old boy got in the way of money. He did fix himself chocolate milks shake while he was there and left his fingerprints on the glass. He got 5 years out of that. I guess Mama knew what she was talking about. Anyway, everybody in town knew Ernest didn't leave money in his cash register.

None of us were interested in drugs he might have had. If we wanted to "Get high" we climbed the windmill.

Lying too was a mortal sin. We all believed that story about George Washington and the cherry tree. We were pretty safe there. There wasn't a cherry tree on the place and if we cut down a mesquite, we didn't have to lie about it.

I guess I grew up in a pretty good time and had a good teacher. Mama has been gone a long time now but I still remember all she taught me.

If she could read a newspaper today or watch one of our nightly TV shows, she would have what she called a "Wall-eyed fit." Things have changed a lot in the past 75 years. She wouldn't like any of it.

It appears to me that a lot of folks today didn't listen to their mamas.

Certainly not one like mine.

PULLING THE TAB ON CULTURE IN TEXAS

I have a friend who is totally nuts about auto racing. He watches every race he can find on TV and if he goes to sleep in his recliner and misses one, he's mad for a week. As for me, I lost interest several years ago when a kid in a VW Beetle flat outran my Buick somewhere between Fort Stockton and nowhere. Anybody who has ever had any reason to be in that country is aware that there is a lot of nowhere out there. Today, they call it "No Country for Old Men, or Old Women either."

Maybe that's where auto racing started, seeing as how there's not much else to do there. Since the legislature passed the law on open containers, there is even less to do on long trips and in that country, they're all long.

It has always been the custom while driving those long unending highways for the good old boys driving pickups to pull the tab on a cold one for entertainment. It is difficult to read the latest Harry Potter book while driving. In that country, if stopped by a State Trooper while engaged in reading Harry Potter's latest, the penalty might be severe. State Troopers out there are rather severe to start with. They had much rather be working between Austin and San Marcos.

My friend was once a race driver of sorts. His racing was confined to those castor oil burning drag racers which burn up a set of back tires in a quarter mile. He finally got older and wiser and quit while he still had both arms and legs. His eyebrows, however, never grew back.

Auto racing these days is big business from Daytona to Fort Worth. Folks drive thousands of miles to attend one. Most take their entire families along in the family motor home, duly packed with a supply of crackers, Vienna sausage, and beer. Race fans, for some reason or other are all fond of beer. They are often referred to as "Bubbas" by folks who don't appreciate racing. I have no opinion, one way or the other. If they like that sort of thing, it's fine with me.

We have all been categorized by somebody, whether we fit or not. Texans are all supposed to be rich, reasonably ignorant blowhards, who wear cowboy boots, drink beer incessantly, belong to the NRA and keep assault rifles in their pickup trucks. On the other hand, we have some culture too, in spite of the fact that one of our famous writers named Sidney Porter, did most of his writing while confined in the Austin City jail. In jail, they called him O. Henry.

Texas has always been big on music too. We spawned Bob Wills, the father of Western Swing, Ernest Tubb, who incited us all to "Waltz across Texas," and who once delivered prescriptions for the Coggin Drug in Brownwood on a bicycle, and yes, even Willie Nelson who didn't.

Call us "Bubbas" if you like, but we have had, so far, three Presidents from our state, a singing cowboy, Gene Autry, and some of the best writers in the business including Larry McMurtry who gave us "Lonesome Dove." None, as far as I know kept assault rifles in their pickups. Some may have pulled the tab on a cold can of something on a long road in direct violation of our open container law, or read Harry Potter's latest which should be. I don't really care.

SOLVING MURDERS ON TV AND DANCING WITH THE STARS

I don't care much for TV programming these days. I still remember when we had to have a hundred foot antenna to get a snowy picture of Lawrence Welk on one of the three channels we got. Even then, it was better than most of the stuff we get today by satellite. At least, Mr. Welk never killed anybody that I know of.

As bad as the reception was, I don't recall any bodies lying around on the set. Mr. Welk occasionally did dance a polka with his girl singer. I could handle that. Today, we have "Dancing with the Stars" which I can't.

A columnist for another paper which I won't mention recently suggested that the 14,000 prisoners the CIA have incarcerated somewhere for engaging in acts of terrorism should be forced to watch this program for an hour and they would confess to anything.

I didn't say that—he did. Probably the reason I don't care for the show is that all the stars I knew are deceased. I never saw John Wayne, Randolph Scott or Henry Fonda dancing anyhow.

We still have "Law and Order" and I have watched every rerun since Nixon was President. I know the scripts by heart. They always start the same way. A couple is walking down a quiet street when one of them spots a body in the weeds and invariable says, "Oh my God, call 911." Everybody has a cell phone these days.

Then, there is "The First 48" in which the detectives have to solve the murders in the first 48 hours or they never will. Mostly, these murders occur in either Miami or Memphis. In Miami, hardly any of the suspects speak English. In Memphis, they don't do much better. They have a department in Miami called "CSI" which means "Can't solve it."

Another show I watch is "Cold Case Files" which proves "The First 48" is wrong. They often solve their cases 20 years after being committed. They depend a lot on DNA which wasn't available when the crime was committed.

Then, the District Attorney refuses to try the case on DNA results alone, even though the suspect's DNA proves he did the deed. He wants a full confession and two witnesses. After all, District Attorneys are elected. They have to worry about that.

When I was a cop back in the dark ages, the Chief of Police could take the suspect in his office, lock the door and in10 minutes he would plead guilty to signing the Declaration of Independence if accused of it. The chief was elected too.

Yes, law enforcement has changed a lot since I was a kid. Back then, the sheriff only had to drive down the street and folks worried about things they were not even guilty of. We didn't have any DNA. All we had was WPA and it didn't solve anything.

These days, the criminals have all the advantages. They don't have to say a thing and a lawyer is furnished free, paid for by the tax-payers.

Still, our law enforcement officers must be doing something right. The jails and the penitentiary are not lacking for customers, even in Miami and Memphis.

I apologize to all the ladies who love to watch "Dancing with the Stars."

It takes all kinds of folks to make up a freeway.

A CHICKEN-FRIED STEAK AND SOMEBODY TO CALL ME DARLIN'

I have been reading Jerry Flemmon's book, "Curmudgeon in Corduroy", a book printed in 2000, after his death in 1999. Jerry wrote about Texas and Texas people for 37 years and he didn't miss much.

I was attracted to a chapter on chicken-fried steak, my all-time favorite food. Jerry wrote about Doylene Bradshaw, a lady in Anson, who cooked chicken-fried steak for her husband and children every day for over thirty years.

My shirttail never touched my back until I could get to the grocery store and buy some round steak and Crisco, the two necessary ingredients.

I did it exactly as Doylene said I should, but something happened. Mine was sort of a flop. Doylene wouldn't have liked it any better than I did. My gravy though, wasn't too bad, and I still have three slices left to prove it. I really don't think Doylene sliced hers.

Cooking a chicken-fried steak is a true art, found only in Texas. Some cooks can do it, and some can't. Most can't. I have tried chicken-fried steak in half the greasy spoon cafes in Texas, usually the places who make it best.

Finding a good one is like winning the lottery. It seldom ever happens. They should have a nice crusty coating, with the gravy served either on the bottom or the top. I don't care. It can be put in a bowl and spooned on in the amount I like. Bad gravy, however, can ruin the world's best chicken-fry. It has to have the right consistency and flavor and is best cooked in the skillet where the steak was cooked.

Although I took up cooking some twenty-something years ago out of necessity, I'm a long way from knowing what I'm doing.

I have spent hours watching gourmet cooks on TV. I have tried doing what they do—turning the flame up until it appears they are going to burn the whole place down and flipping the skillet to turn the contents over. All I have managed to do is burn everything to a crisp and dump the contents on the stove.

Gourmet cooks however, never cook chicken-fried steaks. To learn this art, it is necessary to spend years cooking in truck-stop cafes, or lonely run-down places off an Interstate somewhere in West Texas where old grizzled ranchers and down-and-out people wander in, hungry and half broke, and the waitress calls you darlin,' hoping for a quarter tip.

In these places, you either get a chicken-fry straight out of heaven, or something you can't eat. It's the chance you have to take. If you get a bad one, you leave your quarter for darlin' and try another place.

Never complain if you're at least 100 miles from home, Bad things might happen. Nobody is perfect.

We never had chicken-fried steak when I was growing up back during the Great Depression. I don't know a single soul who did. Our meat, when we had it, was always pork. A hog, as far as I know can have 19 different kinds of meat, none of which is adaptable to chicken-frying. We were lucky to have that and we didn't complain.

We never had to leave a quarter, and mama always called us darlin'.

OUR JAILS WERE EMPTY AND CRIME WAS AGAINST THE LAW

I always read Steve Nash's police activity report. Since I was a policeman here back in the fifties, it is interesting to note the difference between then and now. Back then, we arrested so few that our jail was empty about 90% of the time. If we had anybody in jail on Friday, we turned them loose so we could catch them again on Saturday night to have something to do.

Our County jail was even worse than the City jail. Absolutely nobody wanted to spend time there. Back then, jails were not inspected by the state to make sure the little darlings being held there were comfortable and well treated. The state didn't care, which may account for our jail being empty most of the time.

The wide use of methamphetamine and marijuana didn't exist here. In fact, meth was unknown locally. It had been widely used in Japan and during WWII; the Germans gave it to their tank crews. This may have helped us win the war.

In Brownwood, I assume that somebody mixed up some up some battery acid, starting fluid, liquid fertilizer and a little Sudafed or Ephedrine and some match heads, the source of red phosphorus and gave it a sniff. "Wow," he said. "This stuff would make anybody crazy as a bedbug. I bet it would sell." It did and we still have it around.

Most of the police activity and subsequent arrests seem to happen after midnight. I'm never out after midnight so I miss all of this action. Since I live alone, I stay at home after midnight so as not to get mixed up in all this stuff that goes on. I wouldn't have anybody to back up my alibi if I swore I was at home.

I'm puzzled by the fact that a large number of the culprits arrested nightly don't even live here. Why would anybody drive over a hundred miles to smoke a joint and get busted? Does it "feel like home?" Do they not sell marijuana and meth in other towns? Maybe they bring it with them and sell a little to pay for the trip. Anyway, as far as I know, we don't have a "catch and release" program going here.

Sheriff Grubbs indicates there have been 400 drug arrests here and still there are nightly arrests both for meth and marijuana possession. Getting out of jail and back on the streets does not seem to be a problem with these people.

In addition to the drug arrests, we have burglaries, thefts, drunks and domestic difficulties. I would imagine that the officers on duty at night can't even have a coffee break. Where do these people come from? I notice that these are not kids, being in their thirties, forties and even fifties.

Back in the dark ages when I worked as a policeman, we had a way to get rid of our undesirables. If they insisted on hanging around and using our jail facilities and causing us trouble, they were loaded in a police car and given a free ride to somewhere else and told not to come back. I'm not sure about the ethics involved but it worked. I guess this was a sort of "Catch here and release there."

Maybe if we had been furnished with pepper spray and stun guns as our modern policemen are, we might not have had to put anybody in jail. Nobody wants a dose of either. Our choice, however, was more permanent.

We had to shoot them.

SELLING THE SAME OLD BALONEY BUT A NEW WINE IS ON THE MARKET

Today, a lot of folks are worrying about things they never had to worry about before. There are few things happening today that I haven't already survived. I have been through recessions, one family size Depression, money shortage, housing shortage, rationing, been personally involved in two wars and at least one gasoline shortage.

I still remember one day back in the seventies the price of gasoline suddenly jumped to forty-nine cents a gallon. People didn't know what to do so they filled up every container they had with gasoline. Then, there was none to be bought.

Two or three weeks ago, gasoline was less than $3.00 a gallon and nobody was lined up at the pumps buying it. Now, with the price nearing $3.50 a gallon, you most likely will have to wait in line to buy it while somebody puts a hundred dollars' worth in a SUV. I haven't figured that out yet.

The best way to stop the high price of gasoline is to stop buying it. I was born and raised on a farm. I know if you can't sell a pig for $25, you can sell him for $15. Somebody always wants your pig and if you keep him, you have to feed him.

Now, there appears to be the beginning of a food shortage. Rice is being rationed in most stores and nearly everything else has gone up in price 10% or more. Rice, I can live without.

If all of this has brought your spirits down, all the spirits that might raise yours have gone up too. The vintners in Napa Valley who produce Pinot Noir, Pinot Blanc and Pinot Grigio are now producing a new wine for elderly folks which contain an anti-diuretic and is marketed under the name Pino More. I found this bit of information on the internet.

A lot of the food shortage can be blamed on using all our grain to make ethanol, a product most people don't know what is used for, including me. One thing it has done is raise the price of corn to $10.50 a bushel, which in turn raised the cost of meal and milk. Dairy cows eat a lot of corn. If any service station in Brownwood is selling ethanol, I haven't found it. I wouldn't know what to do with it if I did. My pickup doesn't run very well on gasoline and I'd hesitate to put ethanol in it.

I remember when gasoline was twelve cents a gallon and I was hoeing cotton for $1.50 a day. I remember several Presidential elections but not one that I didn't have somebody I really wanted to vote for until now. Something is wrong somewhere. I'm reminded of an old quote from something or other that I don't know the origin of that seems appropriate; "For lack of a nail, a horse shoe was lost. For lack of a horse shoe, a horse was lost. For lack of a horse, a war was lost." I think we have lost a horse somewhere.

I am not a philosopher or an expert on politics but I rest my case. As Whitey Ford, a fellow on the Grand Old Opry used to say about 60 years ago, "I'm going to the wagon. These shoes are killing me."

THE DUCHESS OF YORK AND SOUTHERN COOKING

In a newspaper clipping sent to me by Bud Lindsey, a magazine publisher out in the short grass country, it was indicated that Sarah Ferguson, the Duchess of York, has no use whatsoever for grits. At the time, Sarah was visiting in South Carolina, a state where no matter what you order in a café, you get grits with it. She also made a disparaging remark about Southern cooking in general and indicated she had no desire to try fried okra.

From a lady who hails from the United Kingdom where they regularly eat stuff cooked in sheep's stomachs, topped off with a generous helping of blood pudding, such remarks could easily start a riot. However, Sarah, being regarded as a nice lady otherwise, they chose to overlook it as long as she caught the next bus out of town.

Southerners are rather fond of grits. Grits are a part of their heritage, along with the Confederate flag. Sort of like chicken-fried steak in Texas. Most likely, she wouldn't go for that either. Texans, I've been told, have been known to starve to death in London while watching the changing of the guard in front of the Queen's palace.

Grits are plural for the simple reason that it is impossible to cook just one. If you have any doubt, try it sometime. Grits, as far as I've been able to determine, consists of ground corn. Corn is one of the 18 basic foods regularly cooked in the South, along with possum, gumbo, sweet potatoes and pokeweed and turnip greens.

There is absolutely nothing wrong with corn, made into tortillas, canned, eaten off the cob, or ground into grits. However, Southerners, being enterprising folks soon discovered another use. A barrel of it, mixed with sugar and allowed to ferment for several days, then heated over a fire and ran through coils of copper tubing brought forth something better than grits.

They also discovered that this mixture would get a man in more stuff than a 2 year old in a cow pen. Some folks stuck with it, while others stuck with grits. In my long and mostly unproductive life, I've tried a little of both, but never at the same time. Double jeopardy, they say, is against the law.

Having grown up during the Great Depression, my family ate everything they could get their hands on. Grits, however, were missing from our diet, for whatever reason, I don't know. When groceries got really short, we sometimes had cornmeal mush which is a pore folk's version of grits. Had they been available, as hard as times were, mama might have had to learn to cook one of them at a time.

My introduction to grits came in about 1948, when on my way to New Orleans; I stopped for breakfast in the small East Texas town of Jasper. This was long before the existence of Interstate 20, that famous highway where one lane is always blocked by orange and white barrels all through Louisiana. This, I've been told, makes it easier for law enforcement officers to do profiles on Texans. I was served grits and gumbo along with my eggs. Like old "Fergie," I didn't care much for either one. And like her, I left town.

I have never been too particular about what I eat as long as it's not moving when I eat it. The best way to stop anything you plan to eat from moving is to deep-fry it. Nothing, as far as I know ever escaped from a skillet-full of hot grease.

If anything did, it would be too tough to eat.

ON THE ROAD AGAIN
LOOKING FOR A GOOD MOTEL

During my days of traveling around the country, I noticed a lot of cheap motels with a sign out front that proclaimed they had "Clean sheets." It could be that the Four Seasons Hotels are missing a good bet here, not to mention the Holiday Inns.

I always figured that the price of a motel included clean sheets, but no guarantee.

I remember one time several years ago when a friend and I were on our way to Florida. We had driven nearly all night from Texas until we found a motel in a Mississippi town on the banks of the Big River. It was well lighted with neon, making it difficult to judge the place at three in the morning.

We needed a bed bad, or a bad bed. I think we got the latter. I'm not sure how clean the sheets were but it seemed that both the sheets and pillow cases had been washed in embalming fluid. The whole place smelled like the prep room in a funeral home with somebody cooking curry in the adjoining room.

I have nothing against curry. In fact, I like it even though I feel it should be cooked outside over an open fire.

This motel was a good argument for cremation if I ever saw one. A little creation could have helped too. There was no "intelligent design" about this place. I learned that motels with a lot of neon signs and any mention about sheets should be avoided.

A lady in Stephenville, discussing one of their motels said, "They change the sheets every day—from one room to another." Maybe she knew. I had no reason to find out.

A lot of "Good old boys" in looking for a suitable motel for covert purposes choose one with an easy entrance, parking in the rear and an escape route without having to climb through the bathroom window.

I remember when Brownwood had few motels. Most were called "tourist courts." I don't know if any tourists ever stayed there unless they were destitute and down on their luck. One was near the Pecan Experiment station on Woodson drive, which was then the main highway into town. Another, called "The Alamo Courts" was nearer to town at the end of South Broadway.

The Alamo Courts had nothing to do with either Davy Crockett or Santa Anna's army but when I was a cop back in the fifties, a lot of drinking and fighting went on there. I think the owner finally tore it down, or the occupants did. We were glad to get rid of it even though it was a good training area for new officers. They could learn to say "get on the ground" in a loud voice just like on TV.

I try to stay in a nice-looking motel in a nice neighborhood where no mention of clean sheets is made. Some motels even serve a free breakfast which is a good thing. Some even have workout rooms where you can get the kinks out after a long drive. I much prefer getting a good work-out rather than a good working over.

Still, there are times when you may get stuck in something else. It is best to get on the road again as soon as possible. I just read that Willie Nelson, getting up in years like the rest of us may change his theme song to "On the Commode Again."

Sounds like a good idea to me.

DON'T PLAY THAT SONG AGAIN, SAM—I CAN'T STAND IT

The music they're playing these days has me totally confused. There is somebody in my neighborhood that plays something at full volume that sounds like they recorded some organ music and figured out some way to play it backwards. It causes the leaves on trees to wilt and knocks birds out of the sky.

Even country music has evolved into something totally different from what we played when I was playing in a country band. I grew up during the "Big Band" era and now I'm living in the "Big Noise" era. I just don't know what to make of it.

Every night people pass by my house in cars equipped with 5,000 watt amplifiers playing what sounds to me like somebody beating a big bass drum. The walls vibrate and my furniture changes location. They obviously roll down all the windows on their car to prevent broken glass from flying all over the road and to make sure that everybody within a half-mile hears it. It is clear to me that whoever is doing it is totally deaf, or soon will be.

I still remember when I was a teenager attending dear old Blanket High School and Dorothy McIntosh had a class in Music Appreciation. She exposed us to classical music and we found that we enjoyed it. Obviously, this course is no longer on any school's curriculum.

We even have something now called "Rap" where a fellow talks nasty while the inevitable drums beat in the background. Anybody who can stand to listen to this stuff would consider having their fingernails pulled out with a pair of plier's entertainment.

I don't remember exactly when good music started to go bad. It was still good in the fifties. Willie had short hair, wore cowboy boots and was playing in the honky-tonks of Fort Worth. He moved to Nashville where they didn't like his style of singing so he moved to Austin, let his hair grow and got rich. We still had Les Paul and Mary Ford and Lefty Frizell was at the top of the country charts.

Then, Rock bands came along and guitar players all over the country found they only needed to know two chords to be successful. In the sixties my kids were playing the Beatles until I nearly went crazy but some of their stuff was good enough that I could stand it. It was not country and quite a ways off from Willie.

The Beatles broke up, somebody shot John and I guess the rest flew over the cuckoo's nest. No more "Beatle mania" but they still remain the most popular group ever and there was only 4 of them.

I still remember Hank Thompson and the Brazos Valley boys and Billy Walker who "Crossed the Brazos at Waco." When we landed our B-17 in North Africa on our way to Italy in 1944, the first song I heard was Bob Wills playing "San Antonio Rose." I thought our pilot had made a mistake and landed at Big Spring. North Africa looked a lot like West Texas.

In our squadron in Italy, we had one beat-up guitar and I had a harmonica. In our tent, homesick boys from all over would congregate often wanting to hear music from home. I would play "Red River Valley" and "Across the Wide Missouri." Of course, "San Antonio Rose" was at the top of the list.

I have been wondering that if somebody played the stuff we hear today on a deserted desert island, would it make a noise?

You can bet on it.

ERUPTING VOLCANOES ARE BEST SEEN FROM A DISTANCE

At Christmas in 2004, my son Jimmy and my daughter-in-law Debbie gave me several books. Among them was one called "Pompeii." I found it to be a rather interesting book. I was not aware at the time that a TV movie was soon to be released in January.

During my stay in Italy in 1944 and 1945, I made numerous trips to Naples but I never visited the ruins of Pompeii, located only about 6 miles up the Mediterranean coast. I wish now that I had. I did, however, get an unscheduled close look inside the crater of Mt. Vesuvius.

Sometime in the fall of 1944, I came down with a mild ailment the flight surgeon diagnosed as Sand Fly Fever. He sent me to the military hospital in Foggia, mostly to keep me from bothering him.

I spent most of that time listening to a black fellow in the next bed tell me lies about stealing an old man's chickens that he had no use for. He said the old man finally bought a bulldog and tied him to the door of the chicken house. He said he went over there one night, stole all the chickens and left a note on the door which said, "I'll be back tomorrow night and get the bulldog."

When I was released from the hospital, well schooled in the art of stealing chickens, the flight surgeon then sent me to a resort hotel down on the heel of the boot of Italy. Apparently, he still wanted to get rid of me.

As a result of this, I was behind in my flying which was necessary to draw flight pay. One day, I was sent out to the airfield to catch up. Two pilots and an engineer were going to check out a B-17 which had just had a complete overhaul on the engines.

I was riding in the radio room on this flight and I started to have some doubts about the pilots when I looked out the Plexiglas top and saw the ground. The B-17 bomber was not a stunt plane.

At that particular time, Mt. Vesuvius which had totally destroyed Herculean and Pompeii in 74 AD was erupting again for the first time since 1631. The kids flying the plane wanted to see it even though it was 90 miles outside our test area. The thing was, we were all kids back then. It seemed like a good idea to me.

We quickly made the 90 mile trip and they took the plane down to just above Vesuvius. Then, to make matters worse, the pilot put the plane in a steep bank and we flew right down almost in the crater and made about three circles through the smoke and fire.

I was worrying about the engines. Did the ground crew really do a good job on that overhaul? I decided this was probably the most frightening "mission" I had ever flown with nobody shooting at me.

Finally, we flew back to our base near Foggia and I was considering asking the flight surgeon for another trip to a rest camp. On our usual missions the medics met our plane on arrival back and we were all given 2 ounces of good Bourbon. I looked around, but they were not there when I needed them the most.

The pilot told me, as he helped me out of the plane, "Sergeant, it might be best if you don't say anything about where we've been."

I wasn't about to. I didn't think anybody would believe me anyhow.

ESCAPING TORNADOES, HIGH WINDS, HAIL AND TV WEATHERMEN

The annual storm season is upon us. The TV weathermen get so excited they don't know whether they're planting or pulling up. It is only during this season that they become the "stars" while pre-empting the real network stars. Most of the time during this season, it is useless to try to watch NYPD Blue or Law and Order or anything else due to the interruptions. On a recent NYPD Blue program, I never did figure out who killed who. I only knew who I wanted to kill.

One weatherman on a regional station seems to be constantly surrounded by tornadoes and baseball-size hail. He is always telling folks to "seek cover." Where, I wonder, am I supposed to seek cover? Should I crawl under the bed or get in my pickup and drive to Waxahachie? Hardly anybody has a cellar these days.

Back when I was a kid, the storm season hardly ever started before May. Then, it was just one "cyclone" after another. Nobody had ever heard the word tornado. What we had, according to Mama, was cyclones. I'm thankful we didn't have TV in those days to warn us one was coming. I spent most of my childhood in a cellar as it was.

A bad cyclone once almost destroyed the small town of Zephyr. It blew roosters into jugs, they said, and wheat straws through telephone poles. I heard all about it from Mama for years. Distant thunder would be heard and Mama would say,

"Get in the cellar, kids, there's a cyclone coming. You know what happened at Zephyr."

Worse still, there were no trailer parks then to take the full brunt of the storm. The entire purpose of the storm, it seemed, was to get us. And yet, in my entire youth, I never saw one cyclone. Maybe I just missed it, being confined to a dark cellar where we waited the storm out by the light of a flickering coal oil lantern. After all of these years when I hear thunder, I smell coal oil.

Of course, these storms are not to be taken lightly. People die every year and no longer are these storms restricted to spring. They may happen at any time and anywhere. The warnings do serve a purpose if we listen and take some precautions.

If driving on a highway when a storm approaches they warn us not to stop under an overpass. There is a reason for this. The chances are good that there will be no place to stop, this space being already full of folks who were told not to stop there.

"Get out of your car and lie in a ditch," They say. Lie in a ditch? Not me friend. I'm going to put the pedal to the metal and go to Waxahachie. Maybe they have cellars there and coal oil lanterns. If not, they still have that big expensive tunnel there the government built to smash atoms, or smash something. For whatever reason, they never used it.

It should easily hold 5000 people and my 1993 Ford pickup. I sure don't want anything to happen to it. Cyclone insurance is hard to get these days.

BEER BOTTLES, CHICKEN WIRE AND 40 YEARS OF COUNTRY MUSIC

My Dad was a fiddle player and mostly, he liked to sit on the front porch and play for his own amusement. I tried to learn but all I ever accomplished was scaring hens off their nests in a two block area.

Back during the thirties, he often got called to play for country dances when their fiddle player sampled too much white lightening and fell out of his chair, or the hair came out of his bow.

Somebody would always come to get Dad to take over, sometimes at two in the morning. He would always go because the money he earned might buy our groceries for a week. Times were hard back then and a dollar was hard to come by. A man had to do what a man had to do.

Good guitar players were scarce and Dad needed one to "second" for him while he played so he took a hard look at me.

When I was about 17, I bought a guitar and a friend taught me the three necessary chords to play the old time fiddle tunes. I wasn't good at it but I tried. Dad was known to "cut corners," changing chords before I was ready. While I was still in "D", he would be in "A." He wasn't happy about it.

I guess a more experienced guitar player might anticipate the coming change but I couldn't because it wasn't supposed to happen anyhow. We finally gave it up as a bad idea.

Ira Nelson, Willie's dad, a bass player, told me one time, "I can't play with Willie. I never know where he's going, how long it will take him to get there, and when he's going to stop." I understood completely. I had the same trouble with my dad.

Willie, however, is still doing it that way and it seems he has been rather successful with his unique style of singing and guitar playing. I wasn't.

After WWII, I finally bought a steel guitar, took lessons in Nashville and got a job playing in a band, mostly because every country band had to have one. They didn't know if I was good or bad because there were no other players around to compare me with.

We started making really good money. Sometimes we drove over 200 miles and made $7.50 apiece. That wasn't bad considering that gas was thirty cents a gallon, hamburgers were a quarter, cokes a nickel and beer was $2.40 a case. Anyway, we did it because we liked to.

We played in one West Texas dancehall where they had chicken wire stretched across the bandstand to protect the musicians from flying beer bottles. There was no "road rage" then but a lot of "dance floor rage." Too much beer and cowboys didn't mix well.

Country bands are scarce these days. I know of only four good ones in the entire state. Some of the bands with 2 guitars, a bass, drums and a 5000 watt amplifier may call themselves country but they are not. Would a country music lover drive a hundred miles to hear a band called "Cross Canadian Ragweed"? I think not, but they drove further than that to hear Bob Wills and the Texas Playboys.

I played in country bands off and on for forty years until I decided I had rather go to bed at ten, instead of three.

At a certain age, a man no longer has to do what a man has to do.

FIGHTING A WAR FROM THE BOTTOM OF A BOMBER

A number of people have read in my columns about my exploits as a ball turret gunner on a B-17 bomber during WWII. Others, I have told about it when I was asked.

Still, hardly a week goes by that somebody doesn't ask, "Was the ball turret located on top of the plane?" No, it was underneath the plane. Had it been on top, the only people I could have shot would have been the radio operator, the engineer and both the pilot and the co-pilot.

Such action was prohibited as we needed them all to carry out our mission.

The ball turret, as the name implies, was a round ball, made of magnesium, aluminum and Plexiglas. The Plexiglas allowed the gunner to see outside. Inside the turret, other than the gunner, were two fifty caliber machine guns, a large, Sperry automatic computing sight and the electro-hydraulic motors it took to run it. About 75% of the turret extended outside the plane with the other 25% inside, holding the thing up. It rotated up and down and 180 degrees around.

It was often referred to as a "death trap" because the ball turret gunner was the only crew member who couldn't wear a parachute. There wasn't room for one inside.

I have to admit, this bothered me somewhat. The waist gunners above my turret had their parachutes all buckled on when things got rough with one hand on the escape door handle. Mine was inside the plane.

We were not alone. Tank crews had the same problem, with not much chance of surviving a direct hit with a German .88 millimeter shell or an anti-tank weapon.

This was a real, board-certified war we were in and the generals in charge were not running it from the Pentagon. Maybe this had something to do with the fact that we won it. By the grace of God, some of us survived.

When we landed our bomber in Southern Italy, we were taken by truck to the place where we would spend most of the next year. One look and I was ready to go back home. The place looked like a camp for the homeless with a bunch of old tents with dirt floors scattered among the trees in an olive orchard.

The director of operations, or whatever he was, told me, "I'm glad to see you. We have a shortage of ball turret gunners." "What happened to them?" I asked. "They were washed out." He said.

I had heard of pilots being washed out in training for various reasons, but never gunners.

"How?" I asked. "With a hose," He said. I didn't appreciate his humor and I learned later there wasn't a water hose in the entire 414th bomber squadron.

The only water we had was hauled in by tank trucks and for drinking purposes was put in something called "lister bags." Then, they dropped in a few Atabrine tablets to keep us from getting Malaria. This made the water bitter and almost undrinkable.

I knew then why the Italians drank wine. It was a wise choice.

Somehow, I managed to survive it all for 50 missions, probably due to my survival lessons back in Blanket during the Depression.

As Minnie Pearl used to say on the Grand Old Opry every Saturday night, "I'm proud to be here." I'm proud to be a veteran and I salute all of our veterans everywhere and those who are still fighting for our freedom, all of whom are volunteers.

FISHING FOR MEMORIES AND CRAWFISH IN COGGIN PARK

Back when I was about 12 or 13 years old, it was absolutely necessary that I go to Brownwood every Saturday, rain or shine. I had things to do there. I had to buy a foot-long hotdog at the Yellow Squeeze-In cafe across from the courthouse and check on Roy and Dale at the Gem or Queen Theaters.

Having done all these things, I would check on my friends at the Santa Fe Railroad roundhouse and watch the steam locomotives for awhile. It was a good life and a lot better than what I'm doing now.

The next thing on my schedule was to walk to Coggin Park where I usually found Alan Spence and Ronald Gray fishing for crawfish in the little pond that is no longer there. Since all three of us were Bulletin carriers, we knew each other well. My route was in Blanket and theirs were in Brownwood.

The only equipment needed to catch crawfish was a string and pieces of bacon. If anybody caught any, they were put back to catch again the next Saturday. There was no shortage of Saturdays back then. They came along regularly and at our age, they were apparently never-ending.

There were more Saturdays than there were crawfish but that never bothered us a bit. We had plenty of time.

When the Bulletin came off the press, somewhere around three or four in the afternoon, it was sort of a riot. The newsboys who sold papers on the street were all trying to get their papers before anybody else. The route boys were trying to get theirs at the same time and get them delivered.

My papers were delivered to Blanket on a bus around six so I didn't have to join in the fray but it was fun to watch.

The papers then were delivered on a bicycle, unlike today where they are flung from the window of a car going 30 miles an hour giving the subscriber a bit of entertainment trying to find it. Unlike Easter, this hunt comes every day.

My subscribers expected me to carefully place the paper behind the screen door, a necessity in those days to keep the flies out of the house since there was no air-conditioning. Apparently, none was needed as we all survived.

Over the years, a lot of changes have come about. The building where the Bulletin was located has been torn down, the Yellow Squeeze-In is gone along with the Gem and Queen Theaters, steam locomotives are but a memory and there is no longer a pond with crawfish in Coggin Park.

My old craw fishing friends and I reluctantly grew up, with Ronald Gray sticking to the newspaper business, eventually becoming publisher of the Bulletin and Alan Spence became a doctor and returned to Brownwood to practice.

Like the pond in Coggin Park, they are both gone too, like the never-ending Saturdays of our youth we thought would never end.

I have a lot of memories of happenings in the old park, of W. Leo Daniel and his Hillbilly band appearing there when he was running for the office of governor and Lyndon Johnson landing there in a helicopter when he was running for the senate.

Most of all, I remember the little pond, the crawfish and my friends Alan and Ronald when we were all in the newspaper business a long time ago.

As my old friend Hondo Crouch used to say, "Don't forget memories."

I MIGHT HAVE FLOWN ON
UNSAFE PLANES IN WWII

There has been a lot in the news recently about several airlines pulling their planes out of service to inspect them for various safety violations. Passengers have been rather unhappy about being stranded in Wherever, South Dakota or Coldernhell, Minnesota. The airlines were not enthusiastic about it either.

It started with Southwest Airlines for flying their older model 737s without being inspected for cracks in the fuselage. Personally, I had rather fly Southwest Airlines with cracks in the fuselage than any other airline that didn't.

One time I flew from Phoenix to Austin on another airline and we sat at the airport for 40 minutes before taking off. I ordered a glass of grape juice and it took so long to get it, it was fermented when I did get it. Good things, they say, come to those who wait. The flight attendant then disappeared into the first class section and never did come out.

I sort of like the Boeing 737 plane. It has one fault that I can see, having only two engines. Back during WWII, I flew 50 missions on a Boeing B-17 which had four engines. It was a rare occasion when we returned from a mission over Germany with all four still operating. Still, I never saw a crack in the fuselage.

Any safety infractions that we had were caused by the German ant-aircraft gunners. Actually, they were doing their best to knock us out of the sky and if we had any cracks in our fuselage, they caused it. No FAA inspector ever came around to check.

The B-17 did have a few faults but if they affected the safety, I don't know. I really don't recall anybody mentioning safety during my entire 50 missions over Germany and the Balkan countries. No FAA inspector ever came out and said, "Boys, what you're doing is totally unsafe."

The B-17, among other faults, had no bathroom. Considering the various methods we may have resorted to could have been a safety factor. There were two open windows on the plane used by the waist gunners where their .50 caliber machine guns were mounted. Not a really good place to seek relief.

In my ball turret, there was a funnel attached to a hose that went outside but at an altitude of 29000 feet, it froze up and was of no help. The bombardier often used an empty K-ration box which he dropped out the escape hatch and it immediately bounced off my turret. We often had words about this.

The B-17, unlike the 737, had no heaters. We were forced to wear an electrically heated suit under our regular flight suit. The average temperature at 29,000 feet in the winter was 65 below zero. The suits were never inspected by the FAA to make sure there were no short circuits which might have electrocuted us.

I remember one occasion when our number two engine was hit by antiaircraft fire, knocking it out. The oil in the engine poured out on the wing and immediately froze. The pilot attempted to feather the propeller to stop it turning. The prop refused to feather. Then the shaft kept getting hotter and hotter until all at once it broke and the prop went whizzing off into the wild blue yonder. Had it hit the plane it would have been regarded as a safety violation. Had it hit me, I wouldn't be here.

I guess that if I had it to all do over again, I'd pick the B-17 to fly in. Two things I would request though—a bathroom and a heater.

A FEW MEMORIES OF FT. SAM HOUSTON WHEN THEY PAID THEIR ELECTRIC BILL

I recently read that Fort Sam Houston in San Antonia is having trouble with their electric Company. It seems that their electric bill hadn't been paid in three months and they owe a whopping $4.2 million electric bill. Apparently, somebody had been leaving the lights on.

All this is blamed on a budget shortfall. They didn't get their money. Most likely, FEMA got it. They have been passing money out to anybody with their hands out to the tune of over one billion dollars. FEMA, as everybody knows stands for Federal Emergency Mismanagement Authority.

One recipient in San Antonia bought a $200 bottle of Dom Perignom champagne. At least, he had good taste. The owner of the Hooters restaurant chain in Atlanta has offered to pay for it. They said that they would take it, being happy to get anything at all back.

I'm well acquainted with Fort Sam Houston, one of the oldest army posts in the country. During my military careers, they took me away from my happy home twice and brought me back once.

I came back from Italy in 1945 on a slow boat from Naples with 10,000 crap games on the deck After landing in Boston; we spent one night at an army post then put on a train to San

Antonio. For some reason the train went to New York first. This was an old trick to keep us guessing where we were. The Germans no longer cared.

We followed the Hudson River, eventually crossing the Mississippi and arriving at Fort Sam Houston. I was given a new set of uniforms and a 30 day furlough to visit the home folks. Then, it was back to Fort Sam again where they gave me a train ticket to Santa Ana, California.

Since President Truman had not yet given the order to drop "big boy" on Japan, that war was still a work in progress. I assumed they were going to find a place for me in it. Then, my records caught up with me. Having participated in 8 major air battles and been awarded some medals, I qualified for immediate discharge under the point system.

Another train ride and I was back in Fort Sam again. That time, I was given a small brass pin which they called a "ruptured duck" and sent home forever—I thought.

I was wrong. Having joined the army reserve for what reason I don't remember, a war started in Korea and I found myself back in dear old Fort Sam Houston again. Maybe they hoped to get rid of me for good and I was put in charge of a troop train to Camp Chaffee, Arkansas.

I managed, somehow, to reach there without losing a man, only to find that Camp Chaffee, closed since WWII was completely grown over with poke salat greens. The army cooks had no idea what they were or we would have been served them three times a day. Once we got the poke weeds cut enough that the barracks were visible and things running smooth, we were all sent to Camp Crowder, Missouri to open it. It too had been closed since WWII.

The place was totally devoid of poke salat which made our job easier. The war in Korea seemed to be winding down and one day the Commanding officer told me, "Sergeant, I see no use in sending you back to Fort Sam Houston. You can just get home the best way you can." "And sergeant," He said, "Have a good day."

I think I did.

GOOD LUCK, BAD LUCK, DUMB LUCK OR NO LUCK AT ALL ON FRIDAY THE 13TH

I'm trying to write this column on Friday the Thirteenth. I'm a little apprehensive about how it might turn out. Actually, I have been what we always called "a little under the weather" which, so far, I have been unable to self-diagnose.

I am always reading about the big shots in Washington making an "unannounced" trip to Baghdad. I wonder if they ever tried to make an unannounced trip to their doctor. I have and it won't work.

Most people consider Friday the Thirteenth" an unlucky day. I guess it mostly depends on where they happen to be and the circumstances of their being there. On Friday, September 13th, 1944, I was on a bombing mission on a B-17 bomber, somewhere over Germany. I watched from my ball turret as four of our bombers blew up. Mine didn't.

I have been told that I was lucky. But—it might not have been my luck that got us through it. There were nine other boys on that plane. Maybe we were all lucky. I have been told that our guardian angels and the automatic pilot had already bailed out.

On the plus side, I just received a notification that I have won either a Mercedes or a Porsche, along with a bunch of other stuff. All of this good stuff was foisted on me without signing a thing. I have no idea where they got my name. They probably "Goggled" me. These days, everybody gets "Goggled."

I probably won't contact them as I have a perfectly good 1993 Ford F-150 pickup with about 4 gallons of gas in it. In case nobody noticed, the price of gas recently took a jump in price. The rich folks don't need it and the poor folks have to have it. It's sorta like ice was when I was growing up. The rich folks had it in the summer and the poor folks had it in the winter.

Besides not particularly needing a Mercedes or a Porsche, the tax appraiser most likely would drive by my house and see either one of these cars and double my taxes.

Actually, I hardly think the date or the day of the week has anything to do with misfortune. It is entirely possible to have a flat tire in the rain on any day of the week. However, to be on the safe side, I think I'll stay at home all day and save my four gallons of gas.

The reason I'm stuck with four gallons of gas instead of full tanks is due to my belief that the price of gas was going down. It always has, at least briefly. I was wrong this time. It appears that sooner or later I'll have to make an unannounced trip to a service station. I know that if they find out I'm coming; the price will take another jump.

I guess there are people all over the globe who get a little jumpy on Friday the 13th. It is not just a local thing as everybody has it. No way to get around it. If I worked in a dynamite factory, I'd call in sick. If I had a serious operation scheduled, I'd call it off. There is no way I would even consider getting on a space shuttle or taking any medication without first checking the side-effects.

I don't really consider myself to be superstitious but there are certain things I avoid. I refuse to walk under a ladder and if I accidentally turn a salt shaker over, it is imperative that I throw a handful of salt over my left shoulder immediately.

If a black cat runs across the road in front of me, I immediately stop, turn around and go another way. If necessary, I will drive as far as Proctor to escape the consequences of what that kitty might cause.

There is absolutely no reason to take unnecessary chances on something we can prevent.

I rest my case.

FRIENDLY FOLKS AND BUTCHERING HOGS

Back in the thirties when I was a kid, folks were a lot friendlier than they are now. Of course, circumstances were a lot different. People depended on each other. If somebody butchered a hog, it was the custom to share the meat with his neighbors. It was a reciprocal thing. Everybody did it. If a man was too poor to license his car, he borrowed his neighbor's license plates to go to town. If he had no car, he borrowed that too.

Somebody once said, "We all hang together, or we will all hang separately." Hanging separately was a lonely way to go. This was during the "Great Depression," and things weren't going too well. Companionship was needed, and there was no shortage of it.

If a family happened to be passing a neighbor's house at dinner time, or supper time, they were always welcome to stop and eat. The food wasn't the reason. Nearly everybody had the same thing anyway—just on different days. It was the sharing, and being with friends that counted.

These days, when somebody drives up in our driveway unannounced, we think, "Who on God's green earth is that, and what do they want?"

The wife may say, "Henry, hold them at the door until I get this ratty old robe off and put on some makeup."

That wasn't a problem back then. The wife put on what she had upon arising, and wore it all day. Makeup, she knew little about. What a man seen was what he got. It was rare that a man ever ran off with another man's wife, or stole another man's hog. They all looked a whole lot alike. Beauty then, as it is now, was in the eyes of the beholder.

Unlike in those days, it is not considered in good form to drop by somebody's house without calling first. "We were thinking of coming by sometime soon for a visit," you say.

"Yeah, when?" the wife may ask. "Well, maybe tonight, I just butchered a hog and I thought I'd bring you some." you reply.

"My husband has gone to Afghanistan, and I've got a meeting with—uh—The Sons of Katie Elder" "Hog, you say?" "Maybe another time," she says.

There are still a lot of friendly people around today and even good neighbors. We just no longer have to depend on each other as much. Maybe we should get to know each other better. We all need to depend on somebody at one time or another.

We have all ran across old friends in the supermarket, and for the life of us, we can't think of their names. We hate to ask about the health of their mother, or their kids. Their mother may have "passed away" and their kids may be in the penitentiary. Don't mention butchering a hog either. About all we can do is walk away—fast.

GETTING A CLOSE-UP LOOK AT OUR PAST

I recently spent the good part of a Saturday morning going through the Brown County Museum and the annex across the street. This is a most enjoyable way to pass the time and learn something about our past. Young people will learn a lot and old people will be reminded of things long forgotten.

This tour is not a walk-through thing. One should spend at least a couple of hours there. I found nearly everything I expected to find but a crosscut saw, a wagon sheet and a cotton sack. I have spent a lot of time on one end of a crosscut saw which had to be operated by two people and used mostly to saw logs or cut down large trees.

With my Dad on the other end of the saw which had to be pulled when the other person was pushing, I was often accused of zigging when I should have been zagging. It was hard work too, something I always tried to avoid.

The last cotton sack I saw was around 1946 when a neighbor convinced me that there was a lot of money to be made picking cotton. My previous experience in this pursuit proved him wrong. Maybe, I thought, with age, I had improved.

I went to Shorty the Jew's store, across the street from the courthouse and bought a cotton sack. Shorty had no objection to what everybody in the county called him for two reasons. He was short and he was a Jew. People back then made no pretense at being other than what they were.

When I returned home from WWII, Shorty gave me a new suit. I thought it was blue but when I got home, it was green. I found out later he had the blue light on that day.

My neighbor and I went to the cotton patch where we picked in the hot sun until noon. Then, I weighed in my 25 pounds, hung the sack on a fence post and went home. I didn't make enough to pay for the sack. Shorty, I knew, being smarter than me, didn't give refunds on used cotton sacks.

The last time I remember being in the old jail where the museum is located was several years ago to interview the sheriff when I was investigating a death claim for an insurance company.

A woman had somehow managed to shoot herself in the back with a .22 rifle. I thought this was somewhat puzzling, but my job was not to make conclusions, but to gather facts. If the insurance company paid, it didn't cost me a dime, or the sheriff either.

The museum annex where most of the stuff I was looking for is kept was in charge of Fred Spencer Jr. He is a friendly fellow who knows all about what's in there. He may not know what a wagon sheet is but for his age, he knows a lot. The Brownwood Bulletin has donated all of their old files and chances are you can find a picture of yourself when you were still young and good-looking and not engaged in picking cotton.

The museum has a good collection of World War Two stuff, the war we went into without getting permission from the United Nations. Somehow, we won it too. I can vouch for that because I was there.

I would recommend that anybody who has some spare time on Saturday to visit this place. You might even donate something to their collection or leave them some cash. All I had to offer was an old worn out WWII veteran which they declined.

They don't take anything they have to feed or take to the Vet.

BOXCARS: CORNCOBS AND GETTING AN EDUCATION THE HARD WAY

When I was about 10 or 12 years old, I thought it was great that my older cousin and his cousin who was in no way related to me took a sudden interest in my companionship. I had no idea that their sudden interest in me was to furnish hours of fun and frolic which at the time was pretty scarce around Blanket. They needed somebody, and I was it.

I was not aware that the 12 year old brain was still in a state of development and would stay that way for a long time. It was during this development period that they realized that with a little urging on their part, I would do most anything. I was only trying to grow up and I figured with their vast knowledge, they could help me.

Probably they did. I learned a lot of things that proved helpful to me in later years. I learned never to believe anybody who told me, "This won't hurt much and you'll thank me later", or "This is the best deal you're ever going to get. Just sign right there at the bottom of the page."

After all of these years, I still remember the day when I could see in the distance about a mile beyond the depot, a Frisco locomotive pulling a long string of boxcars fast approaching, while they carefully took a rope and tied me to the track.

Of course, they untied me just before the engineer had a major stroke, along with the minor one I was in the process of having. On another occasion, with a freight train switching cars in the Blanket yards, they locked me in a box car that I had no doubt was headed for Chicago. I knew beyond a doubt that I'd never see Mama again.

As usual, they let me out just as the boxcar was being connected to the train. I was also chosen to see what the effect would be from jumping off a 25 foot high railroad bridge into 12 inches of water in the creek below. I survived, but I took notice that not one of them jumped after I did.

They also taught me all about corncob fighting when the odds were two against one. They always got close to the water trough where they could wet their corncobs giving the cobs extra range and more sting when they hit me. As always, I was on the dry side of the cow lot. I learned that in a corncob fight, never be on the dry side of the cow lot.

My education was hard to come by, as education has a way of being. To get an education, we have to take some hard lumps along the way, but in the end, I guess it's worth it. Education means that you should never allow anybody to tie you to a railroad track when a train is coming. It also teaches you to stay away from older cousins and when you're 12 years old, you're not too smart.

Mama didn't know a lot about what I was doing at age 12 or she would have told me a few things. She didn't have much education, but she was a lot smarter than I was. Mamas always are.

We often wonder in our young years how they got that way.

GOING SIDEWAYS AND LEARING ABOUT WINE AND OTHER STUFF

I don't claim to be an expert on wine. Sometime back a lady in a grocery store told me she was going to cook a duck and wanted to know if I could suggest the proper wine to go with it. "Well," I told her, "The rule of thumb is if you have a red tablecloth, serve red wine. A white tablecloth calls for white wine. The duck won't care which you use."

Back when I was a kid and the wild grapes were ripe on the creeks, we picked several tow sacks full which Mama used to make grape jelly. What was left over, she made into her own special wine which she bottled in fruit jars. This was for medicinal purposes only.

If any of us came down with a sore throat, she would take out our special family crystal, passed on to us by my Granny and made by the Eli Garrett snuff company. We were allowed about a half glass which proved to be enough.

Since nobody in the family spoke French or Italian, we never did come up with a name for it. It was rather potent stuff though.

On October 22, a movie came out called "Sideways," in which a character in the movie raved about the subtle delicacy of Pinot Noir wine. Folks who saw the movie immediately hit the wine shops to buy some. One winery reported a 147% increase in sales in just 12 days.

Due to an excess crop of grapes in California last year and competition from Australia and Chile, wineries were having trouble selling their wine. One company, to increase sales and make up for the loss started bottling something called "Two Buck Chuck" which sold for two dollars.

It was not in the same category as Pinot Noir, made from grapes that are very fragile and hard to grow and is quite expensive. Nobody has ever been observed lying on the sidewalk drinking it from a bottle in a paper sack. The wineries that make it are now doing well.

In the meantime, a lady down in Lake Jackson, Texas has been indicted for causing the death of her husband by giving him Sherry enemas. She couldn't afford Pinot Noir but hoped to if she collected the $240,000 life insurance policy she had on him. Sherry was not mentioned in the movie.

She could probably have obtained the same result with Two Buck Chuck and saved money. The cause of her husband's death was a .47 blood alcohol level. It has been determined that it is best not to try this at home, or anywhere else.

People, as we all know, are apt to do some strange things whether they see the movie "Sideways", or not. My hill country correspondent reports he knows a fellow who bought a new pickup and was trying to see how fast it would run. He says the fellow arrived at the scene of the accident 45 minutes before the ambulance did.

On Thursday morning, Kinky Friedman, a mystery writer and musician from Kerrville announced his plans to run for Governor in front of the Alamo and called for Rick Perry to surrender. Among other things, he indicates he is for Gay marriage, remarking that "they have the same right to be miserable as the rest of us." He didn't mention seeing "Sideways," or Pinot Noir either.

As for me, I'm interested in seeing something. I've been stuck in the house too long with separated ribs. So far, the Pope got better and I didn't.

GOOD DOGS, BEER JOINTS
AND COUNTRY MUSIC

My long-time companion, my Chihuahua dog named Prissy, finally, as we say in Texas, "passed away." After eleven years of constant companionship, I found the situation without her bleak, to say the least. Having faced her death and subsequent burying, which is the really hard part, I debated ever having another dog.

Yet, coming home with no one to meet me with a friendly greeting became more than I could take. Prissy and I had explored the Big Bend together on numerous occasions and driven through Tennessee, Arkansas and Missouri in my old VW camper which she loved. Anytime I opened the door, she jumped in and refused to get out.

She stayed in the old camper without complaint outside beer joints in Nashville while I visited my musician friends. Nashville musicians have an undying love for beer joints where most of today's country songs are written. Willie, in his early days in Nashville, wrote some of his best songs in "Tootsie's Orchid Lounge" on Broadway and sold them for a little of nothing when his bar bill exceeded his entire net worth.

I stood it as long as I could and finally one day, I bought a duplicate of my dog from somebody on a parking lot. I didn't even argue about the price. I took this priceless dog home—priceless because I needed her and priceless because she needed me.

My dog owner friends and a lady who tries fruitlessly to keep me on the right track cautioned me, "Don't ever feed that dog anything but dry dog food." I dutifully went to the store and bought a big sack of dry dog food which compared in price to Russian caviar. Russian caviar would have suited her fine, the stuff I bought didn't.

She wanted what I was having. I couldn't blame her. There is no way I would eat dry cereal three times a day. She regularly sits in front of the stove patiently waiting for whatever I'm cooking to get done. She shows no preference and has developed a taste for mashed potatoes with gravy, chili, meat loaf and Fettuccini Primavera with wine sauce.

Prissy, on the other hand, loved baked chicken. I decided right off not to go that route. I kept Bo Pilgrim in spending money for years, baking three chickens a week. As far as I'm concerned, Old Bo can get out and scratch with his chickens. There is a time to hold and a time to fold.

My new dog, being but three months old, has no more discipline than I did when I gave her a choice on what to eat. She hides my shoes, runs off with my socks and regularly chews on the computer keyboard when I'm trying to write about her. She has found stuff I lost back when Eisenhower was President. When I leave home for any reason, she tries to dismantle the house. Considering her size and weight, she does a good job. Still, a good lick on my hand when I do come home makes it all worth it.

Give me a good dog and I can face the world. Without one, it can be a problem.

HAPPY TRAILS TO US AND YOU AND THEM— WHEREVER THEY ARE

When I was a kid growing up in Blanket, the last day of school in May was reason to celebrate. My buddies and I immediately took off our shoes, tied the laces together, hung them around our necks and picked our way on tender feet to Blanket Creek.

There, we took our first chilly dip in what we called the "deep hole." This was our annual rite of spring. We practically lived on that creek until school started again in the fall. My folks, having moved off the farm into town gave me more freedom to run and play. I had no teats to pull, no hay to pitch, no corn to gather and no cotton to pick. Maybe it wasn't heaven but it was close.

We became the Tom Sawyers and the Huckleberry Finns of Blanket and roamed that creek from the Deep Hole to Bradley's Bluff, about 6 miles south. The creek was our "Wide Mississippi" and we fished for catfish and perch and fried them in one of Mama's old iron skillets and often spent the night rolled up in an old quilt on the ground.

We requisitioned old crossties from the nearby Frisco railroad and built a raft which we paddled up and down the creek. We caught crawfish on a string baited with pieces of bacon and fried them on the spot. We learned from Scott Lanford, our scoutmaster, how to boil eggs in a paper sack over a campfire but we saw no good reason for doing it.

We never ran out of anything to do. If we tired of the creek, we headed for the railroad yard where a long string of boxcars was always parked. We chased each other up and down the tops of the boxcars, jumping the spaces in between. Maybe it was a dangerous thing to do but we were convinced that only old people died and sometimes they took a long time doing it.

We climbed the stairs to the Masonic Lodge over the Levisay and McCulley grocery and tried to see through window to find out what went on in there. John Strickland, a clerk in the store and also a member of the lodge told us confidentially that they rode goats up there on meeting nights.

We would sneak up the stairs on meeting nights in an effort to confirm it. We never saw hair or hide of a goat but we all swore we could hear the clatter of goat's hooves on the old wood floor. We all knew John wouldn't lie.

As we grew older, our interest shifted to John Wayne, Roy Rogers and Gene Autry movies which we saw every Saturday at the Gem or Queen theaters in Brownwood. Both Gene and Roy got into some pretty good fights with outlaws but never hit anybody too hard or they might break a finger which would seriously affect their guitar playing. Neither, we noticed, ever got their hats knocked off or lost the crease in their pants.

In later years, we all spent our time in the military service and even though we knew that our hero, John Wayne had never fired a shot at an enemy in any war, we didn't care. He inspired us while we did.

Old Roy's movies always ended with him and Dale riding off into the sunset singing "Happy Trails." They had no way of knowing it but we had probably been down more happy trails than they ever thought about.

HEAD 'EM UP AND MOVE 'EM OUT, BUT DON'T COME HERE

A lot of folks are moving. There is nothing new about that as a hundred years ago they were leaving St. Louis in covered wagons, heading west to settle our great country. Today, they are leaving Chicago, Pittsburgh, Cincinnati and Boston in droves and mostly going the same direction, but not to settle the country, but to unsettle it.

They are leaving the populated areas to escape high housing costs, crime, and developers. Some are heading south to the land of Magnolias, rednecks and sorghum syrup. One stop-light towns are fast disappearing.

Even the cliff dwellers in California are heading to Arizona after mud slides caused their expensive homes to slide off into a canyon. The great state of Arizona is not known for mudslides. They are however, blessed with rattlesnakes, heat, cactus and Gila Monsters.

They may be disappointed when they get there, finding the same things they left. My old friend, Hondo Crouch, the guru of Luckenbach before his death said, "I went there to get away from it all but when I got there, it was all there."

My youngest son, Ken, who lives in Chandler, a suburb of Phoenix, told me recently. "On my way to work, I pass by a cotton field one day and the next day, $400,000 homes are being built there."

Texas too, is getting their share, crossing all borders. Some even swim to get here. Personally, I think it is worth what trouble they have to go through. The requirements to be a Texan are simple. It is necessary for new residents to drive a pickup, drink Lone Star beer and develop a liking for Skoal, black eyed peas, country music and chicken-fried steak.

Texas may take some getting used to. Our politics sometimes get rowdy and we're set in our ways. We don't like progress much and we talk different. We like Texas the way it is and the way it has always been. We can always tell a Texan but we can't tell him much.

I am no stranger to moving. Before I was 12 years old, we lived on 4 different farms and 5 different houses in Blanket. Dad was always looking for a farm that hadn't been "farmed out" or a better house.

Once we lived on a farm in the "sandy country" where we couldn't raise anything but peanuts, watermelons sweet potatoes and grass burrs. Our diet changed drastically. Then, much to my delight, we moved to town. Town was where the action and the girls were.

Blanket was a thriving little town with a population of 300 which folks said never changed. Every time a new baby was born, a man left town. I was totally happy there. There were no teats to pull, no hay to pitch, corn to gather or cotton to pick.

Dad bought a nice house at a tax sale on the court house steps in Brownwood, and we lived there during my teen-age years until I went off to fight a war. When I was 12, I bought a bicycle, got a Brownwood Bulletin paper route and made more money in the daytime than I could spend at night.

Somebody said, "When things keep coming your way, you're probably on the wrong side of the road." The war took me away from Blanket and the good life and after the war, I never went back except to see my parents. The good life was over. I had to go to work. My "grasshopper" days were over and the "ant" phase had started.

I can never move anywhere now because no truck is big enough to haul my memories.

HEMINGWAY NEVER PICKED COTTON OR DANCED IN A HONKEY-TONK

One of Ernest Hemingway's most famous works was "For Whom the Bell Tolls." I had read all of Hemingway's books before I was in High School. While pulling a cotton sack down an endless row under a blistering Texas sun, I thought about writing a novel I would call "For Whom the bolls toll." It seemed they always tolled for me.

I also had serious thoughts of running off to Spain, writing novels, chasing pretty women and drinking wine from goat skins. None of that, of course, ever happened. I was still stuck in that cotton field.

Picking cotton however, was a boon to education. Anybody who ever did it would strive for an education to get as far as they could from a cotton field and never go back. Everything we do teaches us something.

A few years ago, I observed a bunch of men wearing white coveralls picking cotton in a field near Sweetwater. I assumed they were from the nearby State Jail. I had no idea what their crimes might have been but to me their punishment seemed adequate. Most likely, they gave up crime when they got out.

Even High School football has its educational merits. You learn that when you are being chased by a bunch of big bruisers with mayhem on their minds, you run—as fast as you can. It is best to do that all of your life.

Even Emmitt Smith, a former Dallas Cowboy who has been chased by the best is now a champion dancer, having won against big odds on "Dancing with the Stars," most women's favorite TV show. I prefer reruns of "Law and Order" myself. I never was much of a dancer. I'm still not and won't ever be.

Some folks think dancing is a sin. It was sinful the way I did it. Actually, I gave it up when my partner had to hold me up. It had no educational value anyhow.

I don't think Hemingway did it either. I can't imagine Ernest in a Texas honky-tonk waltzing across Texas. He was more likely to be watching a bull fight in Spain. Texas honky-tonks are not much different.

I have been in more honky-tonks than Budweiser. I learned something there too—keep your mouth shut and your hat on. You may have to leave in a hurry.

In spite of all my dreams and ambitions, I never did write a novel or drink wine from a goat skin. The closest I ever got to Spain was going through the Straits of Gibraltar during WWII.

I left the cotton field at an early age and the bolls no longer toll for me. I have no regrets about it.

I no longer have dreams about writing a novel or going to Spain and drinking wine from a goat skin. I spend a lot of time reading novels other people have written. Larry L. King, a Texas writer now living in Washington keeps me well supplied with books.

At the recent Texas Book Festival in Austin, a theater on Congress Avenue was named for him and two of his plays, "The Night Hank Williams Died" and "The Kingfish" were playing there. He was also both "roasted" and "toasted" by writers and celebrities at the theater.

I recently went to Putnam where he was born and took some pictures to send him. He said, "When I die, my ashes will be sprinkled there to make the journey a full circle."

It will be one heck of a circle.

GENEALOGY OR MYTH

My grandfather on my mother's side, William B. Green, and his wife Nancy, came to Brown County from Hamilton County. Beyond that, I have no knowledge. I was too stupid to ask questions, or too young to know that I should have.

I remember mama saying they camped out on the Bosque River and ate wild grapes. They made the trek in a wagon. Not a covered wagon, mind you, just a plain old wagon. Poor people in those days didn't possess covered wagons. The fact is, they didn't possess much of anything. If they had, it would probably have been repossessed by somebody.

They raised a large family after reaching Brown County. A total of 13 kids, one of whom died in infancy. They were my mother, Myrtle, brothers Callie, known as "Doc," Orville, Ed, Bud, John and Jimmy, who also died at an early age—from what ailment, I do not know. Other girls in the family, other than my mother were Connie, Sarah, Ollie, Maude and Roxie.

Old Bill Green, it was said, made the best ribbon cane syrup in the county, which he freely distributed to any and all who came to assist him on "syrup making" day. It is also said, that his home brew, which he kept cool in the cellar was unequaled. I was much too young to try it, although I had a hankering to do so.

It was also said that it was a foolish idea to loan Bill Green anything other than a Tom cat, which would make its way home as soon as possible. Old Bill would borrow anything, whether he had any need for it or not. He met his demise one evening late, riding one of his plow horses home from a day in the fields. The horse shied at something crossing a creek and in the resulting fall, Bill's neck was broken. I do not recall the year, but it was sometime in the thirties.

My grandfather, Tom Marlin, and my dad, Jesse Marlin came to Brown County, settling near Blanket when my dad was two years old. They came from Palestine in Falls County. My grandmother's name was Martha Caroline and she is buried in the Rock Church cemetery north of Blanket in the family plot. Tom, who was a "horse doctor," moved to Midland with his daughter and son-in-law when they "starved out" on the farm northwest of Blanket, and is buried in the Midland cemetery in what I've been told, in a section reserved for paupers. This was in the middle of the Great Depression and paupers were as common as Johnson grass.

Tom Marlin's daddy, my great grandfather migrated down from Cape Gierado, Missouri, where, according to my dad, he ran a shoe shop. He left Missouri in rather of a hurry when he killed a man, for what reason, I don't know. Possible because the man's shoes were not repaired on the day they were supposed to be.

He apparently hung a sign on the shoe shop, sometime before dawn, which proclaimed that he had "Gone to Texas" As far as I can find out, he detoured by way of Oklahoma and married a "full-blood" Cherokee which gives me some degree of Indian blood. I have noticed that during a full moon, I have a burning desire to make a raid across the Rio Grande and bring home some Tequila.

His father, I have heard, was a sea captain in Maine, and being afflicted with sea-sickness everytime he got on a boat, migrated to Alabama. I don't know this for a fact. History is mostly a myth, repeated over and over by folks who weren't even there.

I probably won't ever know, and it might be best that I don't. Texas, after all, was settled by outlaws and misfits. Sam Houston, it is said, didn't send Jim Bowie to San Antonio to defend the Alamo. He told him to go down there and blow it up so Santa Anna couldn't get it.

HOG KILLING DAY AND GETTING A GOOD SCALD ON LIFE

I recently read on the internet that a fellow down in Georgia killed a wild hog that was 9 feet long, weighed a thousand pounds and had tusks that would bite through the bed of a Ford F-150 pickup.

I am not aware that folks in Georgia are prone to stretch the truth or even outright lie. However, with our population constantly shifting the way it is, there is a possibility that a few Texans have moved down there, and they will. As far as I know, the fellow who shot the hog was not a Texan.

When I was a kid growing up on farms around Blanket, everybody had hogs. Hog meat was a necessary part of our diet. I think we made use of all of it. On hog killing day, the kids even washed out the bladders and blew them up, being the only balloons we had. Hog killing day back then was far more important than the fourth of July. Nobody, however, had a hog that weighed anywhere near a thousand pounds.

Probably the reason they didn't was due to what we fed them. Our hogs ate what we called "slop." Slop consisted of what might have been left from supper, or anything else we could find to put in it. Hogs will eat anything. I remember that Bob Wills once recorded a song about a fellow who was "Sitting by the window, singing to his love when a slop bucket fell from the window above."

Such an event would break up a romance quicker than anything I know, considering the content.

Hog killing day was a community affair and was always held on the first cold day of winter due to our lack of any refrigeration. The men killed and butchered the hogs and scalded the hair off. The water had to be a certain temperature. If the hair came off easily, it meant that they had "got a good scald on it." Today, it means something was done right.

The women cut up the meat and made the sausage. Sausage was always served for dinner. Nobody, as far as I know, including Jimmy Dean, has ever made sausage that tasted that good. I doubt that anybody ever will. Like a lot of good things I remember about my youth during the Depression, hog killing day is gone forever.

We buy our sausage in the supermarket along with the $4.00 bacon that will fry down to nothing if you don't watch it close. The sausage has stuff in it that the women in the thirties didn't know about.

At the end of the day, the participants all went home with a good supply of meat which included hams, bacon and sausage which was placed in the smokehouse, mostly cured with salt. If it turned a little green with age, nobody paid much attention to it. Folks back then were a hardy bunch. When the Good Lord made them, He got a good scald.

If there are any 1000 pound hogs around today other than in Georgia, they must be in Washington. I'm always reading about our elected Congressmen sending a lot of pork home.

I'm still waiting for mine.

THE HOME BREW THAT
NEVER FOUND A HOME

My dad was what is known as a teetotaler. He didn't drink alcoholic beverages and didn't think anybody else should. He would have, if necessary, voted a county dry and then moved. Our county was already as dry as the Sahara, so he never had to move.

Of course, back in those days when I was a kid, as it is now, any prohibitive substance, whether it was in a liquid form, or grown in the woods, had a certain attraction. I once found a case of beer hidden under a railroad culvert. I immediately loaded it on my bicycle and hid it on Blanket Creek.

A buddy and I took a pair of pliers and pried the caps off and sampled it at different times until it was all gone. The stuff in small amounts did seem to make the grass greener and the sky bluer, but also had a downside. It made the road narrower, causing us some difficulty in keeping our bicycles between the bar ditches. We did, however, save the bottles.

After the demise of the case of beer, and it being a hundred miles in any direction where a new supply might be obtained, we decided to make our own. My granddad had done it for years and I had some idea of the formula.

Since our only transportation was pedal power, we found it necessary to bring another buddy in on it that had an old Model A Ford. We needed stuff available only in Brownwood, 13 miles away. One day, we drove over there and bought a can of Pabst

Blue Ribbon malt, a cake of yeast, five pounds of sugar and some bottle caps. We were about ready.

I sneaked a 5 gallon crock jar out of the house that mama used to make pickles in. We then took our supplies and the crock jar down to Blanket Creek where we mixed the stuff up with water from the creek, blowing the green scum off the water as best we could.

We then put one of mama's cup towels over the jar and hid it in some weeds near a fence. Then, we patiently waited. After about ten days, we decided to try it. We found that somehow, several grasshoppers and some unidentified species of bugs had invaded our brewery.

We took turns holding the crock jar up so the other could blow the bugs back and sample the brew. We decided it was time to bottle it. I borrowed a bottle capper from a fellow I knew who occasionally ran off a batch of his own.

We then carried our five gallon crock jar to a remote stock tank in somebody's pasture to bottle it. The stuff seemed to taste about like it should, so we would drink one bottle and then cap a bottle.

Shortly thereafter, we began to have some rather severe stomach cramps. It was then that we discovered we couldn't get our pants down fast enough, and then we decided there was not much use in pulling them back up again.

We poured the whole mess in the stock tank and went home. The Milwaukee breweries were no longer threatened. I forgot all about returning the bottle capper until the fellow told Dad to tell me to bring his capper home. Dad had no idea what he was referring to. When he asked me, I told him I didn't either, but I did feel a twinge in my lower abdomen.

After some discussion, we decided the cause of our failure was due to either bad water or bad bugs. Maybe even both.

ASHES TO HOMINY
AND LYE TO SOAP

One of our most valued possessions when I was growing up back during the thirties was a large cast-iron pot. It probably held 15 or 20 gallons of whatever mama chose to put in it at the time. It was kept in the yard, being much too big to place on our wood-burning cook stove.

To use this pot, it was necessary to build a fire under it, or around it, to heat whatever it was being used for at the time. It had multiple uses. On washday, it was used to boil the clothes with a liberal amount of homemade lye soap. Mama used a big stick, maybe the handle from an old broom to stir the clothes with.

It was also used to make lye soap, rendering out the hog lard and adding the necessary amounts of lye. When it "set up," I have watched her take a butcher knife and cut the soap out of the pot in large bar-size amounts.

The same pot may have been carried to a local creek for the annual family get-together, and used to make a big pot of stew. I think the same stick that was used to stir the clothes and make the soap was also used to stir the stew.

It was perfectly safe. Lye soap would wipe out any germ known to man. The Surgeon General, had there been one, would have voiced his approval. The Center for Disease Control in Atlanta would have approved. None of us, as far as I know, had ever heard of Atlanta, the Surgeon General, or such a center. The center of our universe was on that hundred acre farm northwest of Blanket.

Mama controlled our diseases the best she knew how, or if she failed, called on Dr. Yantis in Blanket. Dr Yantis knew all about diseases, the symptoms, and the prognosis.

There were times, however, when he was unable to do anything about it, with his limited medications. He provided hope though, and in those days, hope was about all we had.

On hominy making day, the iron pot was again brought into use. The husks of the field-corn were removed using a combination of ashes and lye, neither being friendly to the inner-workings of our gastrointestinal systems. After this treatment in the old iron pot, the corn had to be rinsed repeatedly, using water hauled in from somewhere in 55 gallon barrels. Our little farm had no well.

After the cleansing of the corn of all residues of the ashes and lye, it had to be cooked in the old iron pot until it was done. We all loved the hominy, and after all of these years, I still do. In those days, having hominy meant a hard days work for mama. Today, when I get a craving for hominy, a quick trip to the supermarket and a can opener is all that is necessary.

Somehow, it doesn't taste the same. I assume the places that make it have running water and a cleaner pot, where never a pair of dirty overalls have been washed. Maybe they even remove the last taste of the ashes and the lye.

Maybe they don't use ashes and lye these days. Maybe these items are not available to them and scientists have come up with something better. Mama had plenty though, having to build a fire around that pot on a weekly basis, and a good supply of lye for making soap.

Maybe things are better now, and maybe they are not. Mama, if she was here, would know.

HOT TAMALES, CORN SHUCKS AND NOISY MATTRESSES

I have always liked tamales as far back as I can remember. Back during the Depression, we didn't have them often. Maybe once a year after hog-killing time. Real tamales were made from the meat in a hog's head. In those days, they were called "hot tamales," not because they were served steaming hot but because of the hot chile peppers used to make them.

When I was a kid, we used to recite a little poem about those tamales when some were being made.

Hot tamales, two in a shuck,

One fell out

And the other stuck.

Making tamales is a chore anytime but making them on a wood-burning stove in a hot kitchen was enough to discourage any housewife from tackling the chore. Mama did though. Mama did everything.

Spreading the masa on corn shucks was no easy job then and it still isn't. The one thing we had back then was plenty of corn shucks. Nobody in their right mind would ever enter the Levisay and McCullough grocery store in Blanket and ask for corn shucks. They had no masa meal either but the meal we had ground at Chris Switzer's mill was a reasonable substitute.

We substituted a lot back in those days. A substitute is as good as the real thing if you didn't know any different and we didn't. Neither did we care. What we cared most for was any substitute Mama could come up with for beans and cornbread, our usual diet in the winter.

The corn shucks used in tamale making were also used in those days to stuff mattresses. Not only was a corn shuck mattress worse than sleeping on the floor but they were noisy too. Absolutely nothing ever happened on one that everybody in the house didn't know about. The mere act of turning over woke up every hound dog on the place.

Finally, for whatever reason I don't know, corn shucks were restricted to making tamales. There are many things we can be thankful for these days besides air conditioners and credit cards.

Being a life-long lover of tamales, I still remember back in the late forties and early fifties a man named Marshall Castro sold hot tamales from a little cart up and down Center Avenue. He also ran a café on Fisk.

I don't know if he used the meat from hog's heads or not and I really don't want to know. I know for sure that he made the best tamales I have ever found anywhere.

I remember when I was about 17, a kid named Bernard and I had somehow got dates with a couple of high-class Brownwood girls. Bernard was sort of a nerd but he had a car and I didn't.

We had on our best clothes and Bernard even had on a white shirt. We spotted Mr. Castro with his hot tamale cart on the way to pick up the girls and bought a dozen. Bernard, being rather inexperienced in hot tamale eating took the shuck off one. The tamale slid down the front of his white shirt and the shuck stuck in his lap.

He looked a lot like he had just rode in from San Saba on a load of cedar posts but he girls didn't seem to care and everything worked out all right.

We still had nearly a dozen tamales left in case it didn't.

BE IT EVER SO HUMBLE,
HOME IS WHERE THE HOUSE IS

Back in the thirties during what folks called "The Great Depression," we left our little farmed-out hundred acre farm more than once to seek something better. It seemed that no matter where we moved, we found the same thing we had left. And yet, the old houses we moved into became home, the minute the wagon was unloaded. There was just something about home.

There is no word in the English language more precious than the word home. It can be anywhere, and it pulls us back like a magnet. It's where we belong, and we can't escape it.

A mansion on the hill, or a shack in a poor section of town—it's ours, and we can't wait to get there. We have fought wars in distant lands with one thought uppermost in our minds—going home.

A friendly dog greets us at the gate, a loved one waves from the front porch, and we know that we have reached the one place in the world where neither poverty nor trouble can touch us. We are home.

During WWII, I was about as far from home as I ever had been, flying as a ball turret gunner on a B-17 bomber in the 15th Air Force in Italy. We all knew that when we completed our 50 missions over Germany, we were going to that magic place called home.

We all looked forward to that last mission but there were many times I had doubts that we would ever make it. There were days when I thought we would never even make it back to our base in Italy.

I watched more than one B-17 being blown out of the sky by the German Anti-aircraft fire but ours wasn't. We were blessed by flying in the best aircraft ever made and the best pilot and co-pilot and crew in the 15th Air Force.

It was also obvious that somebody who outranked even our generals was looking out for us

In early 1945, I finished gunnery school at Las Vegas. I was given a 30 day delay in route to Buckingham Field in Florida. I was also given $400 in cash to pay for whatever transportation I chose. I decided to hitchhike and save the money. It was a bad choice

I was carrying all my worldly possessions in a B-4 bag along with a parachute. I decided the best way to carry the parachute was to buckle the thing on. I finally caught a ride to Boulder Dam, which has been renamed Hoover dam, I assume after former President Hoover. During the Depression years, farmers called their tractors "Hoover Tractors" as no seats were needed. I won't explain that.

Since it was wartime, there were guards on the dam where the road was I meant to go on. I was not permitted to walk cross the dam. Maybe they thought I meant to bail off since I was wearing a parachute. To get home any sooner, I might have done it.

I finally gave up, caught a ride back to Vegas and bought a train ticket, which I should have done to start with and arrived home, parachute and all.

Gael Montana, a lady barber and a long-time friend of mine who cuts hair in a hundred year old barber shop in Comfort, Texas, usually with a large dog sleeping peacefully beneath the barber chair, once told me, "Home is where the house is."

Gael was right.

HUNTING FOR THE JUMPING OFF PLACE

My friend, Dr. Dennis Wentz, was born and raised in North Dakota, not far from the Canadian border. I don't know this for a fact but there is the possibility that from gazing at that flat landscape during his youth, he may have had thoughts that the world was flat and that somewhere south there was a "jumping-off-place."

Later, while attending medical school in Chicago, I'm sure he probably found out the world wasn't flat and that there was no jumping-off-place, at least around Chicago.

I first met Dr. Wentz in the Big Bend National Park when he was at Scott and White hospital at Temple Texas. We became friends and during his entire time at Scott and White, both of us having a love for the Big Bend, went camping there almost every week-end.

I was determined to show him the actual jumping-off place which I firmly believed actually existed. Texas, where I was born and raised was also as flat as North Dakota in a lot of places. Texas however, was not close to anything, except the Mexican border, which from where we were was almost a day's drive.

While hiking in the Chisos mountains, we sometimes could look far beyond the ability of our eyes to see. I was still sure that we would find that elusive place. After nearly two years of hiking, we never did, but I think we got close a time or two.

Harry Marlin

I still believe it is out there somewhere. Columbus was worried about it too with those borrowed ships from Queen Isabella, who they say was sometimes in a bad humor. He had to get them back one way or another. The queen having not approved of his sailing off the end of the earth. He didn't think too much of it either.

THE ILL WINDS OF TEXAS MAY BLOW US NO GOOD

I grew up in a time when the world was mostly uncluttered. It was possible to stand in one spot, turn completely around and not see a microwave tower or a TV tower anywhere. About all that was visible in any rural area above the skyline was an occasional windmill.

Progress has changed all of that and it never again will be the same, mostly because of overpopulation, both here and all over the world.

These days there are people who find it impossible to spend ten minutes without talking to someone on a cell phone, this being the reason for the microwave towers. I see them in use every day somewhere. In the checkout line at the grocery is a favorite place. I recently carried on a long conversation with a woman behind me, not knowing she was talking to somebody else on her cell phone.

All of these towers sticking up everywhere tend to bother me and I don't like it. A hundred years ago such things bothered the Indians. When telegraph lines were being installed across the West, they proceeded to chop down the poles as fast as they were put up. In addition to the problem caused by the white man cluttering up their world, shooting their buffalo and taking their land, they caused a serious illegal immigration problem. We know how that turned out. We are all still here.

The government eventually solved everything by moving the Indians to the sorriest, driest, most remote land they could find, most of which is in Arizona and New Mexico. Somehow, the Indians won the right to do whatever they wanted on their land and they built casinos. After a hundred years or so, they are finally getting even.

Now, we have another problem staring us in the face, or will have when the "Renewable Energy Systems" build the 10 to 25 wind turbines planned for our county. If people lease them the land, we can't stop them from being built but can refuse a tax abatement they all want and need. Where are the Indians when we need them?

At the present time, at least around my place, there is no shortage of electricity. I flip a switch and a light comes on. I have no wish to see giant wind turbines blocking my view of our rolling hills and green valleys and as one citizen near Abilene put it, "Using up our wind."

The wind turbines are expensive, costing up to $2 million each. If we have any hope of our Texas wind blowing us some cheap electricity, forget it. The wind is free which is about the only thing these days that is. It wouldn't be except for the difficulty involved in taxing it.

I think that both the County Commissioners and the Renewable Energy Systems representatives were surprised at the reception they got at the regular Commissioner's meeting with "standing room only" according to Candace Fulton with the Brownwood Bulletin. Apparently there are people in Brown County who don't want the wind turbines cluttering up our landscape.

If the residents of Comanche and Mills County want them, that's fine with me. Give them ours. We will keep our wind and our uncluttered view of what we have. If we suddenly get an urge to see one of these giant wind turbines, we can drive to Comanche or Goldthwaite and get a good look.

I think I'll just stay here, talk on my cell phone and count the microwave towers.

TRAIN ROBBERS, BANK ROBBERS AND HERMITS

I have often thought about moving into a cave high up on a mountain in the Big Bend Country and be a hermit. There are times that it sounds like a good idea. The problem is that I have waited too long to do it. Just getting me up a mountain these days is more than I can do.

There are other problems too. I would need a Coleman stove to cook on and a coal oil lantern to see by. I have no idea where I could find any coal oil. Then, I would need some ice to keep my food from spoiling or live on canned goods. I like smoked oysters but a week of that diet might be all I could stand. No cold beer either in case I got an urge for one

I would have no electricity to run my computer and without a computer, I wouldn't get any spam. After all, I get an e-mail from somebody named Lisa at least twice a day. I don't know who Lisa is but I think she wants to sell me something I don't need. Anyway, I'd probably miss her.

The only cave I have ever been in was littered with some kind of bones. I don't know if a cougar had made a meal from some other hapless animal or a hermit. Maybe both. That's something else that bothers me but I didn't find a coal oil lantern.

It might be best if I just stay here and live out my days with Lisa on the computer. Maybe I'll find out what she's selling.

Back in the seventies when I made frequent trips to the Big Bend area, I met an old fellow named Tull Newton who was pretty close to being a hermit. He lived in an old rock house, formerly occupied by the quicksilver miners at Terlingua. The old one room house had open windows and no door.

Somebody had started the story that Tull was a former member of the notorious Newton gang that had robbed banks and trains from Texas to Canada during the period from 1919 to 1924. He emphatically denied it. He told me, "I didn't rob no damn trains or banks or hold anybody's horses while they done it."

As a result of the stories, tourists flocked to his shack. He developed a dislike for all tourists. "Every day", He told me, "They stick their cameras through my windows trying to take my picture."

Tull had little to do with anybody. Some friends who lived in the area introduced me to him or he wouldn't have talked to me. He was a tough old coot but whether he was a member of the train-robbing Newton gang, I don't know. There is no Tull Newton listed among the four who robbed trains and banks but they were all from Uvalde and he could have been a younger brother. He didn't like to talk about the subject.

Sometime between my trips to Terlingua, Tull was admitted to a nursing home in Alpine and I never saw him again. I guess he died there. I'm sure if you looked long enough somebody could be found who would point out the remains of an old rock house and tell you, "A member of the notorious Newton gang lived right there" Maybe one did. I don't know.

ACROSS THE RIVER AND INTO THE FENCE

I just read that the Supreme Court met and made an important decision. Since the Second amendment to our constitution was ratified in 1791, they decided that it was good enough for folks back then it was just fine with 5 out of 9 of them to remain the way it is now except that we no longer have to be member of a militia to own a gun. Also, anybody in Washington D.C. can now own a gun. I thought they already did.

Since I don't have a law degree, the best I can make out about their decision is that it is perfectly legal now to arm bears. Too, we can now keep a gun on our premises and shoot anybody who violates our territory.

The Supreme Court also gave the go-ahead to building 670 miles of fence along our southern border which has been plagued with lawsuits filed by environmentalists and City mayors along the Texas border. They are calling it "The Great Wall of Texas" and claim among other things it seriously affects the lives of two cats, the Ocelot and the Jaguarondi that regularly swim the Rio Grande to mate. As far as I can determine, neither have cost the tax payers a penny so far. The two-legged variety that swims the river cost us a lot.

Of course, there are always dissenters in the court for good reason. Supreme Court justices are appointed by the President in power at the time. If he happens to be a Republican, the dissenters are all Democrats and vice-versa. A president only gets to appoint a Supreme Court justice when one dies. They seldom ever die and they are appointed for life. That doesn't mean your life or their life but life on earth.

Of course, they have to be approved by the legislature and they seldom ever die either. Want to live a long and happy life? Get elected to something. The average Senator, they say, becomes a millionaire in only 2 years. That's nice too but the average citizen never does.

With the price of gasoline approaching $4.00 a gallon and the daily temperature reaching triple digits, it gets harder and harder to find a good subject to write about. Well, except for one thing. It is now fresh black-eyed pea season. I love fresh black-eyed peas. I'm sure that if the Good Lord ever made anything better, He kept it.

The peas, however, are getting hard to find. With the population shift that is happening, there are people moving into Texas these days, coming from far-off places where black-eyed peas and okra are regarded as poison, and not as many farmers are raising any. In some states, black-eyed peas are used for cow feed. That should be a felony, at least, punishable by 10 years in a lockup.

I was lucky. A nice lady in a fruit and vegetable store looks out for me every year and if they get any peas, she calls me. A few years ago, a friend told me, "I've got 30 acres of black-eyed peas and you can have all you want". I followed his directions, took a big sack and was happily picking peas when an irate farmer showed up. "What are you doing in my pea patch? He asked. I hastily explained. "Well," He said, "That old boy don't own this land or the peas either but since you're here, go ahead and fill your sack."

My "friend" thought that was the funniest thing he ever did. I didn't.

I MIGHT BUY IT IF I KNEW WHAT THEY WERE SELLING

I must be getting too old to understand the ads on TV. Something is wrong. Most of the time, I have no idea what they're selling. I do like the little green lizard with the British accent, and I know what he is selling. How the cavemen got into the picture, I haven't a clue. They always seem to be mad because the ad indicates that lizard is smarter than they are. Most likely, they don't even own a car. I hope not.

It seems to me that if this company spent a lot less money on ads promoting cavemen, their insurance would be a lot cheaper. The lizard does an adequate job of promotion. At least, I understand him, or her, as the case might be.

One auto insurance company advertises that you can have all the wrecks you want and your premiums won't increase. Are they promoting reckless driving, or what?

Another ad that puzzles me is the one for the Ford Edge. The car apparently, according to the ad, has the ability to drive on the ledge of 40 story buildings and up and down stairs. The fellow driving it and his passenger both have the appearance of either being "On something" or their parents were cousins. Then somebody, either a man or woman, says "Edge", making it a 4 syllable word. They can't even do that in East Texas.

Anyway, I just read that a bunch of these cars are being recalled. Maybe somebody found out the hard way that they couldn't be driven on a building ledge or go up and down stairs.

Since the car is a Ford, I'm sure it's a fine car but the ad agency they use is a little weird.

Then, there are those two fellows who eat all of their meals at a drive-in but always with their seat belts firmly fastened. Are they afraid they might be rear-ended?

I have found that I have to unbuckle my seat belt to reach the speaker to place my order. Due to my hearing impairment, I can't hear a word they ask on that speaker. I just always agree with them. I never know what I'll get.

Anyway, I know some folks who weigh a little too much for their height that couldn't eat a hotdog with their seat belts on.

I still remember some of the radio ads from when I was a kid. They didn't beat around the bush. What you heard was what you got. The Pepsodent toothpaste ad informed us all that "You'll wonder where the yellow went if you brush your teeth with Pepsodent." None of us had yellow teeth that I recall but why take a chance?

These days on TV we get ads for teeth whitener. Put it on before you go to bed and the next morning you can dazzle your friends and blind other drivers with a smile on the way to work. I wonder if it works on dentures.

I no longer pay any attention to the ads for various medications advertised on TV. Any one of them, according to their disclaimers, might kill me. "Ask your doctor," they say. How am I supposed to do that? I have enough trouble just getting in to see one.

I have decided that the best thing to do is what most TV watchers do. When the commercials start, head for the kitchen for a beer or a sandwich and stay there until they're over.

Let the lizard and the cavemen handle it.

I MISSED BEING NAMED HARRY POTTER BUT NOT MUCH ELSE

My foreign correspondent who lives down in the Hill Country told me the other day that with all the Harry Potter book publicity, I could have made a fortune if my middle name had been Potter. I could have named my last two books, "Harry Potter and The Last Train to Blanket," and "Harry Potter and The Lonesome Bull."

I agreed, but told him I would most likely have personally met J.K. Rowland or one of her lawyers before the sun went down. Besides that, my books were not over 600 pages long and hers are. At my age, I didn't have that much time. Anyway, if I was ever a "Boy Wizard," I outgrew it.

Actually, my middle name might have been Potter as my Grandmother was a Potter before her marriage. Dad, however, was not fond of that name. One of Granny's cousins used to ride his horse around the country looking for her relatives so he could get a few free meals and feed for his horse. He never wore out his welcome as it was already worn out when he got there.

He was a sort of sleazy-looking fellow who slicked his hair back with hog lard or axel grease, the only two things available back then anybody could do it with.

Dad had no use for anybody who didn't work, play a fiddle or follow the hounds. That pretty well left Potter out of my name.

Back when I was born, folks sometimes didn't name the new arrivals for two or three weeks. One day, Dad was in Blanket and ran across Harry Bettis, a prominent businessman. "I hear you have a new boy, Jesse. What did you name him?"

"Well," Dad said, "I guess Harry Bettis would be fine with both of us." Mr. Bettis immediately gave Dad a five dollar bill, which in those days would fill the bed of a wagon with groceries. Being three weeks old at the time, I wasn't worried about groceries.

Of course, J.K. Rowland with 5 best-selling books already wouldn't know how important that was in 1924. It took me awhile too but by the time I was 6, I found out. The Great Depression was getting in full swing and our sunsets were starting to be in black and white.

I have been reading since I was old enough to read. I received every gold star the Blanket school library had for reading. Some stuff I learned, I'm sure is invaluable and other stuff just clutters up my mind. Still, there are times when I know stuff I don't remember learning. I guess, like the hard drive on a computer, it stuck in there somewhere.

Kids, these days have not been known to read much with all the other distractions they have but the Harry Potter books have them reading again. This is an unbelievable accomplishment for J.K. Rowland, or anybody else.

I have never read a Harry Potter book and I doubt I ever will but I'm sure if the content of the books should warp young minds, they will outgrow it. They will learn that though there are lizards running around everywhere these days, wizards are in short supply.

I never did take a course in Creative Writing. Maybe I should have but it just never came up. The fact is, I was older than rope before I ever made an attempt to write. This came about at the request of Shelton Prince, a former publisher of the Bulletin who somehow got the idea that I should write a column.

I NEVER WROTE A BEST SELLER OR LEARNED TO JUGGLE CATS

I have been trying for a week to think of something to write and had little luck at it. I could write about the rain but I'm afraid if I do, it will stop. When it stops raining in the spring, it might not rain again until October. Actually, by now, I should have a bunch of tomatoes set out in the garden but due to the rain, I don't. I had hoped to get them out before the first hail storm.

I was having a new roof put on and about the time the roofers got started, the rain started. A week later, it stopped long enough to finish the job. I did learn one thing though. They removed one layer of shingles before the rain and it didn't leak which leads me to believe I didn't need that roof anyhow. I sure don't know.

I have been occupying my time during the rainy days reading a number of books, all of which were written by New York Times bestselling writers. I wasn't impressed. I have noticed that every book I have read recently was written by those bestselling writers. I wonder if any of them ever wrote something that didn't sell.

I have. I still have a whole box full I wrote that didn't sell and the New York Times didn't even mention it. Anyway, I had a lot of fun doing it and I sold enough to pay the printer. I'm a sort of rural literary carpenter. I like to take a bunch of words, put them together and build something that somebody, sometime, might read whether the New York Times does or not.

I have written a lot of stuff that those New York Best Sellers wouldn't touch with a 10 foot pole. I don't recall any of them ever writing about buzzards, but I did. They also never wrote about going on a rabbit drive or standing around watching the government shoot cows.

Of course, most of them are not as old as I am or have been through half the stuff I have. Most likely they never picked cotton on a hot day, or saw the inside of a ball turret on a B-17 bomber and been shot at with .88 millimeter guns over half of Europe while freezing my rear off at 30,000 feet.

Maybe they were at Harvard or Yale learning to write while I was doing those things but I still write whether I know how or not. I never did even learn how to juggle cats. I once took a course in bookkeeping and learned how to juggle books.

There is a lot more to writing than sitting at a computer and hitting the keys. First, it helps a lot to have something to write about before you start. It does make it a lot easier if you have a little knowledge about the subject you're writing about.

Like I said, this is one of those weeks I couldn't think of anything to write, which reminds me of a story I heard. A woman woke her son up one morning and said, "Get up. It's time to go to church." "I'm not going," He said," They don't like me and I don't like them."

"There are two reasons you're going" His mother said. "You are 59 years old and you're the preacher." I'm writing this for two reasons. I'm 83 years old and I'm the columnist.

WATCH OUT FOR THE
SIDE-EFFECTS OF SIDE-EFFECTS

I recently came down with an ailment I quickly self-diagnosed as a sinus infection. Sometimes my self-diagnosis of my various ailments is nowhere near correct. There is a reason for this. My entire medical training was obtained from Google on my computer. Well, at least it is a start.

Anyway, I gave my ailment a day to get well and it didn't so I had to resort to a trip to the drug store. I picked out a box of 24 capsules which promised to give me a fast cure. I can truly vouch for the fact that they did.

I was cured before the day was over, mostly because I read the information on the box and never took a one. After reading all the warnings, I decided that it might be best to stick to a simple sinus infection rather than die from a serious side-effect. There were a few on the list that would interest Dr. Kevorkian who was released from prison on June 1, and may go back to doing what he was sent up for in the first place.

Every time I read the warnings on various medications, I think of what Albert Einstein said many years ago when his mother insisted he take a dose of Castor Oil. "For every action, there is a reaction." It is those reactions that bother me.

I have several prescriptions around my place that I never took, and never will. The bad part about prescriptions is that you don't have a clue what's in one until you get it and read the warnings.

If there are not sufficient warnings listed, a quick check with Google will give you some more.

I realize why the drug companies are forced to list all these possible side-effects and hope that somebody doesn't sue them over one they forgot to list. If they do forget one, most likely somebody will come down with it and immediately call a lawyer.

I grew up in an era when few medications were available. What there was, we were glad to get when we needed it. I don't ever recall going into Ernest Allen's drug store in Blanket to get a prescription filled and have Ernest say, "Harry, if I was you, I wouldn't take this. Dr. Yantis didn't list any side-effects."

Nearly every medication we take warns us not to "operate machinery." Obviously, the drug companies are convinced that most Americans do nothing but take pills and operate machinery. I have been a resident of this planet since before they dug the Bayou and I don't ever remember operating any machinery. Isn't machinery like maybe cotton gins?

I do recall operating a wheel-barrow one time on a construction job but I quit when they insisted on putting concrete in it. Anyway, I was just about 17 at the time and I didn't need any prescriptions. Nothing I had was worn out then. Now, everything I've got just about is.

I plan on taking good care of the few parts I have left that still work. The last time I checked, 1924 parts were getting hard to find. I even stopped smoking which was the one thing I did really well.

One thing about it though, I wore my parts out in a normal manner doing something constructive. I didn't wear my knee and hip joints out jogging up steep hills or lifting weights or pounding them on a treadmill.

I was forced into picking cotton in my youth and nobody knows what the long term side-effects of that might be. I find nothing on Google under "Cotton picking side-effects.'

I can only hope for the best and prepare for the worst.

MOST ACCIDENTS HAPPEN AT HOME BUT SOME DON'T

I recently had what the medical profession calls a "CVA," which means a "Cardiovascular accident." The reason they call it an accident is that nobody in their right mind would want to have one on purpose. Ordinary folks who never went to medical school call it a stroke.

It first came to my attention when after leaving a local restaurant with my lady-friend and my right leg decided it did not want to ride home in the car with us. It took both of us to get it in the car and shut the door so it couldn't get out.

I thought the action of the leg was most peculiar but things then got worse. I got up the next morning, made a pot of coffee as usual. As I was pouring myself a cup, I noticed that I was missing the cup by about 5 inches and pouring coffee all over the stove. A little while later, I poured orange juice all over the dining table. My right hand had lost direct contact with my brain. My leg still wasn't cooperating either.

My daughter came over shortly after that and asked why there was coffee all over the stove and orange juice on the table. I had no reasonable explanation "Well," She said, "I know somebody who can explain and you are going to see him right now."

We loaded up me and my right leg in her pickup, shut the door good so it couldn't get out and went to see my doctor. He apparently had no difficulty with a diagnosis. His biggest problem was me. I am not a good patient. I have been told that about 90% of people who die are under the care of a doctor.

After some tests to confirm his diagnosis and an agreement to take physical therapy and try to quit smoking, I was allowed to go home, taking my right leg and right hand, the two troublemakers with me.

Since smoking, according to medical science, seems to get the blame for most of our ailments, I thought of all the people I see lurking in alleys and on the sidewalks in front of their places of employment lighting up on their breaks. It seems that smoking is no longer permitted in any building unless the smoker has the deed to it in his pocket.

I can envision at some time in the future, ambulances making regular daily runs like the garbage trucks to pick up smokers on the sidewalks and in the alleys who can't get their legs and arms in gear. I hope that never happens but it did to me. Of course, I'm older than rope and started smoking during WWII when cigarettes were cheap and somebody spent a lot of time trying to kill me.

Mark Twain said, "Quitting smoking is easy. I have done it a thousand times." I have been down that road a few times myself. Once, I quit for about three years. A friend and I were climbing a mountain in the Big Bend Park. We stopped to rest and he lit a Camel. It smelled like an 8 course dinner to a starving man. I had to have one and I did. Later, I gave up mountain climbing as being bad for my health.

Things are looking up. My right leg no longer objects to riding in a car with me and I no longer pour coffee on the stove.

ICED-TEA ON SUNDAY WHERE THE WHEELS STAY ON YOUR BUGGY

My Granddad Marlin was what folks called a horse doctor back in the thirties. I don't think he ever got within 400 miles of a school of Veterinary Medicine, but he did it anyhow. He was much in demand in the north part of the county and every morning he hitched his horse to his buggy and made calls. He knew just where to stand when he stuck his knife in a bloated cow.

My aunt Annie and Uncle Will lived with him and Will did the farming when he felt like it. He also was a big practical joker and played the banjo. I don't know if he played the banjo good or bad. I don't know if anybody does.

A favorite joke among musicians is that "perfect pitch" is when somebody throws a banjo in a dumpster from 30 feet and hits an accordion. Anyway, Will played one when he wasn't farming or aggravating Granddad Marlin.

After Granddad hitched his horse to his buggy in the mornings, Will would sneak out and take the nuts off the rear axle that kept the wheels on. About a hundred feet up the road, the rear wheels would come off. Will laughed until he ran out of breath.

Granddad, being a mild-mannered sort seldom raised his voice. He would say, "Will, you ought not to a-done that." Will might not do it again until Granddad forgot about it, usually not more than a month or so. He would say, "Pa, we've got to check them nuts more often. You might get hurt." He didn't fool Granddad a bit.

Our part of the farm was just south of their farmhouse and I often walked there and ate dinner with them. Nobody ever missed a chance back then to eat dinner with anybody. Folks often timed their visits to arrive at the noon hour. Anything they might have was probably more than they had at home.

One Sunday when I was about four, Granddad Marlin saved my life. I somehow got a chunk of ice from my tea hung in my throat. I was fast turning blue. Granddad picked me up by the heels and hit me in the back. The ice flew halfway across the kitchen.

Somebody picked it up and put it back in my tea. After all, folks had a good supply of kids but ice was scarce. It was a long way to town and nobody ever bought over 25 pounds which cost fifteen cents. It was kept rolled up in a quilt until it totally disappeared.

Anybody who never lived through the Great Depression, to quote the words of a former governor, "Don't know squat about anything."

A lot of folks who lived through it are still here but a lot of them, including Granddad, are gone. Maybe he went to a place where iced tea on Sunday is a regular thing and the wheels never come off his buggy. I might settle for that myself.

IF I'M CALLED BACK IN SERVICE, I HAVE A NEW SET OF RULES

Thousands of former military personnel are being called involuntarily back in service. I'm not sure that somewhere my name is not on their list. After all, they got me during the Korean uprising but that was my fault. In a weak moment, I had joined the army reserve.

I figure I might be a little old to do some of the things I did back in WWII and again in 1951. Still, I might be able to do something and the army always has something for somebody to do. They never ran out the last time I was in there.

In the event they do recall me, it is my desire to set out a few rules that the army would be forced to comply with. I definitely prohibit anybody from coming into the barracks at 4:30 in the morning, blowing a whistle and hollering "FALL OUT". Loud whistles unnerve me and the words "fall out" are two words I don't want to hear. I recently fell out of my bathtub. Sometimes, I fall out the back door.

I would also insist on taking my dog along. She has nobody but me to look after her well-being. During the months of June through August, I would expect fresh black-eyed peas and cornbread for dinner at least once a week. I would never allow wieners and sauer—kraut to be served in any mess hall. I also never cared for the army's version of salmon salad which they served every Friday.

I would also require that somebody pick up my clothes, make up my bunk and shine my shoes. I'm just too old to worry about stuff like that. There would be no such thing as "lights out" at ten at night. I sometimes read until after twelve. I would also require a private room. I can't stand listening to that rap the young folks play these days.

I would not be required to go on 30 mile hikes or run the obstacle course, neither of which is necessary in my version of military service. Also, no close-order drill or standing for hours at retreat. I would retreat from that as I have already done my share.

If the enemy got up enough nerve to shoot at me, I would immediately shoot back. If they should put me in a tank, I would insist that I never be required to drive around in enemy territory with my head sticking out. They have cracks in those things to look through.

I would insist that I never be required to fly 30,000 feet in an unheated plane with the temperature at 65 below zero and stuck in a little plastic bubble under the belly of the plane with no parachute. I have already done that too.

Taking into consideration all of my requests, I doubt very much if the military decides to use me at all. I don't really care but I want them to know that I'm available if they get in a tight.

If it turns out they do take me, the country is definitely in trouble.

IN TOUGH SITUATIONS, ALWAYS TRY TO SAVE YOUR BRASS

I never did take a course in Creative Writing. Maybe I should have but it just never came up. The fact is, I was older than rope before I ever made an attempt to write.

This came about at the request of Shelton Prince, a former publisher of the Bulletin who somehow got the idea that I should write a column. It was then that I discovered that in order to write a column, creative writing was necessary.

Actually, what is involved is taking an idea that doesn't amount to a hill of beans and making it interesting enough that somebody will read it.

Probably, the whole idea originated with sports writers who are experts in the field. They have to be since often they have little to work with. As everybody knows, Friday night football in Texas is big, from little places you never heard of to big places you wish you hadn't.

Everybody in these places expect to read about their team on Saturday morning, win, lose, or draw. Whatever the poor sports writer writes had better be good. He has to answer to the coach, the players and worst of all, the parents. Leaving town is not the answer. They will find you.

My friend, Larry L. King, a noted Texas writer who was born and raised at Putnam in Callahan County was once a sports writer for a Midland paper. He got so good at creative writing, he was hired at Harvard to teach it. I have no doubt that he learned it all at Midland, writing sports.

Since I was never a sports writer, I had to learn my creative writing from other experiences. I still remember an event that happened back in 1943 when I was at the Las Vegas Army Air Base learning to be an aerial gunner.

They were using AT-6 planes, both to pull the tow target and to fly the gunners who shot at it using .30 caliber machine guns. The AT-6 planes had the loudest engines known to man. One could be started at Vegas and heard in Albuquerque. When firing from the rear cockpit of the AT-6, the gunner was supposed to make sure the spent brass cartridges stayed in the cockpit and not fly over the side.

On one occasion, the pilot noticed that the kid firing from the rear cockpit was allowing the brass to fly over the side. He yelled to the kid over the intercom, "Save your brass." Due to the engine and wind noise, the kid, on his first plane flight ever, misunderstood the pilot and immediately bailed out.

The kid became a sort of hero at the base and "Save your brass" became a rallying cry throughout the Army Air Corp. From then on when in a situation when things were looking bad, somebody would get on the intercom and yell, "Save your brass."

I still remember a mission I was on in 1944 when our B-17 lost two engines and our 97th Bomb Group left us over Germany all alone and unprotected. We were trying to make it to Northern Italy and losing altitude by the mile. I thought of what that kid had done at Vegas in 1943. I got on the intercom and called the pilot. "Bob," I said, "Do you think it's about time we should save our brass?"

We did make it to Italy that day and saved our brass. It might even work for sports writers too.

OLD MEMORIES, OLD INDIAN FIGHTERS AND DOUBLE-DIP ICE CREAM CONES

I was recently discussing with my lady-friend the living conditions we had to put up with, including no modern bathroom facilities while growing up in the late twenties and thirties. I grew up thinking "Running Water" was an Indian Chief and his wife's name was "She-who-had-to-go-outside."

My lady-friend disagreed with me about the Indians. "I don't think there were any around back then," She said.

"Well, I said, I seem to remember Dan Pinkard coming over to our house and telling about an encounter he had with Indians on Salt Mountain." The best I remember, he ran them off to Oklahoma where they built Casinos and have been getting even with white folks since then."

"You may be right but I think you've got the wrong time frame. Dan was probably 80 years old when he told you that." "They say," She said, "That happiness is good health and a bad memory and all you have left is the bad memory."

I still remember a lot about those days—some good and some bad. I remember the wagon trips to town on Saturday where we stayed all day.

I remember riding on the tailgate and jumping off to run barefoot through the dirt and then running to catch up. Saturday was a big day in Blanket. Dad would tie the horses to a mesquite tree behind the Levisay and McCulley grocery where other wagons were parked and the horses tied.

Every family that went to Blanket on Saturday stayed until sundown. It was a social event where the men and women got together to discuss everything from crops to who had a new baby while the kids chased each other between the stores or ran up and down the tops of the boxcars on the railroad siding.

I still remember how good the nickel ice cream cones tasted that we bought at Macon Richmond's drug store. A double-dip piled high cost a dime.

I remember on hot summer nights when we moved the beds out in the yard to get what breeze there was. Sometimes a sudden thunderstorm sent us scrambling to get the bedding back in the house.

In the hot summer fields, picking cotton, heading maize or gathering corn when our sweaty clothes was hit by a cool breeze it caused instant evaporation affording the only form of air conditioning we had ever known. These were "the good old days" I hear people say today if they survived.

Trying to "keeping up with the Joneses" was unheard of. The Joneses were as poor as everybody else. It was a time when people who owned cars often borrowed license plates from another neighbor who owned one to go to town.

Then, WWII happened, Camp Bowie was built, people got jobs and started making money but everything was rationed and nobody could buy much, not even a new pair of shoes when they needed them. The speed limit in cars was 30 miles an hour but surprisingly, folks managed to reach their destination as they do today at 80.

Eventually, the young men at Blanket went off to war and some didn't come back. Those that did after seeing the world found Blanket a little too small and dull and they moved elsewhere. For several years now, some have been coming back, obviously looking for a small and dull place to live out their remaining years. Maybe they remember those double-dip ice cream cones for a dime.

Like the Indians at Salt Mountain, they too are gone.

IT IS BETTER TO PROTEST
IN AN ELECTION BOOTH THAN
A DITCH AT CRAWFORD

August is here and the protest season has started. President Bush is taking his annual vacation at the ranch and Cindy and her crew of protestors are on hand. Thousands are protesting in Mexico following the election of the new president.

I'm not protesting. If fact, I'm not physically able to protest, having taken a good fall in my kitchen, doing severe damage to my left hip. "You're lucky," folks say, "that you didn't break your hip."

Lucky? If I had been lucky, I wouldn't have fallen in the first place.

I love to go camping. I have been going camping on a regular basis for years. However, even if I wasn't injured, I have no desire to go camping in a road ditch at Crawford. I couldn't see the President anyhow. Nobody ever sees the President but his aides and Laura and I have no desire to see Cindy. In fact, I wish she would just go away.

I guess I might get on CNN and everybody in the country would think I'm some kind of nut like the rest of the protestors. There are some things I just don't want people to know.

When I was a kid, growing up on a farm near Blanket, nobody, as far as I know, ever protested anything and we had plenty of reason. Occasionally, I heard people complain about the

County Commissioner not grading the roads often enough but nobody ever camped out in a ditch in front of his house.

Anyhow, TV hadn't been invented and nobody would have seen them. People hardly ever protest without a TV camera in front of their face. If the Commissioner didn't do his job, they voted him out of office.

The best place to protest is in an air conditioned building in an election booth. That's where I do it. I'm sure it is just as hot in Crawford in August as it is here.

We were much too busy back during the Depression to do anything but try to survive and along with it, try to find a little humor in everything. People would watch somebody on the street at Blanket crank a Model T. The chance always existed that the crank would backlash and break an arm. That could be interesting. Our three doctors always watched.

A crowd would gather just to watch somebody fix a flat tire. Entertainment was sparse most of the time until the fall when the "Medicine Show" came to town. They usually stayed a week with a stage set up in front of a trailer house with rows of benches for folks to sit on.

They always had a "blackface" comedian called Flapjack who we thought was funny but sure these days to attract protestors. They sold a medicine called "Tate-lax" which they guaranteed would cure nearly anything. It was cheap and folks bought a lot of it.

It might not have cured anything but it did make folks feel a little better temporarily at least, being made mostly of caramel coloring and alcohol. Anyway, nobody ever missed the show and we were sorry when it left town.

Sometimes after the Medicine show left town a fellow would move in on a vacant lot, set up a tent and show old western movies. Everybody went to that too. Usually the film was so old and scratched that it looked like the actors were riding in a driving rainstorm. Still, we didn't protest.

Of course, with no TV cameras, it would have served no purpose.

IT COULD BE DANGEROUS
TO BELIEVE EVERYTHING
PEOPLE TELL YOU

A few years back, three friends and I were on a camping trip to the Big Bend National Park. On the third day, we were camped out near Santa Elena canyon when one of those freak storms blew in from the north. One minute, it was about 85 degrees and the next minute it was sleeting. Then it started snowing.

One of the boys asked me, "What are we going to do?" "Do not worry," I said. "I know a place where we can stay until this is over." I have a friend who is an artist and lives in San Antonio. He had built a nice cabin in the mountains about 5 miles north of Study Butte and about 25 miles from where we were. He told me to feel free to stay there any time the need arose. It seemed to me that a need had arisen.

After driving to the cabin, we found the front door locked. A back window had a large piece of plywood nailed over it as did the back door. One of my friends, being about 6-3 and weighing around 200 pounds, had no difficulty in removing the plywood from the door.

The cabin had electricity and I, being the instigator of this, got the bed and the pleasure of sleeping under an electric blanket. In looking around the cabin, I noticed several T-shirts with Harley-Davidson logos hanging on a makeshift clothesline. It went through my mind that as long as I had known him, my friend Tony had shown no interest in motorcycles.

We all had a good night's sleep while it continued to snow. In the morning, it was clear and warm, melting the snow on the mountains. After a leisurely breakfast, we went back to the park, totally unmolested.

A short time later, I was in San Antonio and found my artist friend Tony selling his prints on the Riverwalk. "Tony," I said, "You saved our lives awhile back. My friends and I were camped out in the Big Bend and it come a snowstorm and we spent the night in your cabin."

He looked at me sort of funny. Then, he laid the news on me. "Harry," He said, "I hate to tell you this but I sold that cabin to members of a motorcycle gang out of Austin about a year ago". I thought about WWII and surviving 50 missions as a ball turret gunner on a B-17 bomber where even angels feared to go. It appeared that I may have just survived again, maybe something worse.

Another time, I was playing in a country band with a fellow who knew about my liking for black-eyed peas. One night he told me, "I've got 30 acres of black-eyed peas. Go over there and pick what you want." He gave directions and I went.

I had picked about a half-sack of peas when a fellow came storming across the field. "What do you think you're doing on my land and in my pea patch?" He asked. My explanation was ignored. It was then that I found out my guitar-playing friend didn't own the land or the peas either. The man reluctantly allowed me to finish filling my sack but I sure never went back. My guitar-playing friend thought it was funny. I didn't. However, I guess I had lucked out again. The man, as best I could learn, never in his life owned a Harley.

IT'S FINE TO FILL GRANDPA'S SHOES BUT DON'T WEAR HIS PANTS

A week or so ago, a fellow called me and asked, "What college did you go to that taught you to write like you do?" I told him that as far as I knew, no college in the United States would teach anybody to write like I do. "In fact," I told him, "They teach everybody not to write like I do."

"Well," He said, "You're a good writer." I quickly obtained his address and fully intended to send him a twenty dollar bill, but found I didn't have one.

I did attend college at Daniel Baker for about 3 months, following WWII but they wanted me to guard the bell tower to keep students from Howard Payne College from stealing their bell. I had just returned from Italy where I flew 50 missions as a ball turret gunner on a B-17 bomber. I felt as out of place as an old maid at a slumber party. Guard their bell tower? Not hardly.

I didn't care if they stole the bell or not. Sometime, after I left college, somebody did steal their bell. I have always felt a little guilty about it. I could have stayed and possibly prevented this theft. I might have even learned how to write. I don't know who stole their bell but somehow, I learned how to not write.

Writing, in my case, was sort of an accident. I wrote a book about growing up during the Great Depression to give my kids some idea of what it was like. They were not impressed. Kids these days are not impressed by much except weird music, weird musicians and wrecking cars and blowing up stuff in the movies. Whatever happened to Randolph Scott?

Judging from what I see around town, the boys also like to wear their Daddy's pants if he happens to wear a size 44 waist and the girls like to wear their little sister's jeans which reach just below their belly buttons.

Back when I was a kid, we were forced by poverty to wear hand-me-down pants, usually from our big brother who didn't wear a size 44 in the waist. Mama would say, "You are not going to school with your pants dragging your tracks out. Let me cut those off about 6 inches."

The pants we were sometimes forced to wear might be about 8 inches too short. They were known far and wide as "High-water britches." We could wade Blanket Creek at its deepest point and never get them wet. Actually, it was an embarrassment to wear pants like that. Had tacky been in style as it is today, we all might have amounted to something other than being called "The Greatest Generation"

Still, our Mama's wouldn't have allowed us to look tacky. Poor people in those days had a lot of pride, that quality that seems to be disappearing among some of the young people of today. But certainly not all of them. Maybe we see the other kind more often. Somebody will have to take our place in the near future and writers will have to learn how to not write and the young people the correct length and waist size of pants. They need to know a lot of things to run our country the way it should be run.

Lord, help us. I hope we still have enough around to do it. I know a few.

WHEN YOU GET OLD, NOTHING WORKS AND YOUR SHOES WON'T FIT

I like greens. I like all kinds of greens but at this time of the year, I like young tender turnip greens. My daughter, Laura, came over and tilled the garden and with me helping as much as possible, we planted some.

In fact, we planted a lot. Turnips are coming up where we didn't even plant turnips.

At this time, they are just at the right stage for eating. I have a problem though. Due to my lack of balance, I can't bend over and pick them without the possibility of taking a header smack-dab in the middle of the greens.

If that happened, somebody would be sure to say, "I hate to bring this up, but I think you have turnip greens stuck in your teeth." "Looks like some in your eyebrows too."

My daughter, Laura, being from a younger generation that missed growing up during the Depression, has never developed a taste for turnip greens. Back then, we put sugar and milk on them and had them for breakfast. My only hope was to coerce my lady-friend to come over and pick me some. So far, she hasn't complained because she likes them too.

My loss of balance is not the only problem getting old has caused me. I can't buy shoes that fit. As far as I know, my lack of balance has nothing to do with it. The last pair I bought in Fort

Worth, I got at a bargain. They were $150 shoes marked down to $80.00.

They fit like a glove in the store but when I got home, they seemed to be about two sizes too big. About all I can do is drive to Fort Worth and wear them in that store.

Sometime back, I decided to buy a new pair of boots. I drove all the way to San Saba to a boot store. A couple of clerks who wore boots and seemed to know what they were doing fitted me with a nice pair that cost as much as an airline ticket to Samoa.

I walked up and down the store a few times and they fit perfectly. But—you know the story. When I got home, I couldn't even get them on. They are resting comfortably in my closet along with the shoes.

I have decided that once you pass 75, nothing ever works out anyhow. Just this past week, I read that Governor Perry had made a deal to put video cameras along the Texas border and they were up and running. Any citizen with a computer could participate in watching the border and call in when illegal immigrants were seen coming across the river.

It seemed to me that this would be much better than watching the current crop of TV shows. I have been watching reruns of "Law and Order" for the past couple of years. Some of the programs are so old the cops are using bows and arrows.

I quickly got on my computer and signed up. I was supposed to receive an ID by e-mail. Then, I read that they were having glitches and nothing was working. I never did get the ID by e-mail either.

By the time this column is printed and the election is past and if the governor gets reelected, they'll have it fixed. Maybe my shoes will fit too.

If not, it's back to "Law and Order" for me.

FROM OKLAHOMA DUST
TO CALIFORNIA WINE

John Steinbeck wrote 25 books and won a Nobel Prize for literature. Of the 25 books, he is best known for "The Grapes of Wrath," written in 1939 when we all were in the middle of The Great Depression.

In Oklahoma the raging dust storms brought on by a drought along with the Depression was more than people could stand. The big corporations that owned the land were bulldozing the tenant's houses, leaving them with no place to go. Strangely enough, they're still doing it. I recently read that in Cleveland, Ohio, there are 10,000 repossessed homes, all vacant. The bulldozers are warming up. None of the former occupants are known to be interested in going to California to pick grapes.

The tenant farmers in Oklahoma and parts of Texas loaded what few possessions they owned in whatever they had that would run and headed for California, the Promised Land, to pick grapes or whatever needed picking. It was about these people that Mr. Steinbeck wrote the book.

I read the book as I read every book I could find back then but I didn't learn much. My family was in the middle of the Depression too. We didn't go to California as we had no car to go in. Making a trip to Blanket in our wagon on Saturday was far enough. Besides, nobody bulldozed our house down. It wasn't much but we owned it.

Anyway, times would have had to be worse than they were before Dad would have left his hounds and his hunting grounds north of Salt Mountain.

In 1940, the movie, "The Grapes of Wrath" was made, directed by John Ford and starring Henry Fonda. This was one of the few movies directed by John Ford that wasn't filmed in Monument Valley. I guess the stark landscape there looked like heaven on earth, compared to the Oklahoma panhandle.

For some reason, there are certain scenes in the movie that stick in my memory after all these years. I remember Mrs. Joad going through boxes of mementos of happier times with tears running down her cheeks trying to decide what to keep and what to throw away and Grandpa, who "damn well didn't want to go to California" anyhow throwing a fit with oatmeal running down his chin. I decided then that when I got old I would avoid oatmeal.

I guess I saw the movie at the Lyric Theater and it was in black and white as all movies were in 1940. Anyway, color would have ruined this movie. We were living in a black and white world back then. Maybe we went to the movie to see what the poor folks were doing.

If I remember correctly, the Joad family drove to California in an old Willys-Knight truck. I remember a fellow at Blanket who went to a mechanic school in Detroit. Unfortunately, he graduated just as the Depression started. Somewhere, he obtained an old Willys-Knight truck and I watched him rebuild the engine. When he was finished, it ran as smooth as a new baby's rear. I guess he could have gone to California but he stayed unemployed in Blanket like everybody else. California was another world then. It still is.

Grandpa Joad had no desire to move to California but they loaded him up anyhow. He made it—well, just barely. He died just over the Arizona-California line without ever picking a grape.

Sometimes fate makes some really good decisions.

THIEVES, METH LABS
AND A MISSING HOUSE

The Associated Press reports that two thieves recently stole an entire brick house in Lindale, a small East Texas town, dismantling it one brick at a time in full view of people passing by on Lindale's main street.

It took them 3 months to do the job and people waved to them as they passed by, probably thinking how nice it was that young people were engaged in such a productive occupation rather than selling drugs.

They took everything including the plumbing, leaving nothing but a big pile of rubble and numerous homeless roaches.

The house belonged to a real estate agency in Dallas. An agency employee drove by one day and noticed something awry. The house was gone. She reported it to a Constable who indicated that nobody in Lindale had ever stolen a house before.

Our Brownwood thieves, up to now, haven't either. I assume it involves too much work. So far, they have stolen everything but a house and a hot poker.

The two culprits in Lindale were quickly tracked down and arrested along with a methamphetamine dealer who was trading the drugs to the boys for the materials from the house. They were all charged with engaging in organized criminal activity.

Meth labs are like fire ants. Officers close one lab and they simply move to another location as soon as they get out of jail. Wherever there is a market, they are to be found. The market seems to be good even though the use of meth has disastrous results to the users in addition to causing the high crime rate in our small Texas cities.

If anybody has the answer to this problem, I'm sure our law enforcement officers would like to know it. Neither educating the users or time in jail seems to have any effect.

Meth is a powerful and destructive drug made from ingredients that nobody in their right mind would even consider ingesting. Yet, they do. Once they try it, they are hooked.

Getting off the drug is like trying to put a raw oyster in a parking meter.

Are they not aware that their teeth and hair will fall out and large bumps will appear on their faces and all over their bodies? Do they not know that they will steal a brick house, one brick at a time to get the drug?

I am thankful that I grew up in an era when drugs as we know them today didn't exist. Sure, we sneaked around and smoked Bull Durham, chewed tobacco and even on occasions tried a bit of Garrett's snuff, but no way would we have ingested anything that contained battery acid and starting fluid. We were smarter than that. Having a coal oil soaked rag tied around our necks to cure a sore throat was bad enough.

Our pharmacist practically worked in a drug-free environment. He had only one drug that I know of and it was dispensed by a doctor to relieve intense pain when nothing else worked.

Back when I was a member of the Brownwood Police Department in the 50's there was an old boy that used to break in the Palace Drug and steal a bit of the stuff now and then. We knew who he was and picked him up.

When I was a kid, a fellow broke into Ernest Allen's drug store in Blanket and stole fifteen cents Ernest had overlooked in the cash register and made himself a chocolate milk shake. Unfortunately, for him, he left his fingerprints on the glass.

If meth had been available then, he might have stolen the entire drug store, one brick at a time.

TRYING TO KEEP UP WITH A WORLD THAT MOVES TOO FAST

I have friends all over the US who keep me informed about things using the internet. Things I normally don't even think about. Vickie in Oregon keeps me informed about happenings there and sends interesting pictures.

Vicki, who is interested in Genealogy, found me about 3 years ago while searching for kin. She indicates I might be her cousin. Maybe, from what I read in the paper we're both cousins of Dick Cheney's wife or Osama Obama, the one running for president, not the other one.

I have a friend who resides down in the Hill Country who writes for a cooking program on the internet. He writes nearly every day about something he cooked. Yesterday, he bragged that he had just cooked the best venison stuffed peppers that had ever been cooked in the history of man. He also keeps a close watch on bridge rail damage, something we all need to know.

Then, there's Bud who keeps me informed on the cotton crop in West Texas and all about bales to the acre. Bud lives in a little town which for years had one stoplight. Now, it seems that I heard it was removed. I recently heard a song on TV during a crime show that featured Bruce Springsteen singing about being stuck at the one stoplight in Stanton. I guess Stanton was famous and I didn't even know it.

Anyway, Bud recently e-mailed; "The cotton on the girl's place east of town has been harvested. They used two eight-row strippers, two boll buggies and two module makers."

I'm not familiar with this stuff. I never saw a stripper in our cotton patch. In fact, the only one I ever saw was at the Fort Worth Stock Show when I was eight. That cost me a whole quarter.

From what Bud says, it looks like the cotton crop in West Texas will make a bale and a half per acre. The good thing about all this is that I don't have to pick it.

Bill, who lives in Nashville, keeps me up to date with the happenings of country musicians. Actually, not much is happening these days. Music has finally progressed to the point that musicians are no longer needed. The words to the songs don't rhyme and the songs have no melody. Anything that can be shook or beat is good accompaniment.

Having thought about the current ages of the musicians and singers whom we loved in the fifties, I arrived at a horrible conclusion—they've got to be eighty. Is Merle Haggard 90? Can Hank Thompson no longer "Spin his wheels at that green light? Porter Wagner is currently dying in a Nashville hospital of an incurable disease. Yep—he's 80. I played Steel guitar in bands off and on for 40 years and I don't feel too good myself. Actually, I don't think I ever did.

Around the rest of my world, things seem to be fine except California. Things are good in Alabama, dry in Georgia, hot and dry in Arizona where two of my grandkids live and everybody is reasonably happy in Houston and Port Aransas. New Orleans had 8 inches of rain and FEMA is passing out money again.

Down in San Antonio, bless her heart, Desi Harlow tells me she is reading my columns to the third grade class she teaches in the inner city school, making me feel a lot better about the whole ball of wax.

I guess I'll just settle for what I've got instead of what I might get.

KICKING THE SANDS OF TIME

Charles Atlas, when I was a kid, was some sort of body builder, maybe the first ever. His full page ads in magazines and the "funny books" which we avidly read always showed Charles with his unbelievable muscular body, holding up the entire universe with no effort at all. The ads further showed a 90 pound weakling having sand kicked in his face by a large Neanderthal with a body exactly like his.

We vowed that nobody would ever kick sand in our faces on any beach, anywhere. In order to achieve this, it was necessary to order his book, which we all did. After carefully reading the book, we noticed no change at all. We still weighed in at around 90 pounds on really good days. Nobody, however, ever kicked sand in our faces on the beach.

There was a good reason for this. There wasn't a beach within 375 miles of Blanket, and we had no hopes of seeing one. Most of us never even saw a beach until we were at least 18 years old when World War II broke out, and the military gave us a good close-up look at a number of beaches around the world. Nobody ever even thought about kicking sand in our faces then. We were well-armed, and loaded and locked. It became obvious to us that we had wasted our money on those Charles Atlas books.

By then, I suppose that somewhere, 90 pound weaklings had shoveled sand in old Charlie's face when they laid him to rest in some designated place, unknown to us all. Things changed in our lives, and it seemed to us all, that they changed a little too fast to suit us. The good old days were going, and then, before we could kick sand in anybody's face, they were gone.

My friend, Bud Lindsey, who lives out in the short grass country at Stanton, was recently reminiscing about catching crawdads with a piece of bacon and his mother's tea-strainer, in the fish pond at Coggin Park. I too, with the able assistance of Alan Spence and Ronald Gray, caught those crawdads, a long time ago. We all had paper routes with the Brownwood Bulletin then, theirs in Brownwood, and mine in Blanket. We would sometimes meet there on a Saturday morning, after I hitchhiked from Blanket.

Later in life, Alan became a doctor, and Ronald eventually became the publisher of the paper we delivered. Bud Lindsey edits a magazine called "The Old Sorehead Gazette," and I, not previously ever having amounted to much, now write a column for the Bulletin. The fish pond and the crawdads in Coggin Park are gone now, along with both Alan and Ronald. All of which has left an emptiness that we can't ever fill.

Nobody, however, as far as I know, ever kicked sand in our faces, on any beach anywhere, and for that, maybe we can credit Charles Atlas. One thing for sure though, I doubt that old Charles knew anything at all about catching crawdads in a fish pond in Coggin Park.

ARMING BEARS, PLAYING DIXIE AND BUTCHERING SONGS

The internet, I find, is a great place to get news, information and entertainment. I often get more entertainment from the news than I do information. I use this story from the Roanoke Times as a prime example:

A man who called himself Boraq Sadiyev from Kazakhstan persuaded producers to allow him to sing the national anthem at a rodeo in Salem, Virginia. He said he was touring America making a documentary and had his camera crew with him. Instead, the crowd of 4,000 was treated to a mangled version of the "Star-Spangled banner", along with some rather nasty comments about "killing every man, woman and child in Iraq, including lizards." This went over like a skunk at a church picnic.

Obviously, he is not, by far, the first person to ever mangle the "Star-Spangled Banner" It has been going on since Francis Scott Key wrote it and probably will be forever. Mr. Key obviously couldn't sing a lick.

The singer, along with his film crew had to be escorted out of the arena to keep him from being shot. There is a suspicion that the fellow was actually a British comedian who gets a kick out of doing such things.

There are song lyrics to which music should never have been written. Another one besides the national anthem is "The Lord's Prayer." Back during my wedding photography days, I have suffered through more butchered renditions of that song than "The Star-Spangled Banner." It seems to me that it runs the entire musical scale and few people have the vocal range necessary to sing it. They still try, anyhow.

And then, up in Wisconsin, according to Fox News, State Senator Spencer Coggs is "irate" that a High School band played a few bars of "Dixie" at the Senate inaugural ceremony. He was not only "irate" but was also "dismayed" and demanded an apology. Apologize for a good southern song like "Dixie"? What happened to the First Amendment? At least, people with ordinary vocal chords can sing it. I don't remember all the words but it does mention wishing to be in the land of cotton. That part, I don't like. I have been there.

Back when I was a country musician, there was always some girl in the audience who wanted to get on the bandstand and sing. The band leader, having a mean streak, would let them. They invariably picked "I Fall to Pieces," a song made popular by Patsy Cline and only Patsy could sing it. They never knew what key they sang in and usually by the second verse, they fell to pieces. On the third verse, the band fell to pieces.

Somebody else who was not credited, put this bit of knowledge on the internet; "They keep talking about drafting a Constitution for Iraq. Why don't we just give them ours? It was written by a lot of really smart guys and it worked for over 200 years and we're not using it anymore."

Personally, I'm in favor of keeping it. Surely, sooner or later, we'll start electing somebody as smart as they were 200 years ago and we'll need it again.

I do hope they keep the Second Amendment. I like that part giving us the right to arm bears. Or something like that.

LAUGHING OUR WAY THROUGH THE GREAT DEPRESSION

Living on a farm back in the thirties was a lot of fun. Going to town on Saturday and not having any money to spend was funny. We all laughed a lot about it. We didn't have much choice in the matter. Cotton picking time was an exhilarating experience. We laughed all up and down those long rows with the hot sun beating down on our backs.

When Dad told my brother and I it was time to head maize or bring the corn crop in, we rolled in the floor, laughing with pure joy. There was not much else we could do about it. Life on a farm in those days was just one big funny adventure to us. Sure it was.

We were swatted in the face with a cow's tail full of cockleburs, while trying to squeeze out a gallon bucket of milk and somehow saw humor in it. We couldn't help but laugh about it. Not everybody got to experience stuff like that. I think our milk cow's name was Bossy but we called her something else.

Then, when the cow, not liking what was being done to her, kicked the bucket over, it was hard to suppress our laughter. It meant we were all going to drink well water for supper. Mama always laughed about it and Dad was so overcome he would take out his fiddle and play "Sally in the Low Ground" for our listening pleasure.

Getting dressed for the first day of school was always good for a few laughs. Our last year's pants struck us somewhere between out ankles and our knees. We couldn't help growing but our pants didn't.

Arriving at school was even funnier when we all compared the length of our pants and the girls all looked as if they had just come straight from a cotton patch. Most of them had. The teachers were well dressed though, being paid as much as a hundred dollars a month. They all knew J.C. Penny personally. Old J.C., as far as I know never had a "roll-back."

President Roosevelt, in an effort to put the unemployed to work instigated the WPA which meant Works Progress Administration but everybody called it "We Piddle Around." We all laughed about that and the several hundred other WPA jokes, most of which I can't mention.

The Great Depression brought the country to its knees but laughter helped us to walk tall again. We were all poor when it started and still poor when it ended and hardly knew the difference. We had far more freedom than we do today and now they call us "The Greatest Generation." Maybe we were, but then, we would have laughed about it.

In 1941, the Japanese attacked Pearl Harbor and then a former house painter in Germany had an idea he could take over the world and changed our world forever. They didn't know about "The Greatest Generation", but they soon found out. We didn't "piddle around" about it either.

We loaded our bombers with bombs and went to far off places. They didn't know we were going to drop them. We were all just nice people who laughed a lot. We can still do today what we did then to protect our freedom.

All that the government has to do is just turn us loose like they did in WWII. I flew 50 missions over Germany and not once did anybody say, "You boys be careful and don't upset anybody."

NEVER RUN WITH THE
SCISSORS IF YOU CAN'T RUN

I have been reading recently about the dangers of young children being poisoned by lead paint from their toys. One large toy company has lost millions by having to take back the Chinese painted toys. None of this is my fault. I didn't send the toys to China to be painted, nor did I sign a contract for the toys to be made there.

When I was a kid, I didn't have any toys, painted or unpainted. Fisher-Price and Mattel hadn't even been heard of. If they had gone broke from selling Chinese toys with lead paint, nobody would have cared. Everybody else was broke. I did have a Garret's Snuff bottle that I could push around in the dirt and pretend it was my car. It worked pretty well.

One day it was a Chevy, the next day a Ford and then a Chrysler. That's all we had back then and as far as I know, all we needed. They were built right here in the United States.

Anyway, for the past two months I have had adequate time to read newspapers and suffer through daytime TV. The Bulletin has been nice enough to do reprints on stuff I wrote long ago and only a few noticed the difference. I even missed it a day or so myself. I received several e-mails congratulating me on my columns and noting how much they had improved since August. It made me feel real good.

What happened was that like Humpty-Dumpty, I had a good fall on the 28th of August. Worse still, I broke a vertaebrae which seemed to be an important part of my ability to stand or walk. As a result of all of this, I was stuck in the hospital for 5 days and even now, I'm not allowed to go hiking in the Big Bend or operate a wheelbarrow.

What started all this in the first place is that I got to thinking about something my Mama told me about 80 years ago. She said, best I remember, "Son, don't ever run with the scissors." I was never sure what might happen to me if I did, but for my entire life, I've remembered her words and wondered about it.

August 28th dawned clear and hot and seemed inclined to stay that way. Except for my dog Bitsy, I was alone. It seemed to me to be a good time to run with the scissors. I went to the drawer in the kitchen, got the scissors and then took a good run toward the back door.

I had forgotten one important thing—I couldn't run.

I bounced off the back wall a couple of times and somehow got turned completely around and landed on my backside against the wall. I knew immediately that something was broke and it wasn't the scissors. Incidentally, I haven't found them yet. Running with scissors is one problem I no longer have.

I don't have any lead paint on my toys either. Eighty years ago I didn't have any toys and today, I still don't. I still remember when my brother Ray and I found the old car battery in the dump ground. We took it home, broke it open with a hammer and played with that lead for a week or. We even tasted of it. If we had any ill effects, I don't know of it.

I still remember though at Sheppard Field at Wichita Falls during basic training in 1943, that drill sergeant would yell at me, "Marlin, get the lead out."

How did he know?

LEARNING ABOUT GIRLS
AND THE FICKLE FINGER OF FATE

Back when I was a kid growing up in the small town of Blanket, my buddies and I knew practically nothing about girls. We did wonder a lot and one thing we wondered about was what they looked like without clothes. I was aware that such thoughts would have been prohibited by our mama's but we still thought about it.

About as close as we ever got to solving the mystery was the time we spent checking out the ladies underwear section of the Sears and Ward's catalogues. However, we learned practically nothing there except the current prices and we had no interest in that.

You must understand that back in the thirties morals were very strict. All the girls we knew were pure as the driven snow and none, as far as we knew, ever drifted. The mystery went unsolved.

The boys all spent the summer swimming in Blanket Creek as "naked as jay birds" we called it. This was acceptable for boys but not for girls. If they ever went swimming, we didn't know about it and we kept a close watch on them.

Finally, one of the good old boys in our group figured out a way to solve the mystery once and for all during basketball season. The girl's dressing room and shower occupied the right front portion of the gymnasium at the High School and a lot of the fans parked their cars against the gym while attending the games.

The "good old boy" discovered that by standing on a car bumper, the proper height could be reached after cutting a hole in the wall to get a front row seat, so to speak. A number of holes were quickly whittled through the wall. At night, the bumper standees were not noticeable in the dark.

Back during the thirties, cars had some real bumpers. They were designed to take a good hit on whatever the driver drove into with no damage to the car. Plastic was yet to be invented. The bumpers were well constructed of steel with adequate standing room for at least three boys to the car.

On basketball nights there were a number of boys standing on the bumpers, each with their own peep hole. For reason I don't know, one boy in the group told one of the girls about it and the show was about to be over.

The girl was not happy about the situation and carried a kitchen knife to the dressing room one night and stuck one of the boys in the eye with it causing a loss of his eyesight. I really don't think she meant to harm the boy but it happened.

I sometimes think about what happened and I guess I was as mixed up in it as the others but being only 10 or 12 years old at the time, I was about 6 inches too short to look through a peep hole and get a knife stuck in my eye.

However, about ten years later I was just the right height to be assigned as a gunner in a ball turret under the belly of a B-17 bomber and drop bombs on the Germans while they were doing their best to shoot it down. In the Army Air Corp, we had a name for it. We called it "The fickle finger of fate"

There was absolutely no way to escape it either then, or now.

LEARNING NEW WORDS AND GETTING SCAMMED AT ANY AGE

There seem to be a lot of new words in use today that are totally strange to me. I find it interesting that having lived in these parts for 82 years, I managed to miss them. Some, of course are words of the times, like "download "and "upload."

Actually, I was familiar with the meaning—I just didn't know it. I once downloaded a boxcar full of cement. When I was a kid, I once uploaded grain from trucks into boxcars, using a number two scoop.

Both the downloading and the uploading were, no doubt, the hardest work I ever did. I sincerely hope I never become involved with this type of labor again. It is my intention to avoid it at all costs.

Then, there is that word "cyberspace." I have decided that it is the empty space between my ears that has anything at all to do with computers. I am familiar with the fact that all book stores have books for sale on this subject for "dummies." I bought one, only to find it much too complicated for me.

It seems that all of the young newspaper writers recently discovered the word "venue." One writer in Austin where a recent music festival was held used it four times in one story. What he was trying to do was explain what was happening from one honky-tonk to another. Why didn't he just say so?

I was familiar with the word when used as it was meant to be. If a man was being tried for a heinous crime and his defense lawyer felt that due to the number of rednecks living in the county his client couldn't receive a fair trial, he asked for a "change of venue" to another county. Judges, being the way they are and not wanting to lose a good case, usually turned him down.

I know of one prominent case where the lawyer asked for a change of venue and it was duly changed to a county full of rednecks and his client was convicted. Lawyers need to know the territory.

Last week in the Bulletin, Dr. Paul Butler, whose writing I admire, used the word "sobriquet" in his column. He really threw me a curve there. I had to look it up only to find that it was a nickname. Also, in medieval French, it meant a tap under the chin, probably with a ball peen hammer. Didn't they burn Joan of Arc at the stake over there?

Politicians often use what is known as "doublespeak." This simply means that they say one thing but mean another. We are all well acquainted with that. Indians, years ago said "White man speak with forked tongue." They still do.

"Scammed" is another word that has shown up in recent years, along with "spam." Spam is what you get on your computer where folks are trying to "Scam" you. People are getting scammed every day somewhere.

If you choose, you can get scammed at any time on a supermarket parking lot. Scammers are everywhere. I know of one lady who got scammed at a garage. They charged her $5.00 to put fluid in her turn signals.

When I was a kid, a few scammers were around but we had a different word for it. We called it "getting skinned." If somebody cheated you out of something, you had been skinned.

I have to admit, I have been "Scammed" and "skinned" in several different venues over the years.

Being 82 years old, I'm learning though, along with some new words.

ROMANS, COUNTRYMEN, ROCK CONCERTS AND LEFT-OVER RABBIT

I just read recently in the news somewhere that archeologists, digging in England, had unearthed a meal that the Romans were having 2000 years ago. I was amazed. They were having rabbit for supper, or maybe dinner. The story didn't say which. Apparently the Great Depression started long before I thought it did.

I was fortunate to just get in on the tail-end of it. Like the Romans, we had rabbit for supper too and sometimes for dinner. It was a welcome respite from pinto beans and fried potatoes. It went good with hot biscuits and gravy. Maybe the Romans had some too but a pan of hot biscuits and a skillet of gravy doesn't last long. A tough rabbit, we now know, lasts 2000 years.

Anyway, the Romans were lucky to have rabbit, which I'm sure may be an improvement over blood pudding and Sheppard's pie they have in England today.

Not being an authority on ancient times, I have no idea what the Romans were doing in England. Apparently, they roamed everywhere. They had no "Roman charges." I was always under the impression that they were all in Rome at the Coliseum watching the Christians being thrown to the lions while drinking the product of the grape and eating pasta.

The times haven't changed much in 2000 years except neither we nor the Romans eat much rabbit. Today, there is football, hockey, NASCAR races, beer, and Frito pie. Not much different.

It's just our modern way of doing what the Romans were doing but leaving the Christians and the lions out of it.

A lot of folks go to these events in the hope of seeing a race car slam into the wall at 200 miles an hour, a hockey player get soundly bashed with a hockey stick and the quarterback get sacked and carried off the field.

This of course depends, on whose quarterback it is or on whose team the player gets bashed with a hockey stick.

Americans, like the Romans, crave excitement that presents no danger to them, sitting at a safe distance in the stands with a cold beer and a Frito pie. It's just the way we are and always have been.

Of course, this doesn't include everybody. Some folks find excitement by attending the opera or going to rock concerts. The Romans were lucky. They had no rock concerts or their empire might have fallen sooner than it did. Worse still, they would have all been deaf as posts 2000 years before the invention of the hearing aid.

Today, we have both rock concerts and hearing aids and sooner or later, the twain shall meet. I try to avoid both. Rock concerts hold no interest for me and I don't have a hearing aid. Due to my advanced age, I've heard nearly everything anyhow.

There is a possibility that our fate has already been decided long before we arrive kicking and screaming into this world, not knowing if we'll be eating left-over rabbit or be thrown to the lions. The Romans didn't know either.

We just have to do the best we can with what we've got and hope for the best. This might include staying away from both the Romans and rock concerts. We can do that.

HANGING AROUND
A FILLING STATION MIGHT
CAUSE A LIGHT STROKE

When I was a kid, growing up in and around Blanket, we all hung around what was known as "Filling Stations." Today, they are called "Service Stations" although any kind of service is unheard of. Back then, you could always depend on somebody coming out to grease your windshield if you stopped at one.

We hung around these filling stations because there was no other place to hang out. Anyhow, if a kid ever expected to learn anything, it was a good place to do it. Most of what I learned, I didn't need to know but I thought I did. The best place to learn to cuss was in a garage. We had a couple of those too and over time, I learned some real zingers.

Back then, when a wrench slipped off a nut, the result was some really good mutilated knuckles which couldn't be covered by the normal accepted use of the English language.

I guess it is traditional that in small towns, kids and even grownups still hang around filling stations. When I was growing up, due to the unemployment brought on by the Depression, there wasn't much else to do. When the cotton was picked, the corn and grain harvested, it was hanging around filling station time.

We could, if we desired, hang around with our three doctors in front of Ernest Allen's drug store. Doctors, however, proved to be pretty dull company. They never had the rather unusual contests that we did at the filling stations. A lot of the gas in filling stations didn't come from the pumps.

On February 22nd, I was honored by the company of two friends from the Hill Country who came to celebrate my 84th birthday, if such events should be celebrated. John Raven, a former stuntman from Johnson City who at one time was regularly shot from a cannon at Luckenbach to entertain the tourists and Scott Conrad who raises Longhorns near Hondo.

Raven, formerly known by his stunt name as "Bad McFad" switched from being a stuntman to writing. He indicates he took a loss of about $2 a week. Both he and Conrad were raised in Taylor, Texas and were familiar with hanging around filling stations like everybody else.

Raven told about one filling station they hung around in Taylor owned by a man named Homer. Just inside the station, Homer had his desk with the cash register occupying most of the space. Every day, an old man named "Uncle Pate" Davenport came to the station and spent most of the day sitting on the desk. He was in the way of transacting business.

One day Homer drove a couple of nails in the desk, about 6 inches apart, soldered wires to the nails under the desk which he ran to the back room and hooked to 110 volts and installed a push button.

The next morning, Uncle Pate showed up and took his place on the desk. Homer went in the back and hit the button a couple of times. Uncle Pate sort of jerked twice, shivered a little and eased off the desk and left.

Nobody saw uncle Pate for about a month. One morning, he showed up at the station, and took his usual place on the desk "Where have you been, Uncle Pate?" Homer asked.

"We haven't seen you in a month."

"Well Homer," Uncle Pate said, "The last time I was in here I had a light stroke and I've been keeping pretty close to the house since then."

THEY ATE BÉCHAMEL SAUCE AND THOUGHT IT WAS GRAVY

Back during the Depression when I was a kid, folks visited a lot, mostly because they had nothing else to do. Kinfolks were the worst about visiting. My mother's brother and his crew lived up on the plains in a little town that was spelled with a "Q" which I can't spell anyhow. I think it was an Indian word which meant buffalo chips.

Anyway, in the fall after the cotton was picked you could count on them all showing up at our house for a week or so. My uncle had an old flat-bed Dodge truck equipped with sideboards to haul the kids and the mattresses where they all slept.

We didn't have much in the way of anything to eat at our house and they made a serious dent in that. We had to completely replace our chicken crop after they finally left to visit other kinfolks. We also consumed a lot of flour gravy which the chefs today call Béchamel sauce. I grew up eating a lot of that stuff and didn't know what it was.

The kids, all boys, the best I remember, having lived all of their lives on the plains were not familiar with trees. They climbed every tree on the place, leaving a trail of broken limbs everywhere. When they arrived, all of our livestock headed to the back of the pasture and stayed there. I thought about it myself.

Actually, they were good people caught up in the same circumstances that we were. The big difference was that we didn't have a Dodge truck to load up and go visit kinfolks. Besides, Dad didn't care much for Mama's kinfolks, or anybody else's. All he was interested in doing was taking his hounds and going wolf hunting.

Of course, Mama didn't think it was polite to leave company at home and go wolf hunting. It seemed like a good idea to me in view of the circumstances but neither of us went anywhere until the kinfolks left.

Finally, after no more than two weeks, they loaded up the Dodge truck and went to visit one of my mother's sisters who lived about 15 miles away. The last time we visited there, they had even less to eat than we did which included a lot of the Béchamel sauce. Like us, when unexpected company came, about all we could do was stir up another skillet of Béchamel and slice a big onion.

They lived in a tenant house located in the middle of a cotton patch. There wasn't a tree on the place for the cousins to climb. They had no livestock to chase either and my uncle had no hound dogs affording him a chance to leave the premises. He was stuck there eating gravy that neither one of us knew the name of.

Life, as we all know can be cruel and most of the time is.

As fall turned into winter and the nights too cold to sleep in the Dodge, they loaded up the kids and went back to the plains for another year.

Spring arrived, the limbs grew back on our trees, the cows came back home and Dad and his hounds were free to run again. But as fall arrived, and the cotton was all picked, we knew beyond a doubt that the kinfolks were coming from what they called the Plains and that funny-named town that started with a "Q" and we were about to eat a lot of Béchamel sauce again.

I guess it wasn't too bad and I still like it.

LOOKING BACK TO THE PAST AND PONDERING THE FUTURE

Thanksgiving has come and gone and I guess a million turkeys were consumed throughout the United States, along with cornbread dressing, pumpkin pies and all the trimmings. There is nothing wrong with that as far as I know.

When I was a kid, back during the Great Depression, which wasn't great at all, we raised turkeys but I never knew anybody to actually eat one. Every year before Thanksgiving, a man in a truck came by and bought all of ours so we could have a little money for the bare necessities of life and maybe have a little left over for Christmas.

Our turkeys were all "free range" turkeys that ranged far and wide and had to be rounded up to be sold. The man came by again before Christmas to buy the ones we couldn't catch before Thanksgiving. The kids too were "free range." We ranged everywhere. Thankfully, there was no market for kids back then.

Everybody back then had a bunch of kids and one or two might not have been missed until cotton picking time. Nobody called the roll at supper time and their absence would only have been noticed by an empty place at the table. It was a sure thing however that nobody ever missed supper.

Of course, we read about the Pilgrim's first Thanksgiving at school and how they had a big feast and invited all the Indians. I don't, however, remember if they had turkey or not. It is doubtful that they had cornbread dressing as I never knew anybody from that part of the country who knew how to make cornbread.

Another event that comes before Thanksgiving that didn't amount to much for us was Halloween. I was nearly grown before I ever heard of Trick or Treating. I don't know if the pilgrims started that or not. Back then, we could have knocked on every door in Blanket without once getting a piece of candy.

We "celebrated" Halloween, if you can call it celebrating, by pushing over every outhouse in town. Of course, with the coming of dawn the following day, the "usual suspects" were rounded up and we had to put them all back in place again. We accomplished nothing but work and still got no candy.

On Christmas night, we gathered in downtown Blanket and had Roman candle fights and put baby giant firecrackers in each other's back pockets. Back then, it was possible to buy a Roman candle 3 feet long for a quarter. It was similar to a rocket-propelled grenade.

One time, somebody accidentally shot a big hole in the front window of Macon Richmond's grocery, where just on the inside, he had a stalk of bananas hanging. We couldn't quite reach the bananas but we soon found that by punching it with a stick, it would start swinging closer to the hole and with a quick grab, we had bananas.

Again, the usual suspects were rounded up and Macon moved the banana stalk. From then on, we had to pay the usual price of two for a nickel.

I guess what we did back then seems pretty mild today with NBA players having a knock-down-and-drag-out on National TV in Michigan, which we have all seen at least 18 times and a deer hunter shooting other deer hunters in Wisconsin.

I recently heard a fellow on a radio talk show whose name I have forgotten, remark that we are living in the "Idiot Culture."

I don't believe much I hear on the radio these days but I believe that.

THE GOOD OLD DAYS ARE GONE BUT HAVE A LOT TO BE THANKFUL FOR

Since 2006 arrived with brush fires instead of fireworks, it did not make me feel any younger than I am. I haven't bought any fireworks since a nickel package of Baby Giants went up to fifteen cents.

To make matters even worse, the doctors tell me it might be best if I quit my bad habits. "1924 parts," They say, "Are getting hard to get."

Right now, I'm on my fourteenth president and with a year to go before the fifteenth. I'm not sure I'll make it. I'm not even sure I want to. I can see no good prospects coming up. Besides that, I'm on my fifth war, one of which I was regularly shot at and one I was a non-combatant. Still, I would sort of like to stick around and see what happens next.

Some presidents get the blame for what the previous president caused. We had President McKinley until 1929 and then we got Hoover. Mr. Hoover got the blame for the Great Depression, which, I remember, was already in full swing when he was elected.

There were a lot of jokes going around about President Hoover, including the one about the tractors having no seats or steering wheels as the farmers had lost what they set on and had no way to turn.

We had no tractor on our farm and no hope of getting one. Our horses, however, knew how to turn at the end of a row. The tractors didn't.

We had no Medicare, Social Security or welfare. What little we had, we got on our own. We raised what we had to eat or we didn't eat. We never missed a meal. There were times when we had beans for breakfast and beans for dinner and swelled up for supper.

Still, we had some good times along with the bad. Folks helped each other then. If a neighbor killed a hog, he shared the meat with his neighbors. Gasoline was twelve cents a gallon but we had no car. Apples were two for a nickel but I had no nickel. No violins were playing in the background either.

Stealing was rare. I remember the time somebody stole some hams out of a neighbor's smokehouse. He never told anybody about it. One day in Blanket, a fellow asked him, "Did you ever find out who stole your hams?" "Not until just now," The fellow told him.

I do not wish to convey the impression that I'd like to go back to those days because I don't and I hope none of us ever do. When I empty the change from my pockets at night, I have more money than my entire family did in 1930.

Yes, the "good old days" are gone and today, we have a lot to be thankful for. Our memories sometimes play tricks on us causing us to remember those days as the best years of our lives. They were not but we learned things then that make our lives better today.

We learned how to fix things when they were broke and a lot about logic. We had no idea who Einstein was but we knew one of his theories, probably before he did, that "An object at rest, remains at rest," especially at the end of a long cotton row on a hot summer day.

"Return to those exciting days of yesteryear" was the introduction to the Lone Ranger radio show back then.

I believe I'll just stay right here. I have already been there.

SEEKING A ROAD LESS TRAVELED

I spend a lot of my time looking for a street that nobody is driving on. Traffic annoys me whether it is the driver doing 20 in a 40 mile zone or one doing 40 in a 20 mile zone. Up to now, I haven't found what I'm looking for. I cut through what used to be quiet residential streets only to find a car on my back bumper and meeting 6 more. If there is any street in this town not loaded with traffic, I haven't found it. I'm amazed. Where are they all coming from?

Not only that but where are they all going in such a big hurry? I hope the young drivers are aware of the fact that if it wasn't for those old white-haired drivers who sometimes impede traffic a bit, they might be speaking Japanese or German now.

I like things quiet. I would prefer to be "where the rivers flow and cars don't go, where you can ride your horse and shoot your gun and the mail don't run."

Sometime back, The Veterans Clinic in Temple gave me a hearing test and decided my life would be more complete with hearing aids. With the help of a nice young man at the local Veterans Service Office, they gave me two.

The quiet disappeared. The first thing I heard was a fellow smoking a cigarette three houses down. I was told that I would "get used to it." Sure—like I'd get used to a tack in my shoe.

I do find them handy for watching old reruns of "Law and Order" on TV, which seems to be all there is. My favorite actor, Fred Thompson, the hard-nosed DA has quit, having some thoughts of running for president. In the event that he gets elected, crime in this country might disappear.

My favorite place for quiet is the Big Bend National Park. I know places out there that are so quiet if a tree fell, it would be heard in Washington D.C. However, it is doubtful they would know what it was.

Several years ago, I was in the park and met a fellow from Houston who was filming a series on the park for a TV station there. I agreed to accompany him and show him some scenic places off the beaten path. He would set up his camera and check the sound recorder.

"Something wrong here," He would say. "I'm not getting any sound."

"The reason why you're not, "I told him, is there isn't any."

He kept complaining about the absence of something called "white noise" which he says is always present. "When you get back to Houston," I told him, "You can put any kind of noise you want on there."

About 50 years ago, a western movie was filmed in the Big Bend called "High Lonesome." It is that. I have camped in places that were so lonesome the coyotes prowled in large groups. It is nice to be in a place like that. I always had my Chihuahua for company.

Now I find myself living on a 4-lane highway where the traffic never ceases, night or day. I long for the quiet of the Big Bend but I am now too "stove-up" to go. I would love to hear a coyote howl instead of a Ford 150 pickup.

Years ago, J. Frank Dobie wrote, "I'd rather hear a coyote howl than anything I've heard on any man's radio." I have to agree with him.

Or my hearing aids either.

DON'T WORRY ABOUT OLD AGE UNLESS IT MOVES IN WITH YOU

For some reason or other, I remember people I knew 60 or 70 years ago as looking exactly the way they did then. When I accidentally run across one of those folks in the grocery or the doctor's waiting room, I'm shocked.

I went to a High School reunion about 10 years ago and I was amazed that all the good-looking girls I attended school with looked like their mothers.

I can't believe that anybody could age that much in such a short time. I sure didn't. I still look exactly as I looked when I was thirty. I have always managed to take good care of myself, never staying out at night past ten and always eating a good balanced diet.

I have no bad habits at all. Well, maybe I did at some point in my life but I can't remember when that might have been. Was it just last week? Time does fly.

I do admit that something rather strange happened to me about four or five years ago. An old man showed up here one day and moved in with me. He looks a lot like the folks I knew 70 years ago. He has a face that resembles 25 miles of bad road.

I'm not sure where he came from. I just figured one of those government agencies sent him over to sort of look after me and help with the lawn mowing. I had no idea he was going to stay.

Actually, he is rather worthless. He can't start the lawn mower and is not a good cook. With a little assistance from me, he makes a fair pot of coffee if I'm able to get him up in the mornings. He likes to sleep late and I'm an early riser.

He has another fault too—he falls a lot. It is all I can do to get him up from the floor when he falls. Once when I was trying to plant some peppers, he fell in the garden. Luckily, my daughter had just tilled it and the ground was soft and he didn't break anything.

I have tried to be nice to him and once, I let him drive my pickup. He backed into a tree and bent my bumper.

I have enough problems of my own without looking after some clumsy old man. Actually, if I knew where he came from I might call whoever sent him to come by and take him back and send me a later model.

I don't think he would like that. I pretty much let him do what he wants. He reads a lot and I get him the best books from the library and don't say a word when he reads until the wee hours of the morning. I also buy him Blue Bell ice cream.

The most puzzling thing about the whole deal is that nobody can see him but me. I have visitors on occasion and he sits right there at the dining room table and nobody sees him. That, I don't understand. Even my Pet Chihuahua, Bitsy, doesn't see him.

Once, not long ago, he fell in the bathroom and Bitsy went in and licked his face, thinking it was me. Actually, he does favor me a lot except I'm still 30 and he is at least 83. I sympathize with him but I can't do a thing about it.

I guess that one of these days, I'll come home from the grocery and he'll be gone but I'll be here a long time yet.

After all, I'm just 30.

A LITTLE TOO MUCH EXPOSURE AND TOO LITTLE DISCIPLINE

School officials at a junior high school in Odessa recently removed 75 students from class until their parents could bring them some clothes that fit. I'm sure this involved the parents making a quick trip to Wal-Mart, or somewhere, to buy some new clothes. It's a good bet that they didn't already have some.

The boys were wearing pants that came down over their rears and the girl's jeans were at least an inch below their belly buttons, or just shy of falling off.

Maybe the boys were all hoping to eventually be plumbers. What they had showing is known world-wide as "plumber's cleavage." Plumbers, on the other hand, have a good excuse. It is impossible to bend over under a sink with tight pants on. I can no longer do it without any pants on at all.

I was once hired by a plumbing company as a head plumber. I went ahead of the regular plumbers and dug all the ditches. That's the extent of my plumbing knowledge and I wasn't fond of that.

Anyway, I'm glad to see school officials cracking down on this type of attire. Maybe I just used a bad choice of words there. Actually, I don't think the school officials should have to do that. It is the responsibility of the parents, but they obviously are not doing it.

When I was going to school, back in the dark ages, our pants fit fine in the waist but we often showed a lot of leg below the knees. This was a result of having to wear "hand-me-down" pants because we couldn't afford new ones. We called them "high water pants" and we could wade Blanket Creek without getting them wet.

Back then, the girls in my class never exposed anything. I had no idea what a teen-age girl's belly button looked like. It was years before I found out, not that I was really interested as I had one of my own.

Another junior high school official in Odessa was indicted for "carrying a prohibited weapon" to school and firing it in his office. I can understand that. I think school officials these days should be allowed a gun in a holster on their hips and one in an ankle holster just in case.

Instead, the City police department has to furnish protection, I guess, from the students. I can't fathom the sheriff sending a deputy out to the Blanket school and hanging around all day. Back then, he only had two.

We didn't need one. Our superintendent was meaner than any deputy sheriff I ever saw and all he carried was a yardstick. He did, on occasions, fire it off in his office on somebody's rear and when they bent over, nothing showed below the horizon.

I recently shopped for a new pair of jeans. All I could find were size 40 in the waist. I asked a clerk why. His answer; "Well, that's what the kids are buying these days."

This leads me to believe that the kids are running the country with the parents furnishing the money. All along, I was wrong—I thought the lobbyists were doing it.

Personally, I think it's about time to "strike a blow for liberty" and take our country back from the kids, the lobbyists, the illegal immigrants, the politicians and anybody else who threatens our way of life.

I congratulate the school official at the Nimitz junior high school in Odessa who has made a good start.

LOOSE SKIN, SHATTERED WINDSHIELDS AND EXTREME MAKEOVERS

I recently read where a woman in California is suing the TV show "Extreme Makeover" for reneging on her contract. I think the lady was what we used to call "whomper-jawed." Apparently their doctors took one look at her and decided there was nothing they could do.

I know the feeling. I was wondering why they sent my application and picture back. Recently I was stopped by a policeman for some minor offense. It may have been because I was driving from the back seat. I sometimes get confused between the two. He took one look and said, "I'm sorry I stopped you. Did a building fall on your during Katrina or Rita?"

What really bothers me is that my friends say, "You look just like you always did." Friends lie just like everybody else. I know that I was once young and good-looking and I have the pictures to prove it. I had no trouble getting girl-friends after the invention of duct tape.

Back when I was a kid growing up in Blanket, there was a fellow who lived out of town a ways who couldn't have got on "Extreme Makeover" either. Dad and I would be sitting on the bench in front of Ernest Allen's drug store and the man would walk by.

Dad always said, "I know that old boy can't help being ugly but he could stay off the street." I have tried to do that myself in recent years. I felt his pain then and I still do now.

It was rumored that when the fellow walked to town, flowers by the roadside withered. Weeds died as if they had been sprayed with Roundup. He owned a car but couldn't drive it. Every time he got behind the wheel, the windshield shattered and the rear-view mirror crawled under the front seat.

An elderly lady recently asked me, "Do you know where I can sell some extra skin? "All of a sudden I have enough for two women my size. It is hanging everywhere."

"No point in trying the army burn center." I told her. "I have already tried them."

The ravages of age wreaks havoc on our bodies and there is not much we can do about it but grin and hope other folks can bear it. One day you may notice that your body is suddenly making noises like your coffee maker. Don't worry about it. You're still here or you couldn't hear it.

We should feel sorry for our doctors. Every day, they hear about ailments that even Harvard Medical School has never heard of. We expect them to do something about it. They try with wonder drugs and then wonder what the next day will bring to their door. We all do too.

Any kind of makeover we get would have to be extreme but even that wouldn't make us look like we want to look, or the way we once looked. It's not our age that bothers us as much as our memory. We remember when we didn't always have to slip up on the water bucket to get a drink.

I recently tried something new. I pressed my face against the computer monitor and put the computer on "Restore." Nothing happened. I'll take that up with Bill Gates later.

We have to look on the bright side. The checkers in grocery stores seldom ever look up and we still have our driver's licenses.

I still worry about the windshield though.

LUBBOCK, TEXAS THROUGH MY WINDSHIELD

Sometime in the early sixties, I took my wife and two kids on a tour of the West. We saw things we had never seen before, and would never see again. The two kids were not impressed. They sat in the back seat and read funny books across a land that took our pioneers decades to cross, or to conquer.

Driving through miles of Indian Reservations beyond Albuquerque, my wife said, "I sure hope we don't have a breakdown out here." "Those Indians," she said, "sure don't look friendly." "I sure don't blame them," I said, as I pushed the little car to its limit, trying to reach Colorado before dark.

At some pseudo western town by a railroad track, we stopped briefly to gawk. We entered a fake western bar where one might expect to find Matt Dillon, Miss Kitty, Doc and Festus having a beer, with maybe a friendly gunfight going on upstairs, with bodies falling over the railing like pins in a bowling alley. This was, we thought, the Wild West.

Nothing like that happened of course, and the bartender served only Sarsaparilla, and Matt, miss Kitty, Festus and Doc, found only in the imagination of Hollywood's script writers, were not there, and had never been.

We drove on into the vast distances of the unexplored West, at least to us, and found a campground and put up our imaginary Teepee. I inflated our genuine Sears Indian air mattresses, and we went to bed. We thought about posting a guard to watch for hostiles, but after driving 500 miles, we slept, and dreamed about Matt, Miss Kitty, Doc, and Festus, and still wondered what Sarsaparilla was.

The next day, we drove our asthmatic Volkswagen to the top of Pike's Peak where a breath of oxygen could be obtained by putting a quarter in a machine. There was none, however, for our Volkswagen, that seemed to need it worse than we did. We honked and waved at every car with Texas plates who seemed to be our only allies in this strange land.

My wife and I gloried in the sight of the snowfields and the high passes of the Rockies while the Volkswagen suffered from lack of air, and the kids read funny books. This was The Great American West, at least part of it, and we were there.

We saw what we could on our very limited budget, drove over the high passes, gazed at the snow-clad peaks in wonderment, and thought a lot about Texas, and home. Mack Davis, a noted musician and singer from Lubbock wrote a song about "Looking at Lubbock In the Rearview Mirror."

Not knowing any better, Mack, at the time, really wanted see Lubbock in his rearview mirror. At that particular time in our lives, we couldn't wait to see Texas and Lubbock appearing through our windshield. A land where a man can see a hundred miles, where the roads are straight and the people are friendly. Mack was wrong, but it took him a while to find out. It took us a week, a long time ago in the sixties.

STRANGE HAPPENINGS
IN A STRANGE WORLD

I have seen a lot of things happen since I first arrived on this pretty blue planet, when the Big Dipper was just a little cup. From Model T Fords to satellites, cell phones, computers, air conditioning, flush toilets and Japanese cars driven by young people who drive like maniacs and wear clothes that don't fit and listen to weird music and subsist on Big Macs. Strange things have happened and most likely, stranger things will happen yet.

I remember one strange thing that happened to me about 30 years ago as I was driving from Goldthwaite to San Saba. When I shifted gears, the sole of my left boot kept hanging on the clutch.

I stopped in a small roadside park to see what the trouble was. It was then that I discovered that the outer sole on my left boot had worn through to the inner sole which was hanging on the clutch.

I had never noticed this before and I wondered why I hadn't. It appeared to me that I was going to have to buy a new pair of boots. It never entered my mind to ask for divine assistance, even though my money was scarce. Some folks might have prayed for a new pair of boots right there on the spot, but I didn't. God, as far as I knew, wasn't in the boot business.

The strangest part of this story is that on the following morning, there was no hole in my left boot. Somebody, during the night, had healed it, and saved my sole. I thought of the old TV show, "The Twilight Zone."

Several years ago, I went on a junket to Washington to see Senator Kay Bailey Hutchison sworn in for her second term. We flew out of Love Field at Dallas. Most of the folks on the plane appeared to be wealthy Dallasites who all knew each other. I probably wouldn't have gone at all except the plane fare which included breakfast going up and supper coming back was less than a hundred dollars.

We also were furnished a sumptuous meal at noon by Senator Hutchison and had a full day to explore the sights of Washington. On the flight back to Dallas, I sat by a nice couple who said they lived in a town about 60 miles from Dallas.

When the man found that I was from Brownwood, he asked if I knew a fellow who once lived here for years. I admitted that I had known him for at least 25 years. "Well," the man said, "He is my brother." I didn't doubt him a bit and noticed a remarkable resemblance.

Back in Dallas, while trying to phone a cab to take me to my motel, my new friends approached. "Don't call a cab," The man said, "We will be glad to take you to your motel" We got in his new Cadillac and they drove me to the motel. I got his address and later wrote to thank him for his trouble. My letter was returned marked "No such address."

A few months later, I saw the man's old business associate in a local store. I told him I had met his former business associate's brother on a plane returning from Washington. I was shocked when he told me, "I don't know who you met, but he doesn't have a brother."

Now, I wonder who drove me to that motel that night and if being exposed to politicians all day had again put me in the twilight zone.

I still don't know.

LYING MIGHT CAUSE A HOLE IN YOUR BOOT

I have seen a lot of things happen since I first arrived on this pretty blue planet, longer ago than I like to think about. From Model T. Fords to satellites, cell phones, air conditioning, flush toilets and Japanese cars driven by young people who drive like maniacs and wear clothes that don't fit and listen to weird music and subsist on Big Macs. Strange things have happened and most likely, stranger things will happen yet.

I have seen "Lum and Abner," our favorite radio program replaced by some character named Raymond on TV. I don't know who Raymond is, nor do I have any interest in knowing. I have seen a nutty psychiatrist named Fraser and his skinny brother take the place of Matt Dillon, Festus and Doc and Miss Kitty. None of this, as far as I'm concerned, should have ever happened.

I remember one strange thing that happened about 25 years ago as I was driving my 1977 VW Rabbit between Goldthwaite and San Saba. When I shifted gears, the sole of my left boot kept hanging on the clutch.

I stopped in a small roadside park to see what the trouble was. It was then that I noticed my left boot had worn through the outer sole and parts of the inner sole were hanging on the clutch.

I had never noticed this before and I wondered why I hadn't. It appeared to me like I was going to have to buy a new pair of boots. It never entered my mind to ask for divine assistance, even though my money was scarce. Some folks might have prayed for a new pair of boots right there on the spot, but I didn't.

I figured that God, or whoever was on duty that day, had other irons in the fire anyway. The Bible does not mention, to my knowledge, that God has any experience in boot repair or keeps a stock of new boots on hand. He might and I wouldn't know it.

The strangest part of this story is that the next morning, I found no hole in my left boot. Nor is there one now, after 25 years. I still wear them occasionally. Somebody, during that night, had healed it.

Folks who know me might swear that I never lie unless it is absolutely necessary to avoid a traffic ticket or incarceration of one kind or another.

A few years back, I was on my way to the Big Bend National Park for a few days of camping. I was driving my Ford F-150 XLT pickup and had all of my camping gear in the back and my Chihuahua dog in the front seat.

Somewhere in a remote area between Fort Stockton and Marathon, I was stopped by a Highway Patrolman who had obviously been down there checking on his deer lease. He informed me that my inspection sticker had expired. I told him I had not noticed it.

After giving my driver's license a good inspection, he said, "Mr. Marlin, we moved the sticker from the right side of your windshield to the left so you'd be looking right at it all day." "Yes sir," I said, "I sure ought to have noticed it."

He looked over my camping gear in the back of the pickup along with a cooler full of beer all iced down and remarked, "I assume you were on your way to get that inspection sticker".

"Yes sir, "I lied, "I sure was, and I'll take care of it."

"Have a good trip, Mr. Marlin," He said, with a slight grin.

I sure did, and during the whole trip, not one hole came in my boot.

TAKE A LEFT TURN TO THE ALAMO MOTEL

One of my correspondents who keep me abreast of things says I missed out on all the fun one night last week when a number of drivers got their cars stuck on the new "no left turn" curbs the highway department thoughtfully constructed in the middle of the streets around the traffic "T". It seems that at night, the curbs are difficult to see and are all constructed in areas where if anybody might have an urge to turn left, that would be the spot.

My correspondent says the employees of two different businesses were entertained for some time with the "screeching of metal and sparks flying everywhere" from the cars hung up on the curbs. I hate that I missed it but it may turn out to be a regular occurrence.

Anyway, that particular area has been interesting for several years now. I even remember it long before the "T" was there and before the traffic circle was built. One of Brownwood's better motels and restaurants was located just north of the "T." It was called Willow Garden Motel and Restaurant.

If a movie star happened to be passing through town, he, or she would have stayed there. In fact, I think one did once but I don't remember who it was. We didn't have many motels back then and even fewer movie stars passing through. The Grande Courts was located on East Commerce and it was reasonably nice but I don't remember any movie stars staying there either.

One of our motels was an asset to the police department. If they happened to be looking for a particular thief, drunk or prostitute, they could be found at the Alamo Motel. I think they named it after the real Alamo in San Antonio where Texans fought 13 days for freedom. At this Alamo, they fought every night and usually lost their freedom.

As everybody knows, where the "T" is now was a traffic circle for years. This too was confusing to some motorists. Back in the fifties when I was a cop, we carried gasoline to one fellow 3 times in one night. He couldn't find his way off the thing. In England, traffic circles are called "Round-Abouts" and hardly anything upsets the British except missing tea.

Back in the fifties, a local banker donated the money and a large pool with colored lights and a fountain was built in the middle of it. It was a sight to behold. Hundreds of folks attended the grand opening, held at night to show off the lights.

But then, with daylight came the usual Texas wind which blew sheets of water onto the surrounding businesses and soaked the street causing cars to skid. One enterprising woman shucked her clothes one night and took a bath in it causing more traffic problems.

The amount of water pressure was cut down and the effectiveness of the fountain was lost. Eventually, the pumping equipment went bad and the pool was filled in and flowers planted. Maybe back then somebody was thinking, "Hey, let's build a "T" here and put some curbs in the street so nobody can make a left turn."

Progress, they say, comes from new ideas.

I have no idea how this project is supposed to turn out and I'm not worried about it. I know 9 different ways to go anywhere I might want to go, none of which require me to turn left unless I want to. I do miss the traffic circle though.

I miss a lot of things.

THE NIGHT THE SOLDIER AND SAILORS MEMORIAL HALL BURNED

I still remember the night the old Sailors and Soldiers Memorial Hall burned down. I was assisting a photographer shoot pictures of the Brownwood High School graduating class in the old football stadium.

About halfway through the proceedings, a thunderstorm unleashed its full fury with roaring thunder, lightning and a deluge of rain. Several hundred people made a mad dash for the school auditorium, none of whom arrived there dry.

The photographer said somebody stole his raincoat in the stadium and he was mad. He accused me of doing it. How he arrived at that conclusion, I don't know since I was not wearing it and I was as wet as he was.

At some point during the big storm, lightning, they said, struck the Memorial Hall and in spite of the efforts of our fire department, it burned to the ground. I never heard anybody complain. I am sure, had they known about it, musicians all over the state would have celebrated the fact that they would never have to play on that terrible slanted stage again.

At that time, it was used mostly for country music concerts and wrestling matches. In the late forties, the National Guard met there, having no other place. The building could in no way have been regarded as attractive and an architectural triumph, it wasn't.

A City official who had no love for the place was often jokingly accused of setting it on fire. He never admitted to the deed and when accused would just grin. Actually, I'm convinced that a Higher Power also didn't care much for the building either and sent the lightning to get rid of it.

As for breaking up the graduation ceremonies and getting several hundred people wet, that was just "collateral damage." It is hard to do anything constructive these days without that happening. Another example: when they made Austin Avenue four lanes, the concrete driveway entrance to my house was torn out and never replaced as promised.

At least, the burning of the Memorial Hall provided a reason to build our coliseum on the same site. People watched with interest as the construction started. Few could figure out what the end result might be. Herman Bennett, the contractor, was the only one who knew for sure and he watched it all with a worried look.

First, a large dome-shaped pile of dirt was put on the site, and then concrete was poured over the pile of dirt forming the top. Then, hydraulic jacks were placed on steel posts around the concrete dome and it was slowly lifted to the present height.

I was employed at time as an insurance investigator for a firm in Atlanta, Georgia. I took time off to watch the whole operation and in the event the thing fell on somebody I would have first-hand information. Anyhow, I was as curious as everybody else about the final outcome. Large crowds watched the entire procedure.

Also, at the time, I owned a 16 Millimeter movie camera and I filmed any newsworthy event for KRBC in Abilene. I filmed the raising of the dome from the roof of the Brownwood Hotel. It all went smoothly with no mishaps.

I also filmed the first ever Ladies Only chili cookoff at Luckenbach and later, the second cookoff ever held at Terlingua for KRBC.

Video cameras with sound hadn't been invented then which saved a lot of time editing the sound track. As Martha Stewart might have said about the Memorial Hall burning and the lack of sound on my camera, "It was a good thing."

THE GOOD AND THE BAD
OF LIVING IN THE FIFTIES

My short-term memory is getting like a really old elephant's with Alzheimer's. I have been told that this is normal. Personally, after reaching the age of being older than dirt, I don't think anything is normal.

Of all the years that I have fond memories of, I think I like the fifties best. Our civilization was far more normal than it is today. Nobody seemed to be in much of a hurry. It appeared that things weren't going anywhere anyhow. There was no reason to be in a hurry to get there.

The economy was not really good and our city seemed to be dying on the vine, or had already died. During a part of this era, I was a police officer in Brownwood, a job which paid little and there were times when I had difficulty even paying attention.

We lived on 7th street and our house payments were $42 a month, which at times, even that was hard to make. I knew everybody on the street and my two kids played with their kids. All of our kids attended South Ward and walked to school. There were no soccer games to attend because nobody had ever heard of it.

Since the school furnished no lunches as they do today, my kids had to have money every morning for a hamburger, or something, from Mr. Floyd's store at the corner of 7th and Avenue K.

Still, we were as happy as pigs in sunshine. I really can't account for that except that hard times always seem to bring people together.

Traffic too was nearly non-existent in the fifties. The most traffic we ever saw was when the drive-in theaters let out at night. The kids all had loud mufflers on their cars which was illegal then. Our police cars were so worn out, we couldn't catch them.

In fact, we couldn't have caught O.J. Simpson on his famous 35 mile an hour chase on the L.A. freeway. Our police cars had no air conditioners either.

Kids in their fifties now will remember the Dairy Maid on Coggin where they all congregated, or perhaps The Mug drive-in on a triangular piece of land near 4th and Coggin. I remember the Dutch Doll drive-in on the Brady highway and Gilmore's on Center Avenue. Today, there is a bank there.

Then, things got better financially. The sixties arrived, I got a better paying job, bought a new home at 13th and Asbury and our third child was born, a boy who is now a computer engineer in Phoenix. There was a 50 acre vacant field east of our house and Asbury Street stopped at our garage. The fifties were gone, leaving only memories.

We no longer have drive-in theaters but our traffic is horrendous. Brownwood is booming. It now takes me 10 minutes to get out of my driveway on Austin Avenue. Thirty years ago, I could have pitched a tent in the middle of the street and never been bothered.

With our economy apparently in good shape I can't help but wonder if the people driving up and down the streets all day and night are unemployed. Maybe, considering the way they drive, they're all just late for work.

I'm a firm believer in taking life a little slower like folks did in the fifties. I can guarantee you're going to get old soon enough.

My advice is to slow down and smell the carbon monoxide.

HOOKED ON CABLE WITH
THE WRONG NAME

My friend Billy Graham is a musician. Having proved his ability in this medium by playing with Glenn Campbell, Roger Miller and Ray Price over the years, his qualifications can in no way be questioned. Billy is a local boy, but maintains a home in Nashville where he returns frequently to either produce compact discs, or play on one with other noted musicians. He also writes songs, and his imagination in this field exceeds that of an old maid at a wrestling match.

While back in Brownwood, he may often rent his Nashville home out to various itinerant musicians, who are trying to make it big in Music City USA. Since his home is located in an upscale neighborhood, he often finds it necessary to make frequent trips there to see if any of his tenants have built an outhouse in the backyard, installed 6 hound dogs under the front porch, or parked a 1951 Chevy on blocks in the front yard.

Musicians, as everybody knows, often come from backgrounds where such activities are regarded as normal. Billy, being from Brownwood didn't. Nobody here would even think of having over 2 hound dogs under the front porch. Also, it is the preference of most folks here to have a motor home on blocks. It shows how far they have progressed.

As often happens, with our current population being what it is, some folks wind up having the same name. There are two Billy Grahams. One, a noted evangelist who has been blessed by the Pope, and one, a noted musician who hasn't. Neither knows the other.

Sometime back, Billy Graham, the musician, was trying to get one of those cable hook-ups to his computer, but was having little success. He called the company. "This is Billy Graham in Nashville," he said. "I can't seem to get a cable hook-up on my computer."

"Yes Sir, Dr. Graham," the man at the other end of the line said. "It will be hooked up Friday." The call was made on Thursday, on Friday, the musician Billy Graham had a cable hook-up. We don't know what the evangelist Billy Graham got. Perhaps a bill?

There may be certain advantages to having the same name as a famous person, and there may not be. Walking into a bank and telling the teller, "Hi, I'm Clyde Barrow and this is my friend Bonnie. We'd like to make a withdrawal" is not one. Of course, most of us know that Clyde and Bonnie are no longer among the living. The young folks don't. One only has to watch "Who Wants To Be A millionaire" to figure that out. All they know is the latest rock and roll star and who is big in movies these days.

Aging is that undeniable phenomena that happens to us all. It will frequently bring us the knowledge to get us out of tight places and show us how to jump off our cars when the battery is dead. It affects both evangelists and musicians, but it will never get us a spot on "Who Wants To Be A millionaire." It might, however, get us a cable hook-up on our computer if your name is Billy Graham.

A FEW MEDALS, A FEW MEMORIES
AND A LOT OF BRAVE MEN

My friend, Dr. Joe Rushing of Lampasas, Texas recently sent me a World War Two Honoree certificate that he obtained from the internet, complete with a picture of me in my flying suit with a cigarette dangling from my mouth. I understand that part. Back then, you were not considered macho if you didn't smoke.

Even all the movie stars smoked then with the possible exception of Roy and Dale. I never saw them light up in the middle of a gun battle. One thing the stars did do back then was kiss with their mouth's closed. I guess this was on account of the cigarette smoke. I never noticed them back in those days trying to eat each other up like they do today.

The Honoree certificate relates all of my WWII activities, like being a ball turret gunner and flying missions for which I received a number of medals. This includes the Good Conduct Medal which was a mistake. That one, I never honestly earned. My conduct, best I remember, was never good.

When I was discharged from the Army Air Corp in 1945, I received a set of my medals. They were pretty and I kept them for awhile. Finally, I gave them to my kids, Laura and Jimmy, to play with. My youngest, Ken, hadn't yet arrived then.

Somewhere in a back yard where we lived, they are safely buried in cardboard boxes, awaiting what, I don't know. To them, they were but treasures to be buried and like kids do, forget them.

Sometime in the 80s, a nice lady decided I should have a set of my medals. She ordered them from the Army in St. Louis. They made one mistake, sending me a pair of Navy fighter pilot's wings. The commander of the Commemorative Air Force in Mesa, Arizona gave me the proper ones.

Today, they are displayed, safe and sound, in a shadow box on my kitchen wall. Now and then, a young visitor will look at them and say, "You did all this?" "You're kidding—right?" "Were you the oldest man on the plane, like maybe 70?"

They are far more interested in a picture of Willie Nelson and me than my WWII service. After all, Willie is now but that was then. "Then" is fast fading from their memories, but not from mine, and it never will.

The news media tells us that WWII veterans are dying at the rate of 1,000 a day. We may have exceeded that during the war but a lot of us are still here and we're not going yet. We were "The Greatest Generation" and to use an old country expression, we're staying until they pee on the fire and call the dogs.

Of course, we have had several wars since then with a lot of brave men involved but we actually won WWII because everybody in the United States did their part. There were no protestors or activists marching on every corner. The country was behind us and President Roosevelt 100%, whether right, or wrong.

"Hang together" somebody said, "Or we'll all hang separately."

I would prefer not to do that. I might even get another medal.

NEURONS, MORONS, SCIENTISTS AND SHAMPOOING RATS

I just read in the news that scientists, those fellows who wear white coats and poke around in stuff have discovered that there is an ingredient in most shampoos on the market today that cause brain damage in rats. I have to assume that they have been catching rats and giving them a dose of Head and Shoulders.

I'm glad to hear that. All along, I thought the weird antics I have been engaging in lately were caused by aging. They say that after using the shampoo, the rat's neurons were no longer communicating with each other.

My neurons, as far as I know, have not spoken to each other in 10 years. At least, I haven't heard it. Actually, I'm not sure what a neuron is. I'm more familiar with morons.

The world today has a good supply of those. They play that weird music you hear all over town and wear clothes that don't fit.

This might be an indication that George Jones, Merle Haggard and Willie who play the kind of music I like haven't shampooed their hair in years. And what about Dolly Parton? She looks well shampooed. She just played an engagement in Houston to 5000 fans and remarked, "If I pulled a Janet Jackson stunt here, it would wipe out the whole front row." That makes sense to me.

There is always that possibility that those weird folks are normal and we have just been shampooing our hair too often. To save what few neurons I have left, I may start shampooing with Ivory soap and bottled water. Ivory, they say is 99% pure. I'm not sure about the water.

Back in the thirties when I was trying to grow up, the women all shampooed their hair with rain water from a cistern and used lye soap. The male species maybe did it with each change of the seasons. Everybody seemed to be reasonably sharp. We never worried about the rats. Nobody ever shampooed one.

Many common household items, the scientists say, can also cause brain damage. Clorox comes to mind. We should never drink it or mix it with ammonia which not only can cause brain damage but also causes a poison gas that can kill every cat in the alley.

I don't know how we could exist today without scientists who warn us against stuff we've been doing all our lives. Mama told me more than one time that a combination of salmon and sweet milk was fatal. I tried it to prove her wrong and I'm still here.

"Don't smoke," they said. "It will stunt your growth." I did, and somehow grew to normal size. The only scientist we had in town was Ernest Allen at the drug store. He mixed up all kinds of stuff in his mortar and pestle. He never once warned us that it might kill us. None of it did, but nobody ever saw a rat in the drug store.

Still, listening to those scientists can give us a bad case of the vapors and fantoids, both of short duration and causes no brain damage as long as we don't shampoo during an attack. Doing so, we are warned, may cause the dreaded bridge rail damage.

It seems that the best thing we can do is to quit reading that stuff, but I can't. When I see the word "Scientist" in a headline. I read it all.

I wonder what I've done wrong and how much longer I've got.

NEVER CARRY A BLUNT
OBJECT INTO A HOSPITAL

I was missing in action last week due to being confined to the hospital for what I was told was "minor" surgery that wouldn't amount to a hill of beans. Do not believe what people tell you about surgery, or anything else. They lie a lot.

My hospital stay was reasonably short and went smoothly with the possible exception of a problem with the anesthesia which temporarily made me nutty as a fruit cake. What I did was spend a good part of my time trying to overhaul their telephone system. After arriving in my assigned room, I tried the telephone which didn't seem to be working, giving a continuous busy signal.

I quickly noticed what the problem was. The telephone cable was running down my left arm and into a vein on my wrist. I knew that wasn't right and did my best to pull it out with no success. Somebody had done a really good taping job.

I decided that since I couldn't fix that end of it, I'd try the other. I couldn't believe where they had it. It was taped to the bottom of a large plastic bag which was full of some type of clear liquid. It should have been plugged into a wall receptacle.

I spent about 15 minutes trying to pull it out of that bag so I could put it where it belonged. I had no success there either.

Finally, I attracted the attention of a nurse who informed me that what I was trying to change was what I was getting my medication from. I assumed I was getting some new type of broadband antibiotic direct from Verizon. Oh yeah, babe.

Finally, they reluctantly allowed me to go home. As I was being pushed out of the hospital in a wheelchair by a nice nurse, I suggested going out the back way. "I'm sure", I told her, "I must owe these folks a bunch of money."

My doctor informed me that once I got home, "Do not do any heavy lifting." Since I usually spend my days, from the time I get up until I go to bed avoiding heavy lifting, I was sure I'd have no problem.

I have to admit, I did hurt a lot from the incision but I avoided taking the pain pills the doctor had written a prescription for. I felt that I was goofy enough the way I was.

I watched a lot of cop shows on TV which is the kind I like best. I learn a lot from watching "Law and Order," "CSI", "Forensic Files" and "The First 48." I learned that 90% of all murders are committed with a "Blunt object." I also learned that 90% of statistics are made up on the spot.

I learned that no state has a law against carrying a blunt object. We can feel free to carry one anywhere without fear of arrest. We have one problem. Nobody sells them. We can buy any kind of gun we desire nearly anywhere but we can't buy a blunt object.

Even in Texas where we have the "right to carry" law, we can't get a permit to carry a blunt object, even if we could find one.

For the protection of the fine people who occupy our state, I think our legislature should move immediately to pass a law against owning or carrying a blunt object. But first, I suppose, to meet legal requirements, we need to know what a blunt object is.

If I find out, I'll let you know.

NEVER KICK A DRY COW
PATTIE ON A HOT DAY

Back several years ago while I was gainfully employed as an investigator, I was attacked by a fellow in a pool hall with a pool cue. A pool cue, as far as I was concerned is a weapon of mass destruction, depending of course on where you get hit with it. My investigation had to do with a fraudulent disability claim. In the small town where this occurred, being hit with a pool cue was a normal thing. It happened, so I was told, with some regularity.

It seemed that half the people in town had one eye poked out. "In the land of the blind," somebody said, "A one-eyed man is king." There were more kings in that town than in Saudi Arabia. They had little to do but play pool and fight.

Knowing full well that there is a time to hold and a time to fold—I folded. I beat the fellow out the door by about 15 feet. About 6 miles down the road, safe in the confines of my car; I called him a no good bastard.

A man has to do what a man has to do. Anyway, I won the case and came in first on the race. You can't beat that with a pool cue.

On another occasion, I was investigating a fire where the owner of the business claimed he had lost several thousand dollars' worth of carpet. I was busy taking pictures of the interior of the building when the owner sneaked in and attacked me with a hammer. He was what we call in Texas "a board-certified mean son-of-a-bitch."

I did the proper thing. I left. I have always been thankful he didn't throw the hammer. My pictures proved that there was no carpet residue n the entire building. My hasty retreat proved that I qualified for any 10 mile marathon in the country.

I learned a lot as a kid growing up on a sorry 100 acre farm during the Great Depression near the town of Blanket. I learned never to poke a black wasp nest with a short stick, never kick a dry cow pattie on a hot day and never wipe your ass on a cocklebur leaf.

DON'T WEAR A CHICKEN SUIT TO ROB A GROCERY AFTER MIDNIGHT

A fellow in Hilliard, Ohio robbed a Kroger store, wearing a chicken suit. He got $16,000 and 12 years. The robbery of the clerk happened just after midnight and was caught on tape by the store security camera along with a woman in the check-out line talking on a cell phone.

The woman on the cell phone was not under suspicion of anything except possibly escaping from somewhere.

The robber wearing the chicken suit was a former employee who, for whatever reason, occasionally wore the suit as part of his duties in the store. It did not require the services of the Secretary of Agriculture to figure out who the culprit was.

He had previously held up a convenience store while wearing a Santa Claus suit, also a part of his duties at Kroger. Being a regular customer of Kroger, I have never observed anybody in there wearing a chicken suit or dressed like Santa.

However, I have seen bunches of women talking on cell phones in the check-out line. Maybe, while hunting lard, I just missed the big chicken and Santa. Anyway, when I'm buying groceries, I don't like to be distracted. I usually come home with only half of what I went to get anyhow.

Strange things happen all over this great country of ours. Recently, a woman took a vacation to Greece and upon returning home found that a strange woman had broken into her house, ripped out the carpets, bought a new washing machine and dryer and put the city utilities in her name.

I would welcome her at my house anytime, especially getting the city utilities out of my name. I could use a washing machine and dryer too and my carpet was put down when Hoover was president. She could even wear a chicken suit for all I care.

With all this stuff going on, the Democrats are still worrying about how the election came out. Believe me, there is a lot more happening out there.

Having grown up during the thirties in the middle of the Great Depression, I feel somewhat cheated. Hardly anything ever happened back then. Nobody ever broke into our house as there were no locks on the doors. We didn't have any carpet either.

Our washer was a number two tub and a rub board. The dryer was wires strung between two posts. Santa Claus was rarely, if ever seen. Nobody ever took a vacation to Greece, or anywhere else.

If a robber had ever walked into the Levisay and McCulley grocery store in Blanket with a gun and wearing a chicken suit, they would have deeded him the store and threw in a stalk of bananas. Yes, Virginia, bananas did come on stalks back then.

Money was obtained from banks, not by a note demanding money, but by signing a promissory note, which back then meant little except that if the crops were good, it would be paid. If the crops failed, another one would be signed the next year. Banks didn't sell Certificates of Deposits because nobody had any money to deposit.

Still, considering everything, it was not a bad time to grow up. We learned honesty, self preservation, the value of a dollar, and that hard work wouldn't result in death, along with the ambition to strive for a better life.

For better or worse, not one of us ever saw anybody wearing a chicken suit.

NO APPOINTMENT NEEDED TO GET YOUR CHRYSLER THUMPED

I'm not fond of Mondays. I'm in favor of doing away with Monday altogether and starting with Tuesday. Tuesday is not a bad day and with Wednesday coming up, we'll be "over the hump." Nothing seems to work right on Monday.

Last Monday, I was up early, as usual, and when I turned on my faucet to get coffee water, the thing went full force and wouldn't cut off. I had to hunker down, reach under the sink and cut it off. I'm still able to hunker down fairly well but I can't hunker up.

I thought I was going to have to e-mail somebody for help but I couldn't reach my computer. By getting a good hold on the sink, I finally got up, found a washer for the faucet and then had to hunker again to turn the water back on. Stuff like that just doesn't happen on Tuesday. Sunday is usually the day your sewer stops up or your dog gets sick.

Regardless of what day it is, we are now all living in the appointment age. I'm old enough to remember when appointments didn't exist. These days, we have to get an appointment to see our doctor, our dentist and our mechanic. To get a haircut or get my oil changed in my pickup, I have to get an appointment.

I suppose that indicates that our economy is good but I lived through a time when it wasn't. At least, we didn't need an appointment for anything. Back in Blanket, my old home town, there was usually at least two mechanics sitting on a bench in front of Boler's Conoco station if you happened to need one.

My doctor could be found either sitting on a bench in front of Ernest Allen's drug store or sitting in his Chrysler in front with the engine running, diagnosing any strange noises he might hear. He had two cars. If the Chrysler checked out alright, he would go home and get the other one and diagnose it.

I often wondered if the medical school he attended also had a course in auto mechanics. He was pretty good with both humans and cars. He always used the thumping method for his diagnosis of humans but I never saw him thump his Chryslers but he may have.

He never traded a car in. When he bought a new one, he stored the old one in Dossey's garage. When I was a kid, I would spend hours behind the wheel of those old cars, taking trips to far off places I could only dream about ever going.

When I went off into the military, the cars were still there. When I returned, both he and the cars were gone. I know where he went but I don't know what happened to the cars. Today, they might be worth more than he made in a lifetime of thumping chests and backs of our citizens.

Today, there is a restaurant occupying what was then Dossey's garage where he once stored his old cars. I have a lot of memories of the old place when I eat there and a lot of memories of Dr. Yantis and memories of his daughter with whom I climbed to the top of mulberry trees and ate mulberries, bugs and all.

We never worried about the bugs because her daddy was a doctor and I had no doubt he could thump bugs too.

I guess that somewhere, he is still thumping folks and maybe a few old Chryslers too.

NO SUVS OR BEER AVAILABLE BUT WE TRIED IT ALL ANYHOW

Somebody recently sent me a story on the internet that the National Transportation Safety Board, in cooperation with makers of 4-wheel drive pickups and SUVs, installed "black box" voice recorders in an effort to determine in fatal crashes the circumstances in the final moment before the crash.

I don't know if they actually did that but it brought back a lot of memories to me. In certain Southern states, including Texas, it said 89.3 percent of the driver's final words were, "Hold my beer, I'm gonna try somethin'."

I don't doubt that a bit. Back when I was growing up, we had no SUVs and few pickups made would run fast enough that if we ran in a bar ditch at full speed to ever bend a fender, no matter what we hit.

There wasn't a blacksmith in town with the ability to bend the fender on a Model T Ford, using every tool he had at his disposal. He couldn't straighten one either in the event some good ol' boy somehow managed to bend it.

There were no plastic or fiberglass cars around back then. Ours didn't bend or break.

Beer too, was rather scarce. It was a hundred miles in any direction where we could get one. We were too young to buy it anyhow. Even without the beer, we "tried somethin'" at every opportunity. Neither the National Safety Board nor our parents knew about any of this.

In the event of an ice storm that covered the street about a half-inch, we would get up all the speed we could, give the steering wheel a quick left turn and go sliding down the street backwards. It was awesome.

We managed to wipe out half the mail boxes in Blanket, but of course, not intentionally. We would have never done that. After all, recreation in small towns was hard to come by. We had to do something since there wasn't any beer for anybody to hold. We managed to do enough without it.

We would congregate on the large lot by the cotton gin on Saturday night following a good rain and make figure eights in the mud. One kid took the family car, a 1927 Chevy home so covered with mud it was hard to tell the make and model. We had no car washes either.

The Model T Fords were well suited for "mudding." Usually, the brake band on the transmission was worn out so everybody used the reverse pedal. The rear wheels would spin backwards. No other car could do it.

When we drove, we knew only one speed and that was whatever speed the car would do. Buying new tires was unheard of. Our tires were "booted" in the thin spots, throwing the wheels out of balance and causing considerable vibration.

I remember once I picked up a hitchhiker in my old Ford and quickly vibrated up to about 80 which was the top speed of the old junker. The hitchhiker remarked, "I don't remember this road being this rough before."

"It's not the road," I told him. "It's the boots in my old tires." "If you don't mind," He said, "I'll just get out along here. I just live right over yonder."

I guess kids today are no different than we were. They just have better cars. I'm amazed that some of us are still here.

It could be because we had no beer for somebody to hold while we "tried somethin'"

NO BRUSH CUTTING, BICYCLE RIDING OR PROTESTING AT MY PLACE

With the price of gasoline being as high as it is, it seems improbable that people would drive from all over the country to Crawford, Texas to either protest the President, or protest the protestors. But they do—in large numbers.

It all started when President Bush purchased a 1600 acre ranch 7 miles north of this little one stop-light town. Even before the war in Iraq started, a Palestinian named Hadi Jawad purchased a house in Crawford he calls "The Peace House" to give the activists and protestors a place to hang out.

Hard times fell on the place. Nobody was protesting anything. Their telephone was disconnected for non-payment. Then, along came Cindy Sheehan from California who came to confront the president over the death of her son in Iraq. She paid the phone bill and camped out by the road to the Bush ranch.

With the help of the telephone, more activists, news people and protestors begin to show up. Money was donated to pay off the $54,000 mortgage on the house. The President, who is on vacation, hoped to spend his time riding his bicycle and cutting brush on the ranch

Texas in the summer is always a good time to cut brush and ride a bicycle. With all the attention he is getting, he has hardly had time to do either. Even the road to his ranch is blocked with protestors, people who came to protest the protestors and tourists who hoped to get a glimpse of Mr. Bush.

The most the tourists get to see is Secret Service personnel and State Troopers and protestors. They aren't permitted within a mile of the ranch gate, even after paying that big price for gas to get there. It seems to be a losing proposition for everybody.

Well—not everybody. The souvenir shops and the town's one restaurant, I hear, are doing a land-office business along with the gas stations.

I grew up in an era when folks had plenty of reason to protest something. And yet, nobody did. Maybe we didn't have anybody to protest to. We had no TV networks or TV either. I have noticed that hardly anybody ever protests anything unless there is a TV camera in close proximity.

Even during WWII when we all went to war, one way or another, I saw no protestors. As the old saying goes, we all had to hang together or hang separately. Today is no different. We are fighting for the same thing—to keep our freedom and our way of life the way it is.

In every war we have ever been involved in, people get killed. I have been there and personally observed it. In the invasion of Europe on June 6th, 1944, 3000 troops lost their lives on the beaches of Normandy in one day. Any loss of life is always regrettable. Loss of freedom is intolerable.

Protest if you must but always thank God you live in a country where you can. In most countries in the world today, you can't.

I have no desire to drive to Crawford and protest anything. I have already seen President Bush when he was Governor of Texas and even shook his hand. Over the years, I have seen my share of State Troopers. I don't need to do that.

I think I'll just stay here and sit on my back porch. I can protest to my dog if I want to and it's a lot cooler here.

AWARD WINNING MOVIES, GOOD BOOKS AND HOW I LEARNED TO READ

I have been an avid reader for most of my life. I started at a rather young age due to the circumstances of my childhood. We were regarded as poor. In fact, as somebody once said, if anybody wanted to show somebody what poor was, they brought them by our house.

One reason for my early introduction to reading was the cold winter wind. It seemed that we always lived in an old house with cracks between the boards and Mama always papered the kitchen with copies of the Brownwood Banner or the Bulletin, or whatever was available.

Every morning I read the news, or whatever else Mama had pasted on the walls to keep out the cold north wind. If we happened to have visitors, which was rare, conversation was sparse as everybody was busy reading the walls.

I still read three or four books a week if I can find a good book that holds my interest. A friend of mine, Larry L. King, a Texas writer, born and reared at Putnam but now lives in Washington D.C. keeps me supplied with books. When I finish one, I give it to the local library.

Sometime back, he got me hooked on Cormac McCarthy when he sent me "No Country for Old Men." This book has been made into an award-winning movie which was filmed around Marfa and stars Tommy Lee Jones. Actually, the locale of the book is at Sanderson and surrounding towns.

I was especially interested in this book as I am familiar with the locale it was written about. I once knew the sheriff of Sanderson whose character is an integral part in the novel and his daughter Candace is a writer for the Bulletin. Another character in the movie, Tommy Lee Jones, also interested me. When I read the book, I had Tommy Lee figured for the part of the psycho killer.

I was wrong. He plays the part of the sheriff, a really nice, dedicated lawman. I guess the reason for this is that I once had a run-in with Tommy Lee when an insurance company from San Francisco sent me to see him and find out if he really existed and his reason for buying a rather large insurance policy and was he able to pay for it. I knew who he was but insurance underwriters seldom leave their cages and the one in San Francisco did not.

With Tommy Lee, I got nowhere fast. The fact is, I was treated like an illegitimate son at a family reunion. Finally, we had an exchange of words in regard to future travel plans. He told me where I could go and I told him where he could go.

I do admire his acting ability and I do hope he got the insurance. With his attitude, he needs it.

In recent years, Marfa has become the movie-making center of Texas, starting with "Giant" in 1955. During the past year, two award-winning movies have been filmed there, "There will be blood" and "No Country for Old Men."

Watching a movie being made is about like watching paint dry. Film is the cheapest commodity they have and they use a lot of it. Working as an extra is also dull. I once danced all afternoon with a lady who looked like Reba McIntire in a movie called "Baja Oklahoma" at Billy Bob's in Fort Worth. We were so far from the camera that the Hubbell telescope wouldn't have picked us up.

I didn't want to be an actor anyhow.

WHEN THE SUN GOES DOWN, IT GETS DARK IN MARFA

I don't go to movies very often anymore mostly because I don't see well in the dark. The fact is, I can't see at all in the dark. The last time I attended a movie was about 4 or 5 years ago. I noticed that the theater had no ground floor at all. If it did, I missed it. I climbed the stairs in total darkness on my hands and knees. I couldn't tell if there were 500 people in there watching me, or I was the only occupant in the place.

Recently, a movie came out that I wanted to see, "No Country for Old Men", so I rented a DVD so I wouldn't have to climb stairs. It was then that I discovered that not only are the theaters in total darkness but now, they're filming the movies in the dark too.

The locale of the book was Sanderson, Texas and the surrounding area. The movie was filmed in and around Marfa which is 75 miles or so up the road. Movie makers prefer to be in close proximity to a nice hotel and a cocktail lounge or two. I guess Sanderson didn't fill the bill.

After seeing the movie, I decided it didn't make any difference where they filmed it as most of it was apparently filmed in the dark anyhow. One scene showed nothing but a pair of automobile lights driving in the dark. This could have been filmed anywhere. Other than three exterior shots, one being the Rio Grande, nothing else was recognizable.

If I hadn't read the book, I wouldn't have known what was going on. One thing I do know, it gets as dark in Sanderson as it does in Marfa.

I remember the days when movies were shot with large carbon-arc lights which if inside, had to be vented due to emitting carbon monoxide. Good lighting was important and if the actor or actress had a wart on their nose, it showed. Not even a shadow was permitted. If an actress was getting a little old, a piece of gauze was placed over the camera lens. A blue filter over the lens turned day into night but the old actress would have still been visible, warts and all.

Not only are movies being shot in the dark but now the TV shows are. This cuts the cost of building expensive sets as nothing is visible anyhow. One of my favorite TV shows is "CSI Las Vegas." "This is a crime show where they usually have three murders to solve in their allotted hour. Everybody knows that Las Vegas is probably the best lighted city in the entire United States, both inside and out.

When the crime scene investigators enter the hotel room or wherever the crime scene happens to be, they never turn on the lights. They all carry a small flashlight. These flashlights are the only light they use to check out the scene whether inside or outside. On occasions, they may put on a pair of orange glasses. It is absolutely mind-boggling to see what this crew can find with those small flashlights and a pair of tweezers. They might even find Sanderson on a Texas map.

Now, there is another movie out on DVD that was shot at Marfa called ""There Will Be Blood." I'm not sure what this movie is about but if it is guaranteed to have been shot during the daylight hours, I'll rent it.

We all know by now that when the sun goes down it gets dark in Marfa.

No, I'm not going. It is doubtful that they will be overrun with folks. As far as I'm concerned, Luckenbach needs to change their slogan from "Everybody Is Somebody In Luckenbach" to "Everybody Pays Somebody In Luckenbach." I hear they're trying to figure out a way to charge to breathe.

Amarillo's slogan is "Step Into The Real Texas." As for me, I don't want to step into anything around that place. The have about 300 feed lots up there.

NOTHING IN A BIND BUT US

We were blessed with a good supply of characters in Blanket when I was growing up there. We definitely had enough of them to keep us entertained. Maybe we were all characters and just didn't know it.

On a back street from our house lived a couple with a son about 20 that sang and played a guitar. He didn't do either well. His parents, however, admired his singing and wanted to share it with us.

Mama didn't mind going over there but Dad, being a musician himself considered it torture. I went to get along with both of them. Their house was located across the street from our barn where we had chickens and a cow. I had thoughts that the fellow's singing might cause our hens to quit laying and the cow's milk to curdle.

We always sat on their front porch where the concert was held. Best I remember, the boy knew only one song, "She's My Curly-headed Baby." which he sang in a high nasal voice while playing his guitar, usually about one key off from his singing.

Finally, they moved somewhere, much to our relief. I still, somewhere in the dark recesses of my mind, hear that song.

An old man lived in the north part of town about 2 blocks from our house. I don't recall his name, which isn't important anyhow. He had an old Chevy coupe, about a 1932 model. He went to town every day, not having anything more important to do.

When I was a kid, going to town was about the most important thing anybody could do anyhow. His Chevy coupe was in dire need of an overhaul as most cars were then. This was during the Depression and spending money on an engine overhaul was not in anybody's budget. If it ran at all, you didn't mess with it.

When the old man started that engine, mechanics winced. At least the two we had did. It could be heard on a clear day for at least a mile. Every piston rod in it seemed to be about to come through the block with each revolution.

His first stop of the day was at Boler's Conoco station. At least one, if not both of our mechanics was always sitting on the loafer's bench, waiting for what the day might bring. Usually, it brought nothing.

I would ride my bicycle down there and hang out with the grownups in hopes of learning something that might benefit me later in life.

We could hear the old man start the Chevy at his house with a clattering of rod bearings and pistons slapping against the cylinder walls. He goosed that old engine with a vengeance, scaring hens off their nests for blocks around.

We all wondered if the old car would make it to town one more time. By the time he reached Dr. Brown's house, the engine had reached an ear-splitting crescendo and then seemed to reach a quiet climax as he passed the Methodist church, where he cut the switch and shifted into neutral, coasting to the station.

The old man would alight from the old Chevy as if it was the latest model Cadillac, fresh from the factory at Detroit; shift his chew of tobacco to a new cheek and smile.

"You really ought to get that thing fixed," Mose Strickland, one of our mechanics would say, accusingly.

The old man would shift his tobacco chew, spit on the toe of Mose's shoe and loudly proclaim, "Well", "There ain't nothing in a bind."

Well, maybe nothing but us.

OBSERVATIONS WHILE WAITING TO SEE THE DOCTOR

Sooner or later, you will visit your family doctor and he may tell you your blood pressure is exceeding the limits set by NASA, the CIA and possibly the FBI. Of course, this may depend on your age, your weight and whether or not you gave up salt at age four, have no bad habits, ate vegetables all your life and regularly have two apples with your morning coffee.

There is a reason for this. First, you sit in a waiting room for an hour and in spite of yourself, you start diagnosing the other patients who are waiting. The fellow on the end who weighs about 250 and has flushed cheeks obviously has high blood pressure.

But wait—do not be too hasty with your diagnosis. The lady who is sitting by him, probably his wife, is giving him a hard time. "I told you," She said, "We were in a 40 mile an hour speed zone and you were driving 60," "And why?" She added, "Did you call that policeman a Nazi?"

Then, she notices you listening and asks, "What is your trouble Buster?"

Finally, you are directed to a small room where there is nothing to read but an eye chart. You take off your glasses and discover you can read the chart much better without them. Somebody, somewhere, goofed. About $150 worth, you remember.

The doctor finally comes in wearing a white coat like they all do. Your blood pressure jumps up higher than your water bill. Do not worry. This is known worldwide as "White coat syndrome."

It happens to everybody. You may get blood pressure pills anyway. Take them if you do.

Sometime back, I was required by a doctor in a white coat to wear a heart monitor for 24 hours. This happened to me not once, but twice. The thing was in a little black box which was buckled around my waist with a bunch of wires running inside my shirt.

I would enter a restaurant to eat and the place would be empty in 10 seconds flat. In Baghdad, I would have been shot. I'm glad I wasn't there and I appreciate the brave men and women who are.

My next experience was with something called an EKG. It is also hooked up with a bunch of wires and kicks out a long piece of paper with squiggly lines on it like a lie detector. It looked fine to me but I did notice some of the lines jumped off the page.

After an interval of about two months, I asked how it came out. "We don't know yet." I was told. "We had to send it to the CIA in Langley, Virginia and they are a little slow". "The last word was that they think you're some kind of terrorist and you're on a "No fly" list" next to Ted Kennedy.

Being on a "No Fly" list didn't bother me. I did all of the flying I want to do during WWII,

In all seriousness, the doctors we have today, along with our modern technology are responsible for all of us having a lot more birthdays than folks had 50 years ago.

I remember our three doctors in Blanket who in their time were diagnostic geniuses but without our modern medicines and technology, they could do little.

Remember to thank your doctor every chance you get. The odds are, you're here today because of him, or her, as the case may be.

As Minnie Pearl used to say on the Grand Old Opry, "I'm so glad to be here."

WATCHING CHEF EMERIL ON TV AND TRYING TO LEARN TO COOK

Due to the sorry state of TV shows these days, my lady-friend and I often watch Chef Emeril on the food channel. Not only is he a fantastic cook but seems to be a better comedian than most I've seen on TV. His audience is so mesmerized by his show that by merely cracking an egg, he sends them into fits of ecstasy.

When he finishes a dish and puts it on a plate, he says "Bam!" That gets his audience rolling in the aisles. The big difference between Emeril and me, other than ability, experience and lack of an audience is that when I finish a dish and put it on a plate; I say "Damn!" Oh yeah, babe.

My Pit Chihuahua dog who is waiting patiently for a bite of something immediately scratches at the door, wanting out. I consider going with her.

A chef, I'm not. If I watched his show the rest of my life, I would still have difficulty boiling water properly. My soft-boiled eggs are hard as a rock, my gravy requires slicing. My attempts at making bread, if placed on a railroad would derail a freight train and my cornbread would cause a prison riot.

Having grown up during the Depression, we had few culinary delights. Sure, I watched Mama cook what we had, most of which would puzzle even the great Emeril. I doubt he has had much experience at cooking turnip greens, pinto beans, black-eyed peas, fried okra or poke salet. Oh yeah, babe, we had a steady diet of that stuff.

I'm fairly good at cooking pinto beans which doesn't require a degree from The San Francisco School of Culinary Arts and I have the ability to fry anything that needs frying which includes nearly everything. I doubt that Emeril even knows what lard is. Most things I like are fried but I stopped using lard when alternatives became available.

I have heard folks say on more than one occasion" If it ain't fried, it ain't fitten to eat." Fitten is a word you don't hear much these days but when I was a kid its usage was pretty common. Mama used to say, "Them overalls are not fitten for you to wear to town."

I would love to be able to cook like Emeril. I can say "Bam!" as good as he can but that's about the best I can do. I know he must have a bunch of dish washers and assistants who are never shown. I have noticed that when he reaches for something, it's there. When I reach for something, it's not. There's nobody here but me and the dog. Oh yeah, babe.

Emeril has a band that plays while he thinks up something else to cook that he knows all of us poor slobs watching the show can't cook and will never be able to. Some of the stuff he cooks I have never even seen before.

He invents his own recipes, they say. I have tried that myself a few times with disastrous results. Maybe a band is what I need to play while I'm scorching something. Keep the audience distracted, if you have one other than a Chihuahua.

Anyway, I'm going to keep watching his show until I learn how to cook something at least halfway right and surprise the dog. I can't wait until I can put something edible on a plate and say "Bam!"

Oh Yeah, babe.

OLD ACTORS, OLD BUILDINGS AND OLD MEMORIES

I am somewhat distressed that all of my old western actors are riding off into the sunset, or have already departed. The last to go was Dennis Weaver who died February 24th, the day after my birthday. Of course, Milburn Stone, who played Doc and Amanda Blake who played Miss Kitty are long gone too.

Dennis limped through numerous episodes of "Gunsmoke" as Chester Goode, Matt Dillon's deputy. It was never explained why he limped. I wondered about that, but maybe other folks didn't. Had I been around then, I would have asked him.

After Dennis was Ken Curtis who played Festus Hagen until the series ended. He was my favorite but he too is no longer with us. He rode a mule and talked pure country and sounded like a lot of folks I knew.

Back when John Ford was shooting the movie "The Searchers," Ken Curtis was married to Mr. Ford's daughter and had a small part in the movie. He was born and reared in Southwestern Colorado, known as the "Dryland."

One day John Ford told him, "Talk "Dryland" for me Ken." He did and it stuck with him from then on. As everybody remembers who has seen "The Searchers" 18 times as I have, he even sang "Skip to my Lou" in the movie.

He was an experienced singer, having sung with both the Tommy Dorsey and Shep Fields orchestras and was well-known for being a member of "The Sons of the Pioneers."

Harry Marlin

I remember that back in the fifties sometime, the country band I was playing with opened for the "Sons of the Pioneers" in the old Brownwood Memorial Hall. I have no idea who designed the stage in that place, or what they were thinking but it had about a 15 degree slant on it.

I was playing a steel guitar with legs on it and it kept sliding forward with every lick I hit. The drummer had it even worse. Four kicks on the bass drum and it headed for the footlights. I think we were all embarrassed at having that happening in front of that famous group.

The last time I saw Ken Curtis and Doc, they were appearing at the San Angelo rodeo. I drove up there to get to meet them and talked briefly. Then, I drove back to Brownwood. That must have been at least 25 years ago.

About 10 or 12 years ago, I saw James Arness at Bracketville where he was shooting a TV movie. He was still Matt Dillon to me but due to having Rheumatoid arthritis, he could hardly walk. I stood in awe in front of one of my heroes and said little. There was nothing I could say.

We are all but mortals and sooner or later, we all go. Buildings too, go, but sometimes it takes longer. The old monstrosity with the slanting stage known as The Soldier and Sailors Memorial Hall is also gone. I don't remember the year as I've had too many years.

What I do remember is there was a really bad storm with heavy rain and lots of thunder and lightning. The Senior Class that year was having an outdoor graduation exercise in the old football field just off Austin Avenue. I was assisting a photographer to take the pictures. Like everybody else, I got wet. I got really wet.

It was on this memorable night that Mother Nature, with the help of a good bolt of lightning, rid the city of the Memorial Hall. Some folks said she might have had some help.

I doubt it. It was too bad for anybody to be out.

OLD BILL BORROWED EVERYTHING BUT TIME, WHAT HE NEEDED MOST

Bill Green, my Granddad on my mother's side of the family was known throughout both Brown and Comanche counties for borrowing things he never returned. Old Bill would visit a neighbor's farm and if he saw something he didn't own, he would borrow it.

It made no difference to Bill if he had no use for it, he would borrow it anyhow. My dad always said, "Don't loan old Bill anything but a tomcat and it'll come home on its own." Once he borrowed our two-man crosscut saw which he couldn't use but he didn't have one.

Old Bill was known far and wide throughout Brown County and there was not a fishing tank or a creek that folks wouldn't let him fish in if he wanted to. When I was a kid, I have gone on many fishing trips with old Bill. We would loads up the wagon with whatever we needed and stay at least a week.

My two uncles, Bud and John would usually go. They were both expert fishermen. It was common knowledge that either one of them if they had a mind to, could catch a ten pound catfish out of a bar ditch.

On our week-long trips, we usually camped on the Jim Ned Creek somewhere near Thrifty. Bill would build a big campfire and put an old black coffee pot on the fire with a pound of Bright and Early Coffee in it and not much creek water. Bill always said,

Harry Marlin

"Hardly anybody knows how to make coffee these days. They put too damn much water in it."

Old Bill's coffee would make a freight train take a dirt road and grow hair on a two-by-four. Maybe it had something to do with the large number of fish we always caught. There was never any doubt that once the trot lines were set out we would have catfish fried in hog lard in an old iron skillet for breakfast, dinner and supper. My good memories are made of stuff like this.

There was a good reason that folks never complained about loaning old Bill stuff. They knew that a little bread cast on the water always came back tenfold. Old Bill raised a big cane crop every year and made a big vat of syrup. Everybody was invited to the "syrup making.' It was better than free tickets to a circus. Folks who came from the forks of the creek went home with enough syrup to last the winter

The annual "Syrup making" also gave folks an opportunity to look around old Bill's place and retrieve what he had borrowed in months past. It also gave old Bill a chance to look through their wagons to see if they had anything he hadn't borrowed.

All this happened during The Great Depression. Charles Dickens wrote in "The Christmas Carol," "It was the best of times and the worst of times." Maybe he wasn't writing about us, but he hit the nail right on the head. We went through "The worst of times," and didn't even know it.

OLD CEDAR CHOPPERS
AND HEAVENLY BISCUITS

One time, several years ago, two friends and I were returning to Brownwood from Fredericksburg. As we sometimes did, we stopped for a break at the Heart of Texas Rest area, 27 miles south of Brownwood.

We noticed something unusual, at least from the usual folks who stopped there. There was a big campfire burning on the paved parking area, along with an iron bedstead, complete with mattress and box springs set up near the campfire. An old truck was parked nearby. Kids were running all over the place. A man and a woman were busy at the campfire.

"I wonder who that is," Remarked one of my female companions. "If I had to guess, I said, they are cedar choppers from somewhere down in the cedar country." To set the records straight, I have nothing against cedar choppers. They were a poor, hard working people who filled a need at the time, and those that remain still do.

Roy Bedichek, a Texas writer, in "Adventures of a Texas Naturalist" wrote about the cedar choppers years ago and wrote that they often chopped cedar into their nineties. When they quit, they died.

John Graves in "Goodbye to a River" wrote about a recluse who lived back in the cedar brakes around Glen Rose. He was seldom seen except on occasions when he appeared in town dragging cedar posts which he traded for the supplies he needed to exist.

I talked to the man in the group who confirmed my guess. "We live down in the cedar country and we're going to Wal-Mart to buy the kids some school clothes. We just decided to make a camping trip out of it for the kids." His hands were heavily calloused and I noticed an ax lying by the campfire.

I am reminded of a recipe for making good biscuits, passed on by Guich Koock, a former restaurant owner in Fredericksburg, former partner in the ownership of Luckenbach and a former TV actor and long-time friend of mine.

Guich told about the wife of an old cedar chopper who made the best biscuits in Texas. Folks would walk a mile for one of her famous biscuits. One day, she revealed her secret to Guich. "You don't want to ever get the dough too moist". She said. "A mouthful of buttermilk is all you need."

I have had a lot of good meals in his restaurant and I still wonder if Guich used the old lady's recipe. He did make good biscuits.

I have never had any luck at making biscuits. Mine always turn out flat as a fritter and hard as a city banker's heart. Thanks to Guich and the old cedar chopper's wife, I think I know my problem. I've been getting my dough too moist.

Since I live alone, with the exception of a Chihuahua dog, I can try the recipe any time I want to. If it doesn't work out, the Chihuahua gets the biscuits. If it does, I may become famous. The dog, however, may climb the fence and leave.

I may even drive down to the Heart of Texas Park and cook them on a big campfire on the parking lot.

A man has to do what a man has to do.

OLD FIDDLERS, OLD DRUMMERS AND THE DECLINE OF MUSIC

I have been listening to fiddle players, both good ones and bad ones for 84 years. My dad was a fiddle player and on the day I was born, he was probably playing "Hell among the Yearlings" I have a friend who is a fiddle player, as good as they get. He currently lives in Nashville. He has played with Ray Price, Glen Campbell, Roger Miller and even me.

He really appreciated my steel guitar playing I guess because he once told me, "Harry, of all the steel players I have played with, you're one of them."

I recently sent him this e-mail; Bill: After listening for months to what the current generation regards as music, I have some advice. Get rid of your fiddle and buy a set of drums. It is obvious that not one drummer in the entire United States is unemployed. I have even heard at least one band that consisted of only one drum. All I hear, night and day, from the radio, TV, my neighbors and cars passing by on Austin Avenue is Thump, Thump, Bam Bang and Whop. Is there any REAL Music left in the world?

Apparently my friend forwarded my e-mail to a bunch of Nashville musicians and song writers who agreed with me. Some sent me CDs of their songs proving that in Nashville there is some real music still in existence. Nobody sent me a drum solo.

It seems to me that I remember a John Wayne movie where "old Duke" and his sidekick, Walter Brennan, better known as

"Stumpy" were camped out by a water hole which was definitely located in Indian country. Suddenly, drums were heard which seemed to be getting closer.

Old Duke said, "Stumpy, I don't like the sound of those drums." Stumpy says, "Me neither Duke. You saddle the horses and I'll get the bedrolls and coffee pot." Then a voice came from beyond the campfire. "Sorry, fellows but he's not our regular drummer."

Maybe I haven't been listening to somebody's "regular drummer" I certainly hope not because I'm familiar with the fact that even country music bands need drummers but please, not the kind I've been hearing. I once played in a country band that was fortunate to have one of the best drummers I ever heard. One day, he just disappeared as good drummers are prone to do. The next I heard of him, he was in Carlsbad, New Mexico.

As far as I know, nobody goes to Carlsbad on purpose except to see Carlsbad Caverns. Obviously, he was kidnapped. Then, he disappeared again and I have no idea where he is now. Anyway, it is not him I've been hearing lately. I keep forgetting about people getting old. He might be about 75 now.

I grew up listening to all types of music and I liked it all. When I was 12, I was listening to Bob Wills which was broadcast live on KVOO Tulsa from midnight to one every Saturday night. I also listened to the "Big Band" music and I was as familiar with Glenn Miller as I was Bob Wills. I learned about classical music from Dorothy McIntosh who taught it in Blanket High School. I am glad I learned about good music at an early age and I feel sorry for the kids today who have no idea what it is. One thing for sure, it is not thump, thump, bang, bam and whop.

OLD GALS, JOHNSON GRASS AND PROWLING AROUND WITH GEORGE

Back in my younger days before I had sense enough to know better, I frequently kept company with a fellow named George. He was a little older than I was and wise in the ways of the world. I figured I could learn a lot from George to further my education.

I did learn a lot, none of which could help me in my effort to amount to something sometime in the future, if I even had a future. George was the only fellow I ever saw who could sleep and drive a car at the same time. He would wake up now and then, pull the tab on a beer and promptly go back to sleep.

My job, as far as I could tell, when we were prowling around at night was to watch the road. George did a great job. We never hit anything that I know of but one bull yearling and a Great Dane dog. George never even woke up.

One night, we drove over a wide territory and through several small towns. George told me, "I've got money in every bank in every one of these towns". I didn't doubt him a bit. He had a going business that made him more money in the daytime than he could spend at night. He was sort of a hero to me since I didn't have one at the time, or a business either.

One night we were riding around in George's late model car when he got a sudden urge for some female companionship, despite the fact that he was married. He pointed out two or three shotgun houses across a large field which was about waist high in Johnson grass.

"There's an old gal lives over there who is as easy as slipping a nickel in a parking meter." He told me. "She could take on General Patton and the Third Army and never bat an eye," he said.

Although I had no interest in this "old gal," I was quite a piece from home and walking through tall Johnson grass to get there didn't appeal to me. I did notice that there was a dirt road leading to these shotgun houses about a quarter mile from where we were.

George, however, chose to take a shortcut across the field with the waist high Johnson grass. He revved up the engine and we went plowing through the Johnson grass and were doing pretty good until we hit an old oilfield well-head in the grass about three feet high.

We came to a sudden and severe halt. "Well, shit." George said. "I think I'll just go home for supper. If it ain't ready, I'm gonna throw all the furniture out of the house. If it is, I ain't gonna eat a damn bite."

I guess I did learn a lot from George, a friend for some 50 years. He did settle down some as we all do when old age approaches and gets a good grip on us and causes us to stay home at night and lose interest in old gals that live in shotgun houses in waist high Johnson grass.

I was always home at supper time and the furniture was secure.

ONE DAY IN THE LIFE OF
A BALL TURRET GUNNER

When I wake up in the morning, there are three things I am thankful that I no longer have to do—pick cotton, work for somebody from can until can't and fly as a ball turret gunner on a B-17 bomber with somebody shooting at me.

In 1944, I had already done the first two things but then I found myself doing the third in the 15th Air Force in Southern Italy.

The ball turret was round like a ball, made from aluminum and magnesium with Plexiglas on each side and in front so I could see more than I really wanted to. It hung out beneath the belly of the plane and supported by a steel pipe bolted to the top of the plane.

It was operated by an electric motor and a hydraulic system. It would rotate 360 degrees around and up and down until the door was inside the plane permitting the gunner to get in and out. Inside was a large Sperry automatic computing gun sight and two fifty caliber machine guns. There was no room for the gunner to wear a parachute.

For this reason, it was known in the Air Corp as a "death trap." I was always assured of a seat on the plane because nobody else wanted mine.

During the bomb run over the target, the ball turret gunners all rotated the turret putting the door inside where we might, in case of a direct hit, get out, put on our parachute and bail out of the plane. This didn't seem likely to transpire.

On one mission I flew, shortly after the bomb drop, the plane in front of us suddenly got out of position and was directly in our path. Our pilot put our plane in a dive to avoid a collision. I think we dropped about 3000 feet. On recovery, our bomb group was gone, leaving us over Germany alone. This was not where anybody wanted to be.

At this time, our bombardier called me on the intercom and said, "Marlin, there is a JU-88 at 2 O'clock low headed our way. Get on him now." In the excitement, I rotated the turret down, forgetting to lock the door. The outside latch on the turret was snapped off and the door fell open exposing me to a 200 mile an hour slipstream with the temperature about 50 below zero. I was definitely in one hell of a fix. I couldn't reach the door to shut it. No way could I get back in the plane with the door open outside.

Finally, figuring I had bought the farm anyway, I unsnapped my seat belt, got a good grip with my left hand on the side of the turret, hung out over a lot of nothing and caught the door with my fingertips. The slipstream snapped the door shut. The inside latch held it shut.

Then, I thought about the reported JU-88, still fast approaching. Actually, to me, it didn't look like a JU-88, but taking no chance, I gave him a burst from my twin fifties, aiming underneath in case it wasn't.

A very British voice came over the radio, "I say, old boy, I'd rather you didn't do that you know. I'm on your side." It was a British Beaufighter, in the same situation we were. We were both glad to see each other.

We escorted each other back to the safety of the Italian coast and he went on his merry way and we flew back to our base. It was just another day and we faced another mission the next day.

I guess our crew chief wondered about the broken handle on the ball turret but that was my secret. Well—it was up to now.

BUTTERFLIES AND BUTTERCUPS
AND PEOPLE WERE ALL FREE

I have decided that the period known as "The Depression," back in the thirties when I was growing up, wasn't so bad after all. Property taxes, if there were any, must have not amounted to much as hardly anybody had any money to pay them with anyhow.

If a man was lucky enough to own a car, there was no state requirement that he carry liability insurance costing today, in excess of $300 a year. Most people then didn't earn $300 a year. Most folks then drove Model-T Fords, well built under the watchful eye of old Henry himself, and it was possible to drive two of these machines together head-on and do little damage, except maybe bend the crank. I never heard of anybody getting killed in a car wreck during this period. Of course, nobody was buckled in the things either.

There was no inspection sticker required either costing $15.00 which is actually nothing but another state tax and goes up nearly every year. I think it was fifty cents when it started. A driver's license then cost a quarter, if a person had a yen for one. No examination was required. A quarter sent to Austin would get you one by return mail but as far as I know, no officer ever asked to see one.

The few State Police I ever saw rode Harley Davidson motorcycles, both winter and summer and the foremost thought on their minds was to get that monster back to the barn and go home as soon as possible. It was rare when one ventured as far as Blanket.

License fees for cars didn't amount to a hill of beans either, and due to the lack of money of most rural residents, only about one fellow in a five mile radius ever licensed his car. Anybody else finding it necessary to go to town for any reason borrowed his license plates.

Of course, we had a county sheriff who somehow managed to get by without 15 or 20 deputies, and nobody messed with him. Unless a man stole his neighbor's cow, he didn't mess with anybody either. Stealing was rare. If a neighbor had anything you needed, you borrowed it in broad daylight, with his permission.

Wagons and buggies were the principal means of transportation then, and the Texas legislature, if we had one, had never found it necessary to require liability insurance on them either. Actually, buggy wrecks were far more common that car wrecks. Mules, which most folks used to pull them with, would run away at the drop of a hat, or nothing more than seeing a sunflower growing by the road. When this occurred, it was what my granddaddy referred to as "hell among the yearlings." The occupants would usually jump out and let the old mule go until he wrecked the buggy, or quit, or both.

Nobody ever told anybody what they could do, or couldn't do back then. A man's conscience was his guide, and everybody had one, a trait that is seriously lacking in people these days. In rural Texas in those days, everybody, as someone once wrote "Lived by the side of the road and was a friend to man."

It was a kinder and gentler world back then, when folks said "times was hard," and they called it "The Great Depression." Maybe there was something great about it after all.

Maybe it was just the people who lived through it.

PHASE OUT THE LIGHTS, THE PARTY'S OVER

I just read that the incandescent light bulb that we've all been using since who laid the chunk is being phased out. After 2012, it will no longer be available. From then on, it will be the fluorescent bulb, or nothing.

The reason for this phasing out of the old bulb is to save electricity. The old ones created too much heat. Think about the shape we would have all been in without them. We would have been forced to watch TV by candlelight. Willie Nelson could never have written his song, "Turn out the Lights, the Party's over." "Blow out the Candle, the Party's Over" just wouldn't have been the same.

I think that most everybody, me included, has been under the misconception that Thomas Edison invented the Incandescent light bulb. He didn't. A couple of Canadians from Ontario did. One was named Evans and the other Woodward. Didn't they also discover Watergate?

One day they were messing with another invention they were working on which made a spark. They put the spark in a bottle and at that moment, invented the light bulb. It seems that Mr. Edison was, at that time, working on inventing the light bulb so the bought their patent for $5,000 and he got the credit. This was probably one of the first major business scams ever perpetrated.

The best I remember, Edison also invented the phonograph about 15 years before anybody ever invented a record to play on it. For several years, I owned one of his phonographs but sold it at a garage sale. I never could find any records.

I beat the government to phasing out the incandescent bulb by 5 years, my reason being that I could never find one that lasted over 20 minutes. These funny-looking fluorescent bulbs are known to almost last forever. I had one that was so old I had to shoot it down with my bb gun so I could replace it.

I well remember life without electricity. When the sun went down, it got dark. It stayed that way until it came up again. Of course, we had an old coal oil lamp that was so dim we had to strike a match to see if it was burning.

We had no refrigerator to keep things cold. We had more ice than we needed in the winter and none in the summer.

Sometime, around 1936, I think, we moved into a house in which the previous tenant had electricity. Having electricity in your house back then meant having drop lights in each room and no wall plugs. Dad signed us up. The minimum requirement for electricity was $1.50 a month.

We could now have a radio. Dad went to Firestone in Brownwood and bought one for a dollar down and a dollar a week. I was in hog heaven. Now I could listen to Bob Wills from Cain's Academy in Tulsa every Saturday night for an entire hour. Life was good.

Then one day, a refrigerator was delivered. Life was getting better. The man who delivered the refrigerator told Dad the thing wouldn't operate from that drop light. New wiring was needed. Dad told him, "I'll take care of it."

About a month later, I heard Dad tell somebody that our new refrigerator hadn't raised our electric bill a bit. Being rather smart in such operations, I took a look at Dad's wiring job. It was a neat job, the correct wire size was used but with only one glaring mistake. He had wired in on the wrong side of the meter. At that time, such action was illegal.

As far as I know, it still is.

PINTO BEANS MAY
HAVE WON THE WEST

The West may have never been won without the help of pinto beans. Our pioneers, leaving St. Louis for the long trek across the prairies carried a supply of dried pintos. A friend of mine who traps skunks down around San Antonio calls them "prairie whistlers."

They didn't spoil, were easy to cook and furnished plenty of nourishment and on occasions, protection from the marauding Indians

When the wagons circled at night and the campfires slowly dwindled following a supper of these marvelous vegetables with the scientific name of Phaseolus vulgaris, a nauseous gas slowly permeated the camp. The Indians, waiting in the dark to attack took notice.

The chief, sniffing the air, would say, "Much bad medicine here. Best we go elsewhere"

A good bean fart in a saloon would bring a gunfight to a halt quicker than Matt Dillon with blazing guns.

We have all seen old Doc on "Gunsmoke" working on a fellow tied to a table with a stick in his mouth to bite on to ease his pain during surgery while Doc brandished his knife.

Doc is saying to Matt Dillon standing by the table, "Are you sure this fellow was gut shot?" All I can find here is pinto beans."

Pinto beans not only won the west but won the Great Depression too. We would have never survived without them. They were our salvation and our best staple food. They brought us together at the supper table and again as we assembled in the yard for a breath of fresh air. They brought a togetherness that we no longer have.

Back during WWII when I was flying as a ball turret gunner on a B-17 bomber, I would remove my oxygen mask temporarily at 30,000 feet, place it against my posterior and give the other crew members a little gas to keep them alert. Due to the logistics of the oxygen system, they all got it.

The pilot would say, "Boys, we've got to get this war over. I think the Germans are using poison gas." Not only did beans win the West but they may have won WWII too.

POLITICS, RELIGION
AND THE LAST PARKING SPOT
AT WAL-MART

This being election year, I get a lot of e-mail from friends whose political views differ somewhat from mine. Under the first amendment, they have a perfect right to their views the same as I do mine. They can stand on a street corner if they wish and voice them loud and clear. We live in a country where we are allowed to do so and we can be thankful for that.

If everybody agreed on everything, we would have a one party government. That's what they had in Iraq only the entire party consisted of one man. Some Iraqis were happy with it and the ones who weren't are pushing up daisies in the sand. We don't want that.

I have never written about politics or religion which is the quickest way I know of to get somebody on my back. I know just enough about both to get in a serious fight. I have avoided serious fights all of my life and I'm too old to start now. Besides, I think it's a felony to hit a Senior Citizen unless one gets the last parking spot at Wal-Mart. There are loopholes in every law.

A fellow in Houston wanted to know what I thought of our president's State of the Union speech. I told him that I thought Mr. Bush had the appearance of a fellow standing in the middle of the California goldfields in 1860 and he was the only one who knew where the gold was.

He also mentioned a particular senator who has graced the aisles of congress for over 40 years. I told him, "If that old boy got struck by lightning, he would think it was God taking his picture."

My philosophy, as far as making public statements is, "Judge not lest you be judged." Having been a resident on this planet for far too many years, I can't stand much judging. We all have to put up with a lot as it is without running each other down.

There may be a time on some cold morning on the parking lot at the grocery when your car won't start. If a nice fellow comes to your rescue with a pair of jumper cables, it might be best not to ask him if he's a Democrat or a Republican.

Up to now, automobiles can't tell the difference.

When I was a kid, back during the Great depression, I had no idea who the president was. I didn't even care as long as we had plenty of beans and cornbread for supper. I don't think I really found out until I was flying on a B-17 bomber dropping bombs on Germany.

It was then that I heard President Roosevelt say, "We have nothing to fear but fear itself." I decided then that he was a long way from where I was. Still, I never questioned his judgment as to why I was there. I still don't.

These days, I hear people on radio talk shows say, "We should never have gotten in World War Two or gone to Iraq. It wasn't our fight."

I'm still wondering that if it wasn't, whose fight was it.

TEXAS WRITER PUTS TOO MUCH SALT IN THE GRAVY

I read a lot of books, and over the years, Larry McMurtry has been one of my favorite writers. I may not always agree with him, but if we lived in a world where we all agreed with everybody on everything, things would get pretty dull. Differences in opinion are what make the world go around.

In his new book, "Roads," Larry hits the hill country of Texas a sort of low blow, and I quote: "I have always been puzzled by the popularity of the hill country. The soil is too stony to farm or ranch, the hills are just sort of forested speed bumps, and the people, mostly of stern Teutonic stock, are suspicious, tightfisted, unfriendly, and mean. Even the foliage is mean, releasing a steady cloud of allergens into the air. Perhaps the very fact that the country is too stony to farm successfully makes it even more perfectly suited to be an ideal of rusticity. Willie Nelson's famous song, "Luckenbach, Texas, has probably lulled many people into thinking that Luckenbach and its surrounding communities are friendly places, when in fact, they are not."

All this from a man who was born and raised, and is still a resident of a town some folks might regard as one of the most god-awful places on earth—Archer City, Texas. However, we have to understand that home is where the house is, and his house has been there a long time. Still, Larry might be regarded, especially by the hill country folks, as putting too much salt into one bowl of gravy.

Having been to the hill country numerous times and to Archer City more than once, it is my belief that "suspicious, mean, tightfisted and unfriendly" people can be found in both places, or anywhere else the roads lead. They are not all congregated down in the hill country. I even know a bunch of people down there who are not of Teutonic origin.

Texas is blessed with a lot of hills, some prettier, and some uglier than those in the hill country, and some that are a whole lot higher and meaner. Drive from Balmorhea to El Paso and you'll see some really mean looking hills. Probably a lot of mean people live back in there somewhere too. Nobody ever gets off Interstate 10 long enough to find out.

However, thousands of folks flock to Fredericksburg in the heart of the Texas hill country every week-end to prowl the antique shops and sample the product of the local vineyards in the wine-tasting shops. Some brave souls even make their way to Luckenbach, once owned by Hondo Crouch, who prior to his death, was so friendly; his goats followed him to work there.

I have no quarrel with Mr. McMurtry who drove all over the United States to obtain material for his book. It is a notable book, and worth reading, as all of his books are. Maybe he just drove too fast through the hill country in his hurry to get back to Archer City where his house is. I can't blame him for that.

GETTING BY WITHOUT SMOKING
IN AN IMPERFECT WORLD

My Hill Country correspondent says quitting smoking is easy compared to quitting bragging about it when you do. That makes a lot of sense to me. Although I am currently involved in the first stage of quitting, I'm still a long way from bragging. I might, though.

At the urging of at least three doctors, I am trying to comply with their threats—uh, wishes, I mean. It's about as easy as putting a raw oyster in a parking meter. I admit, I'm using a crutch in the form of a small pill which is supposed to stop any urge I might have to spend four dollars for a pack of cigarettes.

Since this little pill affects the brain, one requirement is that the user has to have one. I assume that an IQ of at least 40 is required. I may possibly be close to being borderline on that. The pill contains no nicotine. After all, why take something that hooked you to start with.

When I informed one doctor that I had been smoking since the first tobacco plants were introduced in Virginia, he became interested in my mental history. Being a ball turret gunner on a bomber during WWII didn't help my case any. Nobody in their right mind would have done that.

These days, it seems that everybody and their dogs are trying to stop everybody from smoking. Even the government, which during WWII influenced us to smoke in the first place. Cigarettes were either free, depending where you were, or a nickel a pack.

In every K-ration box we carried on our missions, was a pack of 4 cigarettes. I don't think they meant us to eat them.

Entire cities are going smoke-free, even in the bars. For the first time in history, a man can be thrown out of a bar for smoking. Prior to this madness, it was necessary to shoot somebody.

I'm wondering when alcohol will be banned again. After all, excessive use of alcohol has killed a lot of people and like tobacco, it is legal. Drink all you want in a bar, but don't smoke.

Can you imagine a police report that says, "We believe the cause of the accident was excessive smoking. We found an opened pack of Camels in the car."

I believe it is an individual's right to smoke if he or she chooses to do so. I don't think the government, federal or city should be able to infringe on that right. Anybody who wasn't born under a rock and stayed there knows the health hazards of smoking. We do not need to be beat over the head with this knowledge on an hourly basis.

Somebody sent me a cartoon on the internet. It showed an old man, about 90, humped over on a doctor's examining table. He looked awful. The doctor is saying, "Remember when you got on that health kick and stopped all your bad habits so you could live 20 years longer? "Well," These are them."

We do not live in a perfect world. We never have and we never will. We try to do the best we can with what we've got in spite of government interference and do-gooders on every corner getting stupid laws passed to further their cause, whatever it might be.

Still, our part of the world, with all its faults is the best place on earth. Do not forget it and don't allow anybody to ruin it.

RAW OYSTERS, PARKING METERS AND TECHNOLOGY WE LOST

Henry Ford must have gotten a kick out of building his Model T Fords. Everybody who bought one got a kick too if they pulled the spark advance lever down one notch too many. The engine would kick back, causing the crank to kick back. The result was often a broken arm.

When I was a kid, our three doctors would sit on the benches in front of our two drug stores keeping a watchful eye on anybody cranking a Ford. After all, a broken arm was better than no business at all.

Henry started the assembly line method where one man did one job and the vehicle was passed on to the next man who did something else. He paid his employees a whopping five dollars a day and everybody was happy.

Best of all, due to the price, nearly everybody could buy a Model T and nearly everybody did.

The entire car, parts and all, was built in Detroit. No parts were farmed out to be built in foreign countries. There was a good reason for that. At that time in history, people in foreign countries were still riding camels or donkeys pulling two-wheeled carts. They were plowing their fields with water buffalo.

Our auto industry was not bothered by imports. We built the best and most folks would agree that our Fords were better than donkeys. Both kicked a little but Fords were faster.

Americans invented the technology to do anything we wanted. Then, we spread it all over the world only to watch what we used to build here being built in some foreign country. We brought about our own downfall, causing our manufacturing plants to be move to places we can't even pronounce.

It is difficult, if not impossible, to buy something here that was made here. I don't like it and nobody should. Sometime back, I managed to buy something that was stamped "Made In the US." I forgot what it was or what I did with it but I'll bet if I could find it, it still works. If it doesn't, I can fix it.

Trying to fix something that was made in a foreign country is like trying to put a raw oyster in a parking meter.

We send our raw materials overseas and get back something none of us want. We want it built here with our own labor and I know of nobody who wouldn't be willing to pay a little more for it. We can do it and there is no good reason why we are not doing it.

About the only products we can buy here that are made here are whiskey and cigarettes. It is not surprising that folks drink and smoke after a trip to a store.

Is our National motto "Drink American"? I don't think so.

We can manufacture anything we need here and we did it for years. It is about time we start doing it again and let the chips fall where they may. Henry Ford is gone but the legacy he left behind is not.

THE LORD GAVE US THE LARD
AND GOD GAVE US A LOOPHOLE

Back when I was a kid, trying to grow up during what they called "The Depression," there were two subjects often brought up at our house. One was The Lord and the other was the lard. The lard came from rendering hog fat and we used it to fry stuff. As far as I knew, The Lord furnished us the stuff we fried.

Folks were always saying, "I thank The Lord for that." Folks who gave thanks for the food at the table always thanked The Lord. I guess that included the lard it was cooked in.

I never did hear anybody actually thank The Lord for the lard but they should have.

I learned all about the lard in the winter at hog killing time. This was usually a community thing, or at least involving several neighbors. It involved a lot of work and took several people to do it.

Nothing was wasted. Even the fat was placed in large pots with fires underneath and "rendered" which was when it turned into liquid. Then, when it cooled, it became lard.

Everybody usually got enough to last until the next winter. If they didn't, they would be forced to buy a gallon bucket of Mrs. Tucker's Lard which might not have been as healthy as ours. Her buckets, however, were good to carry our lunch in to the cotton patch.

On the other hand, I learned about The Lord in the summer when Mama took me to the "Big Meetings" held under a tabernacle at Blanket. There were enough of them to last all summer. The preachers who held these meetings were called "hell-fire and brimstone" preachers for good reason. They scared people into religion. At least, they did a good job of scaring me but they scared me away from it. I remember one preacher who somehow managed to get 4 syllables into the word God and called Jesus "Jaysus."

In July and August, it was hot under that old tabernacle with no cooling except cardboard fans furnished by a local funeral home. Some of us would break out in a sweat from the heat while others sweated from what the preacher was saying "If you think it's hot here, you ain't seen nothing to compare with where you're going" the preacher would remind us all. He also had a lot to say about Satan who I was sure must be sitting somewhere on the back row.

Somehow, in my childhood innocence, I just didn't believe that God was as mean and unforgiving as the preachers portrayed Him back then. Surely we were left a loophole somewhere to get out of drastic punishment for the meanness we might get into.

During WWII there was more than one occasion that when the German 88 millimeter shells were bursting around my ball turret on that B-17 bomber and with planes going down and the world seemed to be on fire and about to go upside down that I asked God for a little assistance and he gave me a loophole.

Maybe it all started back in Blanket under that tabernacle with a Funeral home fan to keep me cool and the devil sitting in the back row with the hell and brimstone preachers telling me I was doomed and I was far too young to be doomed.

Maybe it all started back during the Great Depression during hog killing time and Mama taught us the difference between The Lord and the lard and that we needed both to survive.

I don't think Mama knew about the loophole

ONE MORE RIVER TO CROSS
MAY BE ONE TOO MANY

The Rio Grande is one river it is best not to attempt to swim or wade across. It is a treacherous stream that may appear calm on the surface but has the power to bend an aluminum canoe double if caught against a rock.

Still, people do, every day of the year and probably somewhere within the 2000 miles which separates the United States from Mexico. They're doing it right now.

"Within the past week, 5 bodies of illegal immigrants were removed from the river near Falcon Heights. All were fully dressed, complete with their shoes. Authorities are of the opinion they may have been using some type of boat or raft that capsized."

"Between October 1, 2005 and September 6th of 2006, 38 people have drowned in this river section including two Border Patrolmen."

Sometime in the seventies, I had the unfortunate experience of inadvertently exploring the bottom of the river. I will never do it again.

Some friends from Brownwood and I had planned a raft trip through Mariscal Canyon in the Big Bend. We meant to rent rafts from Glen Pepper who had a river guide service.

Upon our arrival, Glen, a longtime friend of mine told me, "Harry, I'm short of guides today and have three doctors and their wives who want to take the trip. Since you've been through

321

the canyon before, if you will take care of the doctors, you and your friends won't be charged." I agreed.

About halfway through the canyon is what is known as "The Slot." The river narrows down to about 5 feet across against the Mexican side and the water becomes extremely swift. I looked back and noticed that the doctor's raft was going to hit the slot at the same time the one I was in. I had to stop that from happening.

I put both feet against the side of the cliff and pushed. This collapsed the raft on my side and I went into the river, immediately being caught in a whirlpool and an undertow. This is when I explored the river bottom and there was nothing I could do about it.

I wondered what happened to my life jacket but when I finally surfaced about 50 feet ahead of the other rafts, I still had it on. My glasses, however, I didn't.

Then, to make matters worse, one of the doctor's wives suddenly fell out of the raft for no apparent reason. We had to rescue her. A short time later, one of the ladies in my group also fell out. Unfortunately, other than me, she was the only one in the group who smoked. My cigarettes were on the bottom of the river and I needed one.

One of the doctors was an ophthalmologist. I asked him if he happened to have a pair of glasses with him. "No" He said, "But I'm glad you consulted me. Now, I can write this trip off as a business expense."

In 1966, four friends and I made a raft trip through Mariscal Canyon. About halfway through, our raft hit an old cedar limb sticking through the water and ripped it from end to end. We had to walk out down the middle of the river in the dark. There was no other way out. All we salvaged from the raft was a foot-long piece of summer sausage. We had it for breakfast the next morning when we got out of the river.

It was the best sausage I ever had.

ROBBING BANKS IN A '34 FORD AND BOILING EGGS IN A SACK

In 1933, the Ford Motor Company built the famous 1934 Ford. It was equipped with an 85 horsepower V8 engine that would run 90 miles an hour and a safety feature included doors that opened backwards using the wind to slow the car down in case of brake failure. It was also easier to bail out of the thing if that didn't work.

The car was made popular by Bonnie Parker and Clyde Barrow who were terrorizing the country by robbing banks all over Texas. Bonnie even started cutting her hair in a new style. The ladies called it "like a boy's behind" She also forfeited what little femininity she had by smoking cigars. News was scarce back then and they gave everybody something to talk about. They were the subjects of conversations in every beer joint and café in Texas.

According to our night watchman, a fellow whose name I think was Steve Nash, they came through Blanket one night, cut the lock off a gas pump and put 10 gallons of gas in their 1934 Ford. The night watchman said he watched the whole thing go down and as they drove off, he took his old thumb buster and put two bullets through the back window of their Ford.

A close inspection of the crime scene the next morning showed two bullet holes through the second story window of the Higginbotham building next door. This building was torn down several years ago, destroying this important evidence.

Harry Marlin

While Bonnie and Clyde were busy robbing banks, my buddies and I were camped out on Blanket Creek boiling eggs in paper sacks. To answer inquiries I received about how to do this, the answer is simple. Fill a paper sack full of water, place it on the campfire and when the water boils, put in the eggs. The water boils the eggs while keeping the sack from catching on fire. It worked fine in1934 but I'm not sure about now. Things have changed a lot since then. Eggs are $2.69 cents a dozen, gas is over $3.50 a gallon and Bonnie and Clyde and 1934 Fords are gone forever.

1934 was not regarded as one of our best years, being in the middle of the Great Depression but eggs were only 12 cents a dozen and gas was 12 cents a gallon. Neither was hardly worth stealing which may explain why Bonnie and Clyde stuck to banks.

I made it through the Great Depression and most of the time not knowing it was happening. One lady remarked, "It was a shame it had to happen when so many people were out of work" Living on a farm helped a lot and we never went hungry.

1944 was somewhat different than 1934. I was camped out in a tent in Southern Italy, a long way from Blanket Creek and people were shooting at me with some regularity. The only eggs I saw were powdered eggs, made especially for military use. There was no way to boil a powdered egg in a paper sack.

Sometimes, it's hard for me to separate the good years from the bad. I think I have reached the point in my life where they were all good. Anytime I wake up in the morning and don't have to build a fire in a wood stove or boil my eggs in a paper sack, things are going to be fine.

Well, if that night watchman doesn't find me.

LIGHT BREAD ROLLS
AND ROSEBUD SALVE

My mama, when I was growing up, made the best light bread rolls in the entire world. The aroma of these rolls cooking would lure hoboes from the Frisco railroad six miles away. For the uninitiated, any bread made back in the thirties, except cornbread, was called light bread. Nobody ever went into a store and asked for a loaf of bread. They always asked for light bread. Anything else was unacceptable.

Everybody always asked for iced tea too, even though it wasn't iced and hadn't even been made. Iced tea was a big treat back in those days. Having iced tea for Sunday dinner was better than new frost on turnip greens. Somebody said back then that the rich folks had ice in the summer and the poor folks had it in the winter. I won't argue with anybody about that.

There were no self-service in stores then, the reason being that they didn't want anybody putting beans in their pea bin. A nice man always got what you wanted if you had money, or your credit was good. Nobody had much money for groceries then and the grocer didn't have much either. Times, they said, "was hard." The best thing about it was that none of us knew it.

I have no idea how mama made her light bread rolls. I have tried for 40 years to duplicate them and haven't even come close. She used something she called "east cakes." I don't know if she imported them from the Far East, or her pronunciation of yeast was a little off. It is doubtful that any deliveries were made to our farm from the Far East.

I once sold 25 jars of Rosebud salve and won myself a guitar which I never got. I had visions of sitting on the front porch and entertaining the livestock After all these years, I swear I saw the mail carrier sitting on his front porch playing my guitar to his livestock. I had no way of proving it, but the guitar had "Rosebud" written across the front. Still, maybe he sold 25 jars too. The competition for selling Rosebud salve was pretty stiff. Every kid in school sold it. I have no idea of the chemical composition of the stuff, but it was guaranteed to cure everything from ingrown toenails to rattlesnake bites. It is entirely possible that it contained some of mama's "east cakes," that elusive stuff that I can't find.

With mama gone, her recipe for the rolls is gone too. It is bound to have been simple. The ingredients she possessed in her kitchen were barely enough to make a thin pie crust. She always had flour, sugar and "east cakes" though. Maybe that's what I need.

Maybe one day, before I die, I will figure out how mama made those rolls. I'm going to keep trying until I do. I'm trying to find the address of the Rosebud Salve Company on the internet so I can sell 25 more jars and get another guitar. My dog Bitsy would love it, and my walking mail carrier is too tired to play one.

ROYAL ALLEGATIONS IN
THE BRITISH EMPIRE

The British Royal family seems to be always involved in some sort of scandal, consisting mostly of allegations that nobody can prove. There is a reason for this. There is hardly anything for the British subjects to talk about but the Royal Family and the weather.

The weather always remains the same—lousy. So, they direct their attention mostly to Prince Charles. Nobody knows exactly what the current allegations against him are but he denies them, the same as any man worth his salt would. In our country, the favorite defense is "SODDI," which translates to "Some other dude did it."

One reason the members of the Royal Family are often accused of stuff they don't do is because they have no gainful employment. Mama always told me, "Son, idle hands pick no cotton." Or, "A rolling stone gathers no corn." She probably never heard of the Royal Family but she knew me pretty well.

One thing for sure, having plenty of money and access to a 747 and a yacht, I would never have gone anywhere near a cotton patch. Allegations wouldn't have bothered me a bit and most likely I would have been blessed with a bunch of them.

They live in luxury in palaces or mansions and never get up before noon. Certainly, they would never be caught in a shotgun house on the Thames. Their every need is handled by servants and valets and nobody in the house ever gets up at five and scrambles eggs.

Their only activity is getting in the Royal 747 and flying to one of their remaining possessions which once the sun never set on. Now, it's hard to find one it comes up on. On off days, they may go fishing on the Royal Yacht. I am totally in sympathy with them. It must be pure torture to be both rich and unemployed. As we used to hope for back on the farm, no teats to pull and no hay to pitch.

To make matters worse, there is a High Court injunction against the British Press from reporting the allegations against Prince Charles. This reminds me of Brownwood where we still, as of this writing, have never found out if the fellow in Wal-Mart really got bit by a rattlesnake. Even Prince Charles might like to know.

As for me, I really don't care what Prince Charles or Prince William get into. Both are old enough to get into whatever they want to. So, for that matter, am I. However, if I do, I want the facts of what I did known, not allegations. Let the good times roll.

To quote a famous Texas writer in a recent e-mail to me and whose name I'd best leave off for fear of serious retribution, "I wish I had sinned more aggressively and selectively in my youth. Sins available to folks my age ain't as much fun."

Take heed to an expert, Charles, and don't worry about the allegations. Maybe the weather over there will get better.

RUNNING BOARDS, HUDSON TERRAPLANES AND DRIVING MRS. BROWN

I have been driving since I was about thirteen and had to look through the spokes of the steering wheel. Of course, my family was too poor to own a car during this period but now and then, a relative or neighbor would allow me to drive.

At age 14, I was allowed to drive Dr. Brown's wife to Brownwood to do her shopping in their Hudson Terraplane. Had Dr. Brown known what I was doing with his Terraplane while Mrs. Brown shopped, I would have lost my job and my discount medical benefits.

I would take that marvelous car out on the nearest straight road I could find and try to find out if the needle on the speedometer would really reach a hundred. I never did, but I tried. With Mrs. Brown in the car, I had to drive a sedate thirty like everybody else.

Of course, I didn't have a driver's license. Few people did. If anybody felt they had a need for one, a quarter sent to Austin would bring one in the mail. Back then, State Troopers were called Highway Patrolmen and were seldom seen in our area. In those days, they rode Harley's and wore caps instead of those western hats.

Caps were less impressive. Country folks were not intimidated by anybody who wore a cap. People who played golf, we heard, wore caps. If anybody did get stopped, unlike today, I'm sure the officer would have said, "Step out on the running board please." "Do you have any I.D.?" "Idee about what?" The driver might ask.

Running boards were apparently made for the kids to ride on and we all did. It was more fun than riding on the tailgate of a wagon.

With all those years of driving experience, I consider myself a good driver but different than most. I drive the posted speed, never run red lights or stop signs or make left turns from the right hand lane. I learned long ago the purpose of turn signals. A used car can be bought nearly anywhere in town but you can bet on one thing; the turn signals have most likely never been used.

I recently heard a story about one lady telling another lady of her experience in taking her car to a garage where she knew nobody. "I felt sure," She said, "that I was going to get ripped off but I was amazed when I only had to pay five dollars for putting fluid in my turn signals."

Remember when the light dimmer switch was on the floorboard where it belonged, and then they moved it to the steering column? It caused numerous wrecks when elderly people got their left leg caught in the steering wheel while trying to dim the lights.

My driving habits totally confuse younger drivers. They don't know what I'm up to. I never drive in the passing lane unless I have intentions of passing somebody which I seldom do. To pass anybody these days would require driving at least 85.

People all seem to be in a big hurry these days to get somewhere they've most likely already been, or have no business going in the first place. It might be best if we slow down and smell the roses.

Of course, if we do, we may get rear-ended by somebody with no sense of smell or no sense at all.

SAUCERED AND BLOWED
AT TWO-BITS A POUND

My Granddad, Bill Green, on my mother's side of the family, was a real coffee drinker. I have heard him say on more than one occasion, "Nobody knows how to make coffee these days. They put too damn much water in it." He would dump a half-pound of Bright and Early coffee in the pot and let it boil until folks in Zephyr could smell it.

Then, he would pour a cup, without cream or sugar and saucer it and blow it and slurp it down. There was little doubt that his concoction would easily kill a 10 day old stand of cotton. I became familiar with his coffee making while on numerous fishing trips when we would spend a week camped out somewhere on Jim Ned Creek when I was about eight or nine.

I almost became a non-coffee drinker. Starbucks, it wasn't. Then, when I entered military service in 1943, I found that they were using old Bill's recipe. I was puzzled as to where they got it. Bill was long-gone by then, having been bucked off a horse and wound up with a broken neck.

Back when Bill was making his version of water and caffeine, coffee was selling for two-bits a pound. At that price, Juan Valdez, or maybe his father or Grandfather, who labored daily picking those coffee beans high in the mountains of Columbia must have been living on one tortilla a day. We weren't much better off ourselves but we always had coffee, thanks to old Juan, or somebody.

A couple of years ago, I was at a bookstore in Granbury trying to sell some of my books. The book-signing turned out being on the coldest day of the year. The customers, most of who lived in Fort Worth were iced in.

We did have a good crowd to start with but one of them left.

The nice lady who ran the book store suggested that I go across the square to a "nice coffee shop" and have a cup of coffee.

My "coffee," which, best I remember, cost me $4.00, was what I would call a hot chocolate milk shake. I'm not sure what it was. Old Bill would have fainted dead away. I almost did myself. I was thinking of how many pounds of Bright and Early that four dollars would have bought. I thought I had wandered into the twilight zone.

Coffee making has changed a lot over the years. There is no more Bright and Early or Eight O'clock coffee at two bits a pound. Coffee drinking can be expensive whether you saucer and blow it or not. I gave up saucer and blowing when Old Bill died. I found it to be no longer necessary.

Awhile back, I was visiting Charles Chupp over in De Leon. Charles is a writer, a former newspaper owner and a board-certified coffee drinker. He took me to a little café there where coffee is still a quarter a cup and that includes all the refills you can stand.

Old Bill would have been in hog heaven even if it wasn't Bright and Early. You can even saucer and blow it if you want to. I still wonder what would have happened if I had saucered and blowed that stuff I bought in Granbury.

I don't think I want to know.

BRIGHT AND EARLY COFFEE

Back when I was a kid during the glorious thirties, smack-dab in the middle of the "Great Depression," folks drank real coffee. There was none of this "latté" stuff that has a close resemblance to a milk shake that seems all the rage today. The coffee served in those days would kill an eight day old stand of cotton

There were no modern-day coffee makers then with filters that somehow take the reason out for drinking coffee in the first place. It was made with a simple process. First, a large pot of well water was put on to boil and when the water reached a temperature that would scald the hair off a large hog, the coffee was added.

Nobody skimped on the amount of coffee, which in those days sold for about two-bits a pound. Usually, about half a pound was added to the pot. When the grounds finally settled to the bottom of the pot, it was ready to drink. There was one popular brand I remember called "Bright and Early." The stuff was put on early and if anybody managed to survive a cup, they were reasonably bright the rest of the day.

Due to the temperature of the boiling coffee, it first had to be poured into a saucer where the drinker blew gently on it until it reached the temperature that melts iron. I learned to saucer and blow coffee at an early age, watching my dad do it at four in the morning. It was the necessary thing to do.

In those days, coffee was always served in a cup, complete with a saucer for blowing. Anybody passing George Bolton's café in Blanket in the early morning hours would hear a sound similar to a cow pulling her foot out of a bog hole. Nobody became alarmed and called 911 which didn't exist anyway. What it was, as everybody knew, was the old men slurping coffee out of a saucer. It was the pure music of the thirties.

I'm proud to have been there when coffee was real coffee and men were men. People these days missed a lot by not being there, but I didn't. I tried my best not to miss anything and I don't think I missed much.

I have a friend I occasionally go camping with in the Big Bend National Park. Being some sort of throw-back to the thirties, he still makes coffee the way it was made then. One time, I cringed as I watched him put the entire pound of coffee I figured on lasting for several days into one gallon of water for breakfast.

He also somehow manages to burn eggs and serve totally black tortillas, and always insists on doing the cooking. When he cooks, coyotes howl, tuck their tails between their legs and head for Mexico. I have noticed that creosote bushes wilt within fifty feet of our camp and Park Rangers take annual leave. Yeah, you guessed it. He saucers and blows his coffee too. We both have to.

SAVE YOUR KNEES AND HIPS
FOR WANDERING IN THE DESERT

I have recently had some health problems which cause me considerable worry. None of these problems were caused by my doctors and I can't blame them. None, as far as I know, were caused by me. I have always tried to take care of myself—well, up to a point.

I never picked too much cotton, gathered too much corn or stayed out in the sun too long loading hay. I never took up jogging because nobody ever told me I should. Besides, I had the idea that I would need my knees and hip joints to hobble around in my "golden years." I also would need to drive.

I would certainly need one leg for the accelerator and one for the brake and I saved them both. They still work fine. The first thing I learned is that it might be best not to take an annual physical where my ailments all first came to light. The second thing I learned is that nobody really gives a big rat's rear about your medical problem.

They may tell you that they have had the same thing for years, or their Aunt Lucy had a bad case of it and lived to the age of 97 and was mean as a water moccasin. She also, they may say, "went roller skating every day and smoked a carton of cigarettes a week."

As you can imagine, their problems are of no interest to me. I'm all wrapped up in mine. That's just the way we are. If we all turn green as a gourd, nobody says a word about it. "You're looking good," they say, knowing full well that we're not.

There is an old saying that "Those who live by the sword, die by the sword." In truth, the sword has nothing to do with it. The very fact that we're living means wer'e going to eventually die of something. Our aim is to put it off as long as possible and refrain from taking annual physicals.

What you don't know won't get you near as quick as worrying about what you do know. There may not be a cure for it anyhow. Just hang on until there is may be the best you can do.

The government has a way of holding back cures for 10 years as a means of population control and all along allowing thousands of immigrants into our country on a weekly basis. Some of those immigrants may have stuff we've never had.

My problem, as I've been informed more than once, is the same that Aunt Lucy had who lived to be 97. I have no intentions of going anywhere until they get up a big load anyhow. Aunt Lucy, I assume, went with the first big load.

Back in biblical days, folks lived practically forever and were known to "wander in the desert" a lot, some for as long as 40 years. Noah was 800 years old when he built the Ark. He must have had a lot of help as I have trouble raising a window and I'm a long way from that.

I have, however, wandered in the desert at various times in my life, but 4 days was about my limit.

Maybe I didn't wander long enough.

CONFUSED ABOUT TAXES
AND A LOT OF OTHER STUFF

Among several things Santa Clause brought me this year was a handy gadget called a "Grabber" With this gadget, if you drop something, you can easily pick it up without bending over. Due to a balance problem I have, bending over can result in my falling flat on my face. As Martha Stewart might say, "That is not a good thing."

I drop things a lot. In fact, the first thing I dropped was the grabber. I had no way to pick it up. Maybe I should have two of them. Anyway, I finally managed to hook it with my cane and I'm back in business again.

Since our legislature has hit smokers with a dollar a pack tax on cigarettes beginning January first, the thing would be handy for picking up butts on the street, should the need arise. This tax money is supposed to go to education, they say. That's what they said when they passed the lottery.

When I was going to school, cigarettes were fifteen cents a pack and the schools were open five days a week and there was no lottery either. Maybe I didn't learn as much as I should have but I learned enough that I'm frequently puzzled by the fact that taxes always go up on something when the legislature is in session.

We have a lot of what is known as "Sin taxes." Anything that our citizens are likely to enjoy is heavily taxed, none of which is illegal. The illegal stuff is not taxed for good reason. None of it is sold in stores. Obviously, our legislators are without sin.

According to an Associated Press story in the Fort Worth Star-Telegram on line, the sales tax in Texarkana, Arkansas is 10 percent while across the state line in Texarkana, Texas, it is 8.25. The Arkansas tax on a pack of cigarettes is .69 cents. The residents of Texarkana, Arkansas, however are not required to pay the Arkansas state Income tax. Other taxes on the Arkansas side except on property are higher. Maybe they don't have much income left to pay taxes on.

Once the dollar tax on cigarettes goes into effect in Texas, business will likely pick up on the Arkansas side of town while the citizens there go to the Texas side for cheaper sales tax. Confusing, isn't it?

At my age, I stay confused about a lot of things anyhow without worrying about the folks in Texarkana.

Another item I got for Christmas was a telephone answering machine. It has a feature on it that answers in either English or Spanish. I know just enough Spanish to get into a fight. I don't, however, know enough about modern electronic gadgets to get the thing set right.

The last answering machine I owned had an electronic woman answering my phone. I couldn't get her off either. Everybody thought I had taken a "live in." My lady-friend got plumb upset about it, with good reason, I guess.

I don't understand why everything has to get so complicated when a person gets older. At the urging of Microsoft, I recently updated the browser on my computer. Now, I can get stuff I never got before but I can't get rid of it. It has no "back" on it. On my previous one, I could hit "back" and it would go away.

I am sure there must be an answer to all of this but I haven't yet figured out the question.

As Martha might say, "That is not a good thing."

SITTING ON A BENCH SOMEWHERE WAITING FOR EVERYBODY ELSE

I recently drove out to Blanket, my old hometown. I was thinking that I might sit on a bench in front of a store and watch the people for awhile. It was a lot different from 75 years ago when I was growing up there.

The only bench I found was in front of Katy's restaurant. Neither the bench nor Katy's was there then. The building the restaurant occupies was Dossey's garage where Dr Yantis stored his old cars when he bought a new one.

Mr. Dossey didn't have a bench but Macon Richmond's drug store next door did. Now his building is no longer there, along with a few others.

Our favorite bench was in front of Ernest Allen's drug store, usually occupied by our three doctors who patiently waited for somebody to crank a Model T and maybe break an arm or somebody to get run over by a runaway wagon and team. The drug store building is gone too, torn down years ago. Why, I don't know. It was in good shape when I went off to WWII. But then, I was in pretty good shape too.

People were generally healthy back then and medical care could get expensive. It might cost as much as $2 to see one of our doctors. But—there was no waiting. Just catch one on the bench and tell him your symptoms.

I guess folks don't do much bench sitting these days as they did when I was a kid, back during the Depression.

They didn't have much else to do then as nobody had a steady job. The farmers all came to town when their crops were planted, or laid back in the fall. There was a lot of good conversation that took place on those benches.

It's a shame that they're all gone, along with the people I knew. Outliving everybody is in some cases, not good. I didn't see a single soul in the entire business section and I wondered where they all were.

I drove around the residential section to look for familiar houses. Our old house at the north end of Main Street has been remodeled and looks habitable. When we lived there, it might not have. Others, I could find and some I couldn't.

I found the Goodwin house where Dan and his family lived. Dan was our barber and had a daughter my age and I'm sure that when Mrs. Goodwin threw her dishwater out, it only missed me by a hair.

Dad had some hounds and he and Dan would often go fox hunting on Sunday morning. Since Dan was a barber, he had access to a lot of really good smelling stuff and he used it all.

I often wondered if when they went into the woods all the wildlife high-tailed it somewhere else or stayed to find out what the strange smell was. I guess the foxes did because the hounds always treed one.

I was glad to find Dr. Yantis's house in good condition but Dr. Cobb's house is falling down. Dr. Brown's house deteriorated and was torn down. They have no further need for them anyhow.

I guess that somewhere in the Great Beyond, all three are sitting on a bench waiting for somebody to crank a Model T Ford.

Maybe I am too.

FEELING GOOD ABOUT
A NEW PORCH AND THE KIDS
WHO BUILT IT

One of life's great pleasures is sitting on your own back porch before dawn, drinking that first cup of coffee and wondering about your future, or wondering if you have one. Willie Nelson wrote a song in which he said, "My future is already behind me." Willie was wrong. His future was just starting when he wrote that song. Maybe ours is too.

My problem was that I didn't have a back porch to sit on. I would sit on my sidewalk outside the back door and try to envision that porch. I couldn't see any way it could be done and I knew I was not capable of doing it even if it could be.

Then, on the morning of July 18, a van load of kids and tools pulled into my driveway with a trailer load of materials close behind. My dream about a porch was about to be realized.

The kids, along with their supervisor were sent to my house by the Central Texas United Methodist Youth Mission from the Dallas-Fort Worth Metroplex, with referrals from the Neighborhood Revitalization of Brownwood. The kids, all volunteers are spending their summers doing things for senior citizens that they are unable to do for themselves. There are around 800 kids in this program, working all over Texas. There were 37 working in Brownwood.

The kids, most of whom didn't know one end of a hammer from the other, quickly learned to operate a skill saw and measure and cut boards to the proper length. There were 7 at my house but sometimes looked like 17.

I stayed out of their way the best I could and kept my advice to myself. No kid in the world wants to be told how to do something by an 81 year old man. There was only one time I was forced, against my better judgment to advise a kid adjusting a gate that a 7/16th wrench would not fit on a 9/16th nut. Now, he knows and he won't forget.

With the help of their supervisor, they learned a lot about logic and I learned a lot about today's kids. They are certainly not all bad. They had boundless energy and seemed to operate mostly on Gatorade and Popsicles. At noon, they had a sack lunch and always brought one for me and my daughter, Laura, who was hauling trash and cleaning up.

There were times when their supervisor deliberately watched while they goofed to see if they realized their mistake. They always did.

I don't know the ages of these porch builders but I would guess their ages from about 10 to 14. For whatever reason I don't know, they all seemed to like me. There were three boys and four girls, I think. They were hardly ever still enough to count.

My Chihuahua dog, Bitsy, confined to the house, barked incessantly for four days. On July 22, with the job completed, I took a cup of coffee to my new porch and let her out. She quickly inspected everything and gave her approval.

It was quiet outside for the first time in 4 days as the sun came up. It was too quiet. I loved the porch but I missed the kids.

Maybe they missed me too.

SLEEP TIGHT BUT DON'T LET THE BEDBUGS BITE—THEY'RE BACK

According to various news services, bedbugs are back. They are showing no preference between $950 Hotel rooms and cheap motels. Their return is blamed on foreign travel. That means that there are countries out there somewhere, who in hopes of getting rid of them are shipping them out with whoever passes by.

They were prevalent in Texas back in the 30s when nobody, that I ever knew engaged in foreign travel. A few folks, out of desperation, may have crossed the Rio Grande to Mexico to find out if things were better over there.

Apparently, they were as the Mexicans didn't come over here. Santa Anna, as far as I know was the last one to try it before recent times. Maybe he brought the bedbugs. Anyway, somebody did. We have a supply of every known plant, animal, and insect or tree that either bites, stings or punches a hole. Bedbugs, however, are not native Texans.

We did, at one time however, have a supply of the little biting buggers.

When I was a kid, back in the 30s, we moved a lot, always seeking a better house or land that hadn't been "farmed out." Almost every old house we moved into already had a supply of bedbugs left by the previous tenant.

Pest control companies today say they are very expensive to get rid of, sometimes costing thousands of dollars. They don't know what Mama knew. With twenty cents worth of coal oil she could rid the place of bedbugs and kill every blue bug on the chicken roosts. Blue bugs too were blood suckers that preyed on chickens but left us alone.

Of course, today, coal oil seems to be in short supply. I haven't seen any in years. Back then, it was our cure all for nearly everything. A rag soaked with coal oil and tied around a kid's neck would cure a sore throat if anybody could hold him or her long enough to tie it.

We stuck our foot in a pan of coal oil when we stepped on a rusty nail and never had an infection or a case of lockjaw. It was good for gunshot wounds and snakebites too and usually both happened at the same time when somebody was trying to shoot a snake.

Another cure for bedbugs that I heard of was to pour cheap whiskey mixed with gravel all over the house. It was said that they got drunk and stoned each other to death. I'll bet the pest control companies haven't heard of that either.

With the population shift we have today and half the world's population moving in with us, bedbugs are likely to be the least of our worries. We're going to get hit with everything they've got. Their motto, like American Express is "Don't leave home without it."

At our airports they are only checked for guns, bombs and sharp objects. How about doing a bedbug check? What about bringing coal oil back? What about closing the borders and trying to live with what we already have?

I have no intention of doing any foreign travel. The military took care of that for me during WWII but I didn't get even one bedbug. I recently visited some friends in the Texas Hill Country but apparently that area is still bug free. I haven't had a bite yet.

Maybe that's the reason land down there is selling for $10,000 an acre.

SMOKE IF YOU'VE GOTTEM

As a former voice-president once said in a speech to the United Negro Colleges, "the mind is a terrible thing to waste." Smoking too is a terrible waste. It is expensive, harmful to your body, the American Medical Association says, and turns everything in your house in close proximity to your cigarette a noxious brownish-yellow color.

Yet all of us old dyed-in-the wool smokers find it impossible to quit. A cup of coffee and a cigarette in the morning is a pleasurable experience. Mark Twain is known to have said, "Quitting smoking is easy. I've done it a thousand times."

Me too, Mark. So have a lot of people. I once swore that when cigarettes went to fifty cents a package, I would definitely quit. I didn't, not even when they exceeded $2.00 a pack. It is getting harder and harder these days to find a place to smoke. One whole country, Bhutan, totally outlawed tobacco within its borders.

Of course, it's a small country, located somewhere between India and China and it wouldn't be a big problem to step across the border and light up if a man got a sudden urge. They must have some bad habits of some kind there.

It is obvious to me that those who don't smoke are hell-bent on keeping anybody else from smoking. That tends to irk those of us who do. I never complain when somebody drives a new Lexus by my house and I don't have one. We are supposed to have freedom to do what we want within our laws and smoking is still legal.

Harry Marlin

When I entered the military fresh off the farm, it seemed that everybody smoked. Cigarettes were cheap and during basic training when we took a break, the sergeant would say, "Smoke if you've gottem" It seemed best to me that you had better "have them."

ALL IS WELL THAT ENDS WELL

Back when I was a kid trying to learn everything I could about everything in case fate decided that I go somewhere other than Blanket, I once went to the bottom of a well. I wouldn't even consider doing it now but at the time, it seemed to be the right thing to do.

Back then, most wells were hand dug, using a pick and shovel. The home owner usually dug the well assisted by anybody he could talk into helping him. An A-Frame was set up at the top and once the hole got deep enough, the diggers went down on a bucket at the end of a rope on a pulley, which was also used to haul up the dirt.

This involved getting somebody else, highly trustworthy, of course, to let them down and pull them up. With a few exceptions, nearly everybody was trustworthy back then. Today, it might be a horse of a different color, as some folks never show up when they're supposed to. They might even wander off somewhere to get a cold beer and not come back.

The well was dug until water was found, usually anywhere from fifty to seventy-five feet and the hole was about five feet in diameter.

A neighbor was digging such a well and I watched the whole proceedings, furthering my education in well digging, should I choose that as my occupation. Actually, it didn't appeal to my better judgment, even at age seven.

When the well reached about fifty feet deep and was getting a little damp on the bottom, I thought I ought to have a look at it. It was one of my earlier mistakes. At my urging, the well diggers decided to let me down on the rope. I wondered why they were laughing so hard.

Anyway, down I went, all the way to the bottom. All sense of direction was gone. All I could see was a little patch of blue sky at the top of the well which had decreased in size to less than the size of a gallon bucket.

It appeared that I could be in deep trouble at the bottom of a well and Mama didn't even know where I was. She would have had a wall-eyed fit if she did, similar to the one I was having at the time.

To make matters even worse, somebody hollered from the top, "Harry, we're all going to dinner. You'll be alright down there, won't you?" I definitely knew that I wouldn't. What if water suddenly started gushing in from some underground stream? What if they drove in front of a Frisco train on their way to dinner? I even thought I heard one whistle.

Hardly anybody ever lied back then but those men did. They suddenly appeared at the top of the well and pulled me out. I will never forget at that moment how good the world looked.

When I got home, Mama asked, "What have you been into now?" I said "Well—" and then she said, "I don't want to hear about it."

In 1944, I was flying on a B-17 bomber in the ball turret, hanging out over 30,000 feet of nothing over Germany. At least, I could see in all four directions and straight down. Even with somebody shooting at me I don't think I was ever as scared as being in the bottom of that well back in Blanket, Texas.

Well—maybe.

SOME SIDE EFFECTS
OF GETTING OLD

I have learned a lot of things since reaching the age of discontent. I call it that because I'm not too happy with the way things are going. I'm also frustrated because there is nothing I can do about it.

Television programs are not what they used to be. The actors talk so fast I can't understand them. After a considerable amount of research, I found out why. After the program is filmed, the audio is modified through a program that takes out all the pauses. The reason for this is to gain more time for commercials.

It is difficult for any human to talk without pausing. It's just a normal thing. Anyway, normalcy is no longer recognized in our society. I even tried using the captions which are provided for the hearing impaired. For some reason, I have a little trouble there myself.

That didn't work either. By the time I read the captions on a cop show which I watch a lot, the action has already gone to another case and I'm left wondering who shot who. Besides that, the words are often misspelled. That bothers me too.

To tell the truth, I haven't seen a TV show since Gunsmoke that I could totally understand. Anybody having trouble understanding Festus is not a true Texan. They didn't mess with what he said. Probably nobody in Hollywood knew what he said anyhow.

Recently, I watched an old movie featuring Paul Newman, one of my favorite actors. I was amazed to hear Paul talking like

Mickey Mouse. Maybe the sprocket holes in the film were worn out or the modern projectors were running at the wrong speed.

I learn a lot on the internet that 20 years ago, I wouldn't have known. I know most of the side effects for any drug on the market, as advertised daily on TV. I fully expect to one day go to a doctor and get a prescription for "Side Effects" with instructions to "Take one pill if you feel normal."

I have noticed that people today drive a lot faster than they used to. Where they might be going in such a hurry, I don't know. We have stores that stay open 24 hours a day and there is no reason to hurry to get there. Even though the liquor stores close early, some drivers appear to have already been there.

One good thing about it, cars today have better brakes. When I pull out in front of one, they seem to stop just fine. The drivers even honk and wave at me. Back when I was a kid, stopping a car was a problem. The brakes were mechanical instead of hydraulic.

When the brake pedal on a Ford was pushed, the whole car vibrated from one end to the other. Folks who drove Fords seldom ever were bothered with kidney stones.

Brakes on Chevrolets, squealed like a pig caught in a gate. When folks killed hogs in the fall, they sold the squeals to General Motors.

There was one advantage. Wherever you were going, folks knew you were coming and there was no doubt when you got there.

Sidewalks back then were about 18 inches high to keep cars out of the stores. Somebody might drive off of a curb but they sure didn't drive over one.

I guess things may be better in some respects. I no longer have to cut wood and build a fire in a wood stove on cold mornings.

The brakes don't vibrate on my Ford either and there are no side effects.

COUNTRY CORRESPONDENTS
AND BIG CITY COLUMNISTS

I don't remember exactly when I started writing a column for the Bulletin. I do remember the night at the Depot during some kind of function when Shelton Prince, the Bulletin publisher at the time told me he wanted me to write a column for the paper.

I know that that Bud Ross, Arnold Herdman and I were the appointed bartenders. I'm not sure when it was. I have a framed copy of a column dated January 3, 1997. I don't know if that was one of the first, or I had written some previously. Then, the columns were called "Viewpoints."

Anyway, at the time, I didn't know what I was doing and I'm still not sure I do. Until I received my first check, I thought I was a genuine columnist. The check, however, had me listed as a "correspondent." I'm still one.

The major difference between a columnist and a correspondent is that a columnist is paid more, having spent all that money and time going to journalism school. There's nothing wrong with that. Education brings big rewards.

At one time in my life, I had hopes of attending journalism school at the University of Missouri. Then, WWII happened and took me away to far places, then I got married and kids came along. I did get to Missouri during the Korean War when I joined the army reserve. I found that they didn't teach journalism at Camp Crowder.

A columnist I read regularly lives in a high-rise apartment overlooking downtown Houston, buys a new pickup every 2 years, flies to New York once a year and then spends 2 weeks in Santa Fe. Correspondents don't do that.

New York is probably the most expensive place on earth to visit and Santa Fe runs a close second. I have a musician friend who formerly played with the Glen Campbell band. They played an engagement in New York and Glen, out of the goodness of his heart took the band members to an upscale restaurant after the show.

He ordered a bottle of "good" wine. It was so good, he ordered two more. Glen, being born and raised in Arkansas, knew that a "good" bottle of wine in his home state was about $15.00.

My musician friend told me that when old Glen got the bill, he turned white as a sheet. The wine was $300 a bottle. No correspondents were allowed in this place or columnists either.

I remember thirty or forty years ago the Bulletin had "Country correspondents," usually elderly ladies who wrote about the happenings in their community. We learned how the crops were doing, when it rained, those who were baling hay, had a new calf born and who was ailing.

I remember one in particular who reported from the Ebony community. She could have been a columnist for any paper. She told in detail how the cow ate the cabbage and whose cabbage the cow ate. She obviously wrote exactly the way she talked and once you started reading, there was no stopping. You read it all and wished for more.

I can't remember her name but I'm almost sure it was Briley. Her readers soon felt that they knew everybody in the entire community. She could have taught writing anywhere, and didn't even know it. I never met her but I wish I had. I think I could have learned something.

Maybe I did, and didn't even know it.

SOMEWHERE IN THE WEST, WHERE THE HAWKS BUILD NESTS

Back when I was about 5 or 6 years old, we moved to a rather remote farm quite a distance from the nearest civilization. Dad always tried to find a place with lilacs growing in the yard. It was a good sign that somebody had been there before us and had survived long enough to plant lilacs.

The old house was built in two sections with a dog-run between the kitchen and the rest of it. Since Dad kept a bunch of hounds, it suited him fine, having shelter for the hounds in the winter and shade in the summer.

The place suited me and my brother fine as there was plenty of room to hunt and two stock tanks to fish in. We had a teen-age sister though who didn't like it much.

She had no social life at all except attending school. When she got off the school bus in the afternoon and walked two miles, it all ended. Nobody ever come calling. As Martha Stewart might say, "It was not a good thing." Martha, of course, was not around to advise anybody.

I knew my sister wanted to be somewhere else by the song she sung. After 75 years, I can't remember all the words but I still can hear her sing it.

> *"Somewhere in the west,*
> *I'll build a little nest,*
> *And let the rest*

> *Of the world go by."*
> *"I'll find peace and rest,*
> *Somewhere in the west,*
> *And let the rest of the world go by."*

At the time, none of us knew exactly where "The West" might be. Mama always told me and my brother not to go too far west. "Always hunt toward the house," She said. "We don't know what's back there."

One day, I was determined to find out. I took my dog and our old single shot .22 rifle with a nail for a firing pen and headed west. I walked far beyond where our cows grazed, crawled over two fences and kept going.

Around noon, I came upon a pretty sparkling stream with large cottonwood trees growing along the banks. In each cottonwood tree, Red Tail hawks had built their nests. They were not happy to see me, the dog, or the old rifle.

I knew, beyond a doubt, that I had found the place my sister sung about. It was about as far west as I could go without crossing another fence. Obviously, it was a good place to build a nest or the hawks wouldn't have built there.

If the world was going by, I didn't notice it. If fact, nobody was going by. There wasn't a road within 5 miles. I decided then that I didn't understand teen-age girls and I don't think I ever did.

Eventually, as usual, we moved closer to town where the lilacs still grew in the yard, as always and my sister found a social life and grew up as normal as anybody.

All this happened in the middle of the Great Depression and somehow, we all grew up in spite of our hardships and became known as "The Greatest Generation." Maybe we were because we had to be.

Somewhere northwest of Blanket, Texas, the Red Tail hawks are still building nests in the tall cottonwood trees on the banks of a sparkling stream as they did then.

Like the song my sister sung those many years ago, "Somewhere in the West."

SPRING IS ON THE WAY
AND THE LIVING IS EASY

I'm pretty sure that spring is just around the corner and winter is gone but I won't know for certain until I set out my tomato plants and they all freeze. I've had that to happen more than once. Last year, a hailstorm got them. I didn't get one tomato.

The reason I believe spring is fast approaching is that the little wren that nests in a gourd on my back porch is back and making repairs to her nest. The two blackbirds that have nested in the hollow of an old elm in my back yard for several years are also back.

Then too, I'm getting a good crop of weeds in my front yard and my mower won't start. I have always had trouble starting anything that has a pull-rope on it. I think the things should be illegal to own. If Henry Ford had put a pull-rope on his Model Ts, the automobile industry would have stopped, right then. The crank he furnished was bad enough.

I well remember one time when the little rope disappeared into the housing on the mower. It seemed to be wrapped around something. I took the thing off and noticed the rope was wound around a spring. I then took something loose allowing about 50 feet of tightly wound spring to release with all the power of a Texas tornado. It went by the side of my head, trimming my sideburns and taking about $15 worth of my hair with it.

I never saw the thing again. I have no idea where it went. I also quit doing any kind of lawn mower repair.

As soon as I'm sure that winter has gone and my garden is doing well, I can devote more time to bird-watching. I have a large bird bath and a feeder and no shortage of birds. When I was a kid, living on a farm, I watched birds a lot. I knew where they nested and when they laid their eggs and about when the baby birds would be in the nest.

Then, when I was about 12, my interest suddenly shifted to girl-watching. Girl-watching is not as complicated as bird-watching. There are hundreds of species of birds but only one species of girls. They come in three general classifications, blondes, brunettes and redheads. Easy to remember and no book is needed for identification.

Another good thing about girl-watching is that anybody can do it for years. I must have done it for at least 70 years but for some unknown reason, suddenly lost interest in it. I think my hormones went west. I doubt I could even be arrested for stalking at my age.

Anyway, bird-watching is practically free. Girl-watching, on the other hand, is not. I must have spent the best years of my life and thousands of dollars doing it. Sometimes, I even found out where one nested, but that rarely happened.

We are fortunate to live in Texas. Our state, other than California, has the most species of birds of all the states. We are also blessed with having the prettiest girls on the planet. We have a choice. We can watch one or both anytime we want to.

I sort of like to watch both.

STORMS NEVER LAST, THEY SAY BUT I HOPE WE DO

In my column A week or so ago, I suggested doing away with Monday as nothing ever went right on Monday. We should start the day on Tuesday as with Wednesday coming up; we would be "over the hump." Little did I know that on Wednesday the second day of May, a real wooly booger of a storm would hit.

I spent half of my youth in a cellar with a smoky old lantern waiting for a "cyclone" Mama knew was sure to come. Even today, when it thunders, I smell coal oil. Is this Global warming, or Global warning?

I stood in my back door late that Wednesday and watched 5 large trees blow down in my back yard. One fell across my garage and a large hackberry fell partially across my back porch. I thought for awhile I was being called to preach.

I thought of my old friend Cecil Holman, a mortician who also operated a grocery on Beaver Street for many years. I don't know what brought it up but one day Cecil told me, "I never did preach but I'm not too good to". Me neither.

I had a lot of conversations with Cecil over the years and it was a bright spot in my day when I went by his store. One day, I was in the store and a kid about 3, not even tall enough to reach the counter top, reached up and laid down two pennies.

What you want, son?" Cecil asked.

"Tater chips" The kid said.

"Go on back home, son." Cecil said. "You ain't got tater chip money."

There have been many times in my life when I didn't have tater chip money either and I thought about buying the kid some. Cecil vetoed the idea. "That kid is in here a dozen times a day with his two pennies trying to buy tater chips. His mama doesn't know he's doing it."

They didn't break the mold when they made Cecil—it was already broke.

With the help of my son Jimmy, Brent Groom, two chain saws and my lady-friend, Bernell, who can do anything, we finally got the mess cleaned up and stacked out front for the city crew to pick up. The city requested the stuff be in 5 foot lengths but the storm didn't know what lengths the city wanted. We did the best we could and a truck did come by and pick it up.

My garden is still flooded and the soil is washed off all my onions. Now, as I write this, the weather bureau is predicting more of the same. To get our planet back to normal again, maybe everybody should sell two of their cars and let the kids walk to school. They won't be the first to do it.

When I was a kid, I walked four miles through thick jungles with unknown vicious wild animals prowling all around me. In the winter, the snow was waist deep. Well, that's what I told my kids. Didn't everybody? Actually, it was only 2 miles.

When July comes around, we will be searching the sky for one little cloud that might bring some rain. In Texas, we all know it either rains too much, or not at all. It's too cold, or too hot, too wet or too dry. Nobody I know owns a raincoat.

Still, few among us would want to live anywhere else. We're tough.

We can handle it.

SUN-DRIED POSSUM, BLACK DRAUGHT AND BABY PERCY

Since writing a column about fried squirrel and white gravy, I have received three messages by e-mail and one telephone call from folks who also have experienced this delicacy.

It is most likely that they also knew the thrill of hanging a flour sack full of clabber on the clothesline for a day or two until the whey dripped out, leaving a good supply of cottage cheese. Clabber, these days however, is hard to find. Our pasteurized and homogenized milk available today turns into something not fit for man or beast. Clabber, it is definitely not.

Milk, when I was growing up, due to our lack of refrigeration, would turn sour anywhere from thirty minutes to a couple of days, depending on the ambient temperature. First, it reached a stage known as "blue john," then the clabber stage was next. Neither one went well on oatmeal.

Our grocery stores in Blanket didn't stock milk as they had no distributors or a refrigerator to keep it in. Ernest Allen sold milk shakes in his drug store and bought his milk on a daily basis from Mrs. Milner who had a cow.

Her son Oscar would deliver it every morning in a gallon container. One morning when Oscar delivered it, the glass container lacked about a pint or so being full. Ernest put the jar under the water spigot to fill it up. Oscar was watching. "Mr. Allen," He said, "If I was you, I wouldn't put no more water in there. Ma has done watered it down pretty good."

Both Oscar and Mrs. Milner were as honest as the day was long but apparently on that day, the cow wasn't.

I finally reached my 81st birthday on February 23rd but due to ordnance against shooting in the city limits, I didn't have fried squirrel for supper. A nice lady did give me a can of "Alabama Sun-dried Possum," made from genuine roadkill, guaranteed to have dried on an Alabama logging road for one full day.

Along with a can of poke salat somebody sent me awhile back, I plan on having a nice meal, along with a pan of good cornbread. I really don't expect many friends to drop by. Some folks wouldn't even be interested in fried squirrel.

My son gave me a bottle of that expensive Pinot Noir wine for my birthday that I recently wrote about. There is no mention on the bottle of it being good with sun-dried possum and poke salat but I'll try it anyway. A man has to do what a man has to do.

Besides having food that today might be considered questionable back during the Depression, the medications we took for any kind of illness was worse. Around our place, Mama gave us nothing but Black Draught, a vile herb that should be banned worldwide.

If I had a test coming up at school and wanted to miss the day, I told Mama I was having dizzy spells and I got a large dose of it. There was a good-tasting medication then called Baby Percy. Since it cost more than Black Draught, we didn't have any.

My daughter who works for the Department of Corrections says she once had an elderly supervisor and anytime she attempted to call in sick, the lady would always say, "Honey," You just take a spoonful of Baby Percy and come on to work."

I might have gone on to school if we had any of it. After a dose of Black Draught, I couldn't leave the farm.

TAKE A CRUISE TO NOWHERE OR CATCH A RIDE ON A TEST TRACK

Cruise Lines seem to be having a lot of trouble these days. They load up two or three thousand tourists and then somebody gets sick. Then the whole bunch does. There is no doubt that when you get that many people together, somebody is going to have something.

I have no desire to go on vacation with two or three thousand other folks on a big boat. My choice is to go camping in the Big Bend National Park and camp as far as I can from anybody else. So far, I have never caught any kind of disease from myself.

The latest problem I've heard about cruise ships is from a story in the Houston Chronicle written by Ron Nisssimov. A cruise ship left Galveston recently with only one engine operating properly. They warned the paying customers that they might be "going on a cruise to nowhere." They did. With only one engine working, they probably went in a circle.

They were supposed to go to Cozumel. They didn't get close. Such things do happen anytime humans are involved. Things are never perfect. They did, however, arrive back where they started from.

Some folks complained loud and long and got half their money back. One couple with 8 kids at home had no complaints. "They could have stayed at the dock," the husband said, "We were just glad to get out of that madhouse for a few days."

I am reminded of an old George Dolan story from the Fort Worth Star-Telegram, I think, sometime in the fifties. At that time, a large tire manufacturer had a tire testing track near San Angelo. The test track was built in a large oval shape where the drivers drove for 8 hours at high speeds to test the tires.

One night, a driver picked up a couple of illegal immigrants, drove for 8 hours at high speeds and let them out where he picked them up.

They thought they were on the outskirts of Kansas City.

T.S. Elliot said this about space travel: "If we continue to explore space, we will find at the end of our travel that we have arrived back where we started from and not recognize the place." It worked for the illegal immigrants.

The only cruise I ever took was on a floating crap game called the U.S.S. Mariposa from Naples to Boston in 1945. I was returning home after completing my missions on a B-17 bomber in the 15th Air Force.

The war with Germany ended about the time we went through the Straits of Gibraltar. The German submarines had no underwater communications and had no way of knowing the war was over. As a result of this, we zigzagged all the way to Boston. This made the trip longer.

Our only food on this trip was wieners and sauerkraut. I did notice that a few members of our armed forces got sick but were unable to get to the rail of the ship to throw up because of the crap games. To use a modern term, they downloaded wherever they happened to be.

The next time I go camping in the Big Bend and the tire testing track is still in operation at San Angelo, I may take a side-trip to Kansas City.

If T.S. Eliot was right, I'll be back.

TAKE MY ADVICE GRANNY—
STAY IN OAK CLIFF

I read in the news that an 87 year old grandmother in Oak Cliff received an invitation to join the army. She was interested in the $20,000 enlistment bonus and the medical care but she said," I don't like to get up early."

It appears to me that she's lucky to be able to get up at all. I have a ways to go before I reach 87 and I'm having trouble already.

The army did admit they made a mistake mailing her that invitation but it's certainly not their first mistake. They took me.

I recently fell off my back porch, bounced off a tree and landed on my back which was already damaged from a previous fall a year ago. I pulled up several small trees in the process of getting vertical again. I'm beginning to think that a horizontal position is my natural state.

Having spent two terms in the military, I can advise Granny that there's a lot more to the army than getting up early. She might have trouble getting over the obstacle courses. I have found that at my age, everything is an obstacle course, including back porches.

They also require that you keep your shoes shined to a high gloss. I can't even reach mine. They also have those 30 mile hikes with a full field pack. The pack they refer to is not a pack of Camels. Once around Coggin Park has become a daytrip for me without a pack of anything.

I also remember during my times in the service that a rather mean sergeant was always giving orders to either "Fall in," or "Fall out." The word "fall" causes my back to start hurting.

Of course, when I was in the Air Corp during WWII, we were not required to do a lot of those things but I had to crawl into the ball turret which hung out from the bottom of our B-17 bomber. I also had to get out.

I'm almost sure that today, if I ever got into the thing, they would have to bury me in it. Of course, Granny wouldn't have to worry about that. There are no more B-17s in use. I think they stopped using them when they stopped using me.

They also didn't pay me $20,000 during my entire time in the military. Things have sure changed a lot in fifty years, including me.

There is a long list of things I haven't mentioned that Granny would have to put up with. They probably still serve salmon salad in the mess halls on Friday. Back then, Friday was the day the post exchanges did a good business in junk food. If you've never had any of the army's versions of salmon salad, you've been living right.

There are other things Granny probably doesn't know about. She can't go home when she wants to, or any other place without special permission. The best I remember, I told the army where they could go a time or two. It didn't help matters any.

Granny was delighted though that the army was sending her a knit cap for filling out the form. Had they accepted her, she might have won some medals to show her grandkids and get free medical care from the Veterans Administration upon release, along with the $20,000.

That sure beats a knit cap.

TALKING MULES AND BORROWING WHAT I CAN TO WRITE A COLUMN

There are days when I can't think of anything to write. The older I get, the more often such days seem to happen. I don't know why. As far as I know, age has nothing to do with it. I'm still sharp as a tennis ball even though there are times I don't remember last Tuesday.

Then, I think of Leon Hale who has been writing a column for the Houston Chronicle since who laid the chunk. To make me feel even worse, he is older than I am and writes three columns a week. I write only one.

Both of us have an entire lifetime of experiences to draw upon. I think, at times, I have already used mine all up. I will admit that some of the stuff Leon writes about doesn't amount to a hill of beans. My stuff doesn't either but his is always interesting and that is what counts. Somebody, including me, always reads it.

He owns an old farmhouse on 10 acres of land near a place called Round Top. I have no idea where that is. I think it must be close to some other place somewhere. Anyway, he frequently goes out there and sits on the front porch and watches birds. I can do that here on my back porch but it doesn't help any.

Leon often encounters a mule in a pasture on the country road leading to his farmhouse. He stops and has long conversations with this mule which he swears, talks back. He always has several apples along in his pickup and the mule always demands one or two.

If a car comes by on the road, the mule immediately shuts up until the car passes. Apparently, the mule doesn't want everybody in the county to know he talks. There is not much telling what that mule would tell if he wandered down to the country store.

I was born and raised on a farm and we always had mules. I have never heard any one of them say a word. If I had, I would have probably caught the first Frisco freight train that came through Blanket and left the country.

I have, on occasions heard Dad use some rather choice words to these mules that no self-respecting mule would repeat. I wasn't even allowed to myself. I did pick up a few good ones that I used later in life to describe various bosses that I worked for.

I also tried a few on a drill sergeant I had in basic training in the army. Even an apple or two wouldn't have got me out of that.

Leon takes a three week vacation every year and either takes a cruise or goes to Santa Fe, New Mexico. As for me, I've been on vacation since 1986 when I retired and there is no place I really want to go. I have already been to Santa Fe and I visited Taos before they paved the streets.

During my military service, I was shown a large part of the world and a lot of it I didn't really want to see. I even went on a cruise from Naples to Boston and the food was terrible. We had nothing but wieners and Saur kraut the whole trip. They seemed to think it would stay down better on rough seas. It didn't.

I doubt that Mr. Hale will ever read my column, being busy as he is. I do apologize for using some of his stuff.

I can't find a talking mule anywhere in town.

TEXAS IS FAMOUS FOR MANY THINGS BUT WE MISSED OUT ON THIS

An Ivorybill woodpecker, a bird that is supposed to have been extinct since 1944, was recently spotted in Eastern Arkansas. The sighting has been more or less confirmed as the real thing. The bird is not easily mistaken for the Double-breasted Mattress Thrasher which may also be extinct. Nobody has seen one for years now.

This famous woodpecker is a large bird with a 19 inch wingspan, a bright red crest on its head and is 19 inches long and has a white underbelly. It can, they say, make kindling wood out of the average utility pole in 20 minutes.

The utility companies are ecstatic that the bird picked Arkansas as its home. It was spotted in a heavily forested and swampy area filled with water moccasins which environmentalists hope will deter bird watchers, giving the bird a chance to become unextinct.

Birdwatchers, however, will go anywhere for a look at a bird that is scarce, not to mention one that is totally extinct. There is nothing wrong with bird watching. It keeps those folks interested in such pursuits out of bars and pool halls where they complain about second-hand smoke.

I remember a story I heard a few years back where a group of birdwatchers stopped at a ranch down in the Hill Country. They asked permission from the old rancher to go on his property and watch birds.

"Watch 'em do what?" The old rancher asked.

I have no objection to people watching birds. Coming to Texas by the thousands every year to watch birds, they contribute a lot to the economy. The economy, which the government is always telling us is good, could be a lot better. The government economists, I suspect, have never bought groceries, gasoline, made house or car payments, or watched birds.

Down in the Big Bend National Park, there is a rare bird called the Colima Warbler. It nests, they say, in the trees at the Rio Grande Village Campground. I have been going to the Big Bend for over 40 years and have never seen this rare bird. What I have seen is a lot of people looking for it. What they do see is a lot of pretty scenery, and like the birds, they keep coming back.

Since the rare woodpecker was spotted in Arkansas, folks have been seeing them in Houston and all over East Texas. Even the rare Double-breasted Mattress Thrasher stays away from Houston.

Do not look for them here, folks. Mesquite trees remind them of barbecue. Maybe barbecue caused them to be extinct in the first place. I have barbecued worse.

Human nature being the way it is, if one person sees a UFO hovering over Dallas one day, you can bet they will be seen hovering over Brownwood, Coleman or San Angelo the next day. Maybe even Waxahachie.

On the third day, they may be observed flying over Loving County, the most remote and sparsely populated county in Texas, and all being escorted by a large flock of Ivory-bill woodpeckers.

It's just the way we are.

THE BIG BUGGY WRECK OF 1930

Back sometime around 1930, my family moved from our little worn-out farm northwest of Blanket to a sandy-land farm at a place called Gap, somewhere north of Sidney. Dad decided that he had rather raise watermelons, sweet potatoes, peanuts and grass burrs than cotton.

My married sister, Lela was visiting us for a week during our stay there when she got word from her husband that he was tired of frying his own eggs and boiling his own beans and wanted her at home. She and her husband lived somewhere around a place called Stag Creek.

It was decided that we should take her home to keep peace in the family. Dad hitched up old Pete, our mule, to the buggy for the trip which was about 5 miles. Lela rode in the front seat with Dad. Since no vehicle ever left our place without me in it, I climbed in the small space behind the seat. Going anywhere was better than being nowhere. Gap wasn't the end of the earth but you could see it from there.

It was late in the evening when we left Gap with old Pete feeling frisky and pulling the buggy along at a good fast trot. For some reason or other, among other things, old Pete hated bridges. Somewhere between our house and our destination, there was a long hill with an old wooden bridge at the bottom which crossed over Stag Creek.

It was almost dark when we started down the hill with the bridge at the bottom. Somehow, old Pete sensed that he was going to have to cross that bridge and was determined not to do it.

He backed his ears, flared his nostrils and made a beeline for the ditch. Shortly after he hit the ditch, the buggy turned over and we all hit the ditch. I, along with everybody else was thrown out of the buggy. I skidded through the grass burrs, thinking for sure that my time had come and I hadn't even started to school yet.

Old Pete, having at least avoided the bridge for the time being, turned and stared at us as we picked ourselves up and checked for broken bones.

Our luck held and we received no serious injuries although it took Mama a week to pick the grass burrs out of my head. My sister was convinced, however, that she was bleeding to death. As it turned out, it was found that she suffered only from what folks these days call incontinence.

We assumed that such things regularly happened to victims of buggy wrecks all over the country. Since this was my first, I sure didn't know.

Dad got the buggy out of the ditch, turned it upright and with a few choice words directed at old Pete, led him across the bridge and we continued our trip. Lela was delivered to her anxious husband safe and sound with the exception of still being slightly damp.

We finally moved back to Blanket and Dad started selling ax handles that he bought for a dollar and sold for fifty cents.

He said it beat farming.

THE BIG DANCE OF 1944 AND TAINTED TURKEY FOR EVEYBODY

On Christmas Eve of 1944, the 97th Bomb Group of the 15th Air Force in Italy held a Christmas dance for the troops. Since I was a member of this group, I was there. It was a gala affair as good as they could make it with limited resources.

A building big enough to hold such a dance was found in Foggia, the nearest town, about 12 miles from our air base. Transportation to and from town was furnished since following the dance; it was felt that nobody would have been able to drive.

Somebody even located a large Fir tree and decorated it just like home.

An Air Force band made up of former professionals who sounded a lot like Glenn Miller and his Texas Playboys was found somewhere. They were good—I think.

Since somebody was needed for dance partners, our enterprising crew rounded up all the WACs, Red Cross girls and Italian girls they could find. Some, I noticed, would have had to slip up on the water bucket to get a drink. Nobody seemed to mind once the band started to play.

Since the Air Force didn't furnish drinks, it was left up to the participants to bring their own. There were no liquor stores in Foggia or anywhere else in Italy. The stuff that was brought into that building on that memorable night would never have been approved by the AMA, the CIA, the FBI or our flight surgeon. It seemed, however, to serve its purpose.

I stood by the bandstand watching the guitar player who seemed to be pretty good even if he didn't know Red River Valley. A fellow who seemed to have more than his share of something or other kept harassing him.

He stood it for awhile, then raised up both feet and kicked that fellow plumb across the dance floor. He slid into the lower branches of the Christmas tree and never did come out.

The guitar player never missed a lick. I assume they found the old boy the next morning when they took the tree down. At least, I hoped so. He may have been a ball turret gunner and we needed all we had.

The next day, the mess hall served turkey which had probably been too long in transit. I didn't have much of an appetite so I didn't eat much of it. That night, A First Lt. who was the group radar operator and I were sharing a bottle of Chianti he found outside somebody's tent. Apparently Chianti no longer appealed to the occupant.

The Lt. advised me that he hadn't eaten much turkey either and was hungry. There was no place to get anything to eat except the mess hall and it was closed. We walked to the mess hall and he kicked the door open and came out with two five pound cans of American Process Cheese. I wondered about being charged with conspiracy.

We consumed nearly all of one five pound can of cheese. I buried the other can behind my tent and woke up Bracey, our left waist gunner with my digging. He said, "Marlin, who are you burying out there?"

The following day, the Lt. and I were the only two people in the squadron who could walk with our legs close together. I don't remember flying a mission that day.

The Germans probably wondered what happened, or maybe they already knew about the tainted turkey and the big dance.

Everybody else did.

THE CAR DAD NEVER BOUGHT BECAUSE OF A GUITAR PLAYING WOMAN

We never had a car when I was a kid, growing up on a sorry hundred acre farm northwest of Blanket. We had a wagon and a team of horses and I guess we were lucky to have been blessed with those.

Some of the more affluent farmers had Model T Fords and in later years they bought Henry Ford's later version which he called the Model A. Neither of which exceeded the pure dependability of our wagon and team. We never had to crank a horse on a cold morning or push one to get it started.

Still, we all wanted one. We thought that just having one parked somewhere on our property, whether it ran or not would make us feel a lot better. This was during what folks called "The Great Depression," and most of the time nobody felt really good about anything. Having something to go to town in on Saturday other than that wagon might have made us feel a lot better.

I remember the many times Dad would take a bath in a number two washtub, shave and put on his best clothes and tell Mama he was going to town to buy us a car. We believed him the first few times, and then we started doubting him because he never delivered.

My brother and I would lay awake at night, waiting for the sound of either a Model T or a Model A. coming down that lane and across the cotton patch, making our dreams come true.

Sometimes, we would hear one coming and our hopes rose, only to find that it was somebody bringing Dad home.

He never did explain why he hadn't bought us a car. On more than one occasion, I asked him about it and he would say, "Not yet son—not yet." I don't think he ever really meant to. He couldn't drive one anyhow.

Mama would always say, "I know where he's been." "He's been down there in Blanket all day settin' around listenin' to that woman play that guitar and sing"

Dad would just laugh and say, "She sings just like an angel too." Mama saw no humor in his remark and I know he did it just to aggravate her a little. I decided then that women were God's most mysterious creatures. After all these years, I still think so.

We never did find out who the guitar playing woman was who sang like an angel, or if she really existed. When we would go to town on Saturday, my brother and I would look all over town but we never saw hide or hair of her.

One day I saw an old man I figured was at least a hundred, all humped up on the curb chewing tobacco and spitting in the street. I thought he might know what I needed to know if anybody did.

"Mister," I said, "Did you ever hear a woman around here that plays a guitar and sings like an angel?

He turned to look at me with a far away look in his tired old eyes and said, "Not yet son—not yet."

WHEN THE RABBITS WERE DRIVEN AND THE COWS WERE SHOT

I have been a resident of this county for a long time. Sometimes, I think I've been here too long. Anyway during my long residence in this area, I have attended various functions that I don't remember all the details of, but most of all, why I attended in the first place.

I admit that when I was a kid growing up at Blanket, I had a lot of curiosity about things. If anything was going on around the county and I could either walk to what was going on or catch a ride with somebody, I went.

I may have been to things that few people today have. I'm sure that somebody in the county who is older than dirt may have been there too but I didn't know them at the time.

One of the events I remember going to was a "rabbit drive." I wasn't very old at the time so some of the details of this memorable event I have forgotten, or never did know.

I remember that the "rabbit drive" I attended was near Zephyr. It seemed to be a rather festive event. Everybody came in every conveyance from Model T Fords to horses and wagons. Wives and kids were in abundance. I don't really remember but we may have had what they called "dinner on the ground." Maybe we had fried rabbit or rabbit stew.

I do remember that the men who participated in the drive all carried shotguns and lined up across the pasture about 50 feet apart. Then, they moved across the pasture, shooting any rabbit that ran from behind a bush or a patch of prickly pear.

The whole thing seemed to be rather hard on rabbits. I don't know if the whole county was being overrun with rabbits which needed to be eliminated or if this was just an annual sporting event, like going dove hunting. Maybe the rabbits were eating too much grass, leaving the cows with little, or none.

I don't remember ever seeing a rabbit eat as much grass as a cow but it might have happened at Zephyr. Best I remember, Zephyr had the only cyclone hit there that has ever hit Texas. I learned all about it from Mama. Every time it thundered, she put us all in the cellar. "You know they had that bad cyclone at Zephyr." She would say.

Another event I attended that I wish I hadn't also involved shooting. This, I think happened in 1934 when I was 10 years old. The government, for reason I don't really know killed a lot of cattle. A farmer took his cattle to a specified place where he was paid for them and then they were shot.

Probably for the same reason the rabbits were shot—too many of them. Anyway, I walked a couple of miles to see this but I didn't stay long. It seemed to be a rather sad situation to me. The country was in the middle of a Depression but the cows didn't cause it. There was no reason to shoot them that I could see.

I still remember the exact place the cattle were shot that day. The corral that held them is gone, as is the house that was nearby. I'm sure that somebody remembers it other than me. I have wished a lot of times that I didn't.

Somebody once said that the older we get, the better we remember things that never happened. I still remember too many things that did.

Anyway, I never drove a rabbit or shot a cow.

THE GOOD OLD DAYS ARE GONE FOR GOOD, OR WORSE

Back when I was a kid, living on various farms around Blanket, people visited a lot. We were always glad to see somebody coming.

Today, things are different. If somebody drives up in your driveway or knocks on the front door, your first thought is, "Now who on God's green earth could that be." Some folks hide the whiskey while others just hide. Sooner or later, they hope, they'll just go away.

Our guests were always welcome, regardless of who they were. Some managed to always get there just before supper or dinner. That too, was just fine. We never had much but nobody else did either. Mama might put on another pan of cornbread, slice another onion and put more water in the gravy.

One of our frequent guests was Mr. Pinkard. Most people just called him "Old man Pinkard." I'm sure his mama gave him a name but nobody seemed to know it. I don't know exactly where he lived but it couldn't have been far off because he always walked.

Most of the time, if he arrived in the morning, he stayed all day. Folks said he was "an old Indian fighter." Being a kid, I thought he probably just fought old Indians. Given a choice, I think I would have too.

In later years, I learned that he really did fight Indians, taking part in one of the last Indian fights in the county at Salt Mountain which was located about 5 or 6 miles from where we lived at the time.

One morning, he arrived at our place just as Dad was fixin' to haul a load of water from Blanket. One of the sucker rods was broke in our windmill. The barrels were loaded in the wagon and the horses already hitched up. Hauling water wasn't easy but it was a lot easier than pulling those sucker rods.

Old man Pinkard got on the wagon seat with Dad and I got in the back with the barrels. About a mile from the house, the horses ran away, taking us on a wild ride with barrels going all over the wagon bed. I thought my time had come. I guess Old man Pinkard did too.

He was hollering as loud as he could, "Saw 'em down, Jesse, saw 'em down." Jesse finally got them "sawed down" before we all got killed. Old man Pinkard didn't show up at our house for a day or two after that.

I loved to listen to the old man's stories about his Indian fighting days, or anything else. Our guests contributed a lot to my education, such as it was. I always hung onto every word.

Another fellow who visited often was Arley Simpson. I don't know where he lived either but it must have been in walking distance.

Arley would sit on the front porch for hours, telling stories and smoking hand-rolled Bull Durham cigarettes. I watched him carefully and if I could someway come up with a nickel, I would buy my own Bull Durham and roll a cigarette just like Arley. His must have tasted a lot better than mine did though.

However, I kept my Bull Durham hid under a rock and Arley didn't. Maybe that made the difference. If I had got caught, they would have tasted a lot worse.

Harry Marlin

In our modern world, folks don't visit as much as they did back then. Everybody is too busy trying to make a living so they can buy a house, two cars, pay every kind of tax known to man and have enough left to buy groceries.

Maybe the days of my youth were "the good old days."

THE GOOD TIMES, THE BAD TIMES AND THE MEMORIES OF BOTH

I recently received an e-mail from one of my readers who mentioned "fried squirrel and white gravy." I assumed by that statement that he had grown up during the thirties. Few people these days are familiar with such stuff.

However, though we often had fried squirrel and white gravy, we also had well-balanced meals like we do today. Ours was balanced between fried squirrel, fried cottontail rabbit, turnips and greens and the old standby, pinto beans. Jack rabbits were a little tough. I have heard people say they could run along beside a jack rabbit and feel to see if he was tough or not.

Of course, when hog killing time came along, we threw the whole thing out of balance by having pork. In those days, a hog could be bought for less than the cost of a package of pork chops in your local supermarket today.

Everything being relative to price and income, maybe they are about the right price. I remember when apples were two for a nickel and nobody had a nickel. Gasoline was .12 cents a gallon and nobody ever bought over 2 gallons at a time.

Possessing all this knowledge might be invaluable today. It might bear putting on your resume when seeking a job. I am almost sure you would be left sitting in the reception room until several policemen arrived on the scene carrying nets.

The good thing about it all was that there was no stigma attached to being poor. Most everybody was. There were practically no thieves around then as nobody had anything worth stealing.

My dad and mother "ran away" to get married, all the way from Blanket to Sidney in a horse and buggy. They were married by a justice of the peace who stood on the ground during the short ceremony while they sat in the buggy.

Happily married, they started back to Blanket but were chased down by a fellow on a horse, sent by the JP who had second thoughts about the legality of the marriage. He said their license was for Brown County and he was in Comanche County.

They continued on to Blanket where they were married again, still sitting in the buggy. If they were lucky, they caught a couple of rabbits on the way for their wedding supper.

Yeah, things were tough in those days but the people were tougher. At their 50th wedding party, Dad told the 130 guests, "We started out with nothing and we've still got it." I have to disagree. Maybe they had nothing of monetary value but after 50 years, they still had each other and something called happiness.

I often hear elderly people talk about the "hard times" and the "good times" back during the Great Depression. We had some of both. People were friendly back then and neighbors shared what they had, even fried squirrel and white gravy.

We had country dances that might last the night unless the hair came out of the fiddler's bow and the guitar player broke his strings. We had "pie suppers" at the one-room Willow Springs school north of Blanket and the "all day singings with dinner on the grounds" at Rock Church.

Today, the school building is long gone and nothing remains but the willows and the memories. Rock Church too, is gone but I can still hear the old piano and the voices of the singers through the open windows, as softly as the wind blowing through the oak trees.

I think of my two favorite people who were married twice while sitting in a buggy in 1903 and I think of the good times.

WE HAVE MET THE GREATEST GENERATION AND IT IS US

I recently corresponded with a lady in Alabama by E-mail who was a neighbor when I was growing up on a farm near Blanket. She lived with her family less than a mile from where we lived. She is a little older than I am but I don't know how much. I have been accused of being older than God's dog. I don't know for a fact that God even has a dog. Everybody has one so He might.

We decided that though we grew up during the Depression, it was still a good time and a lot better than growing up today. People were friendly and everybody helped everybody else. If a neighbor killed a hog, everybody got some meat. Crime was almost non-existent. If you needed something your neighbor had, you borrowed it.

If we got sick, it was no problem to see a doctor. We had three in Blanket and they spent most of their time sitting on a bench in front of Ernest Allen's drug store. If you could manage to scrape up two dollars, you could see one or all three for six.

We didn't get to go anywhere much but when we did, we enjoyed it. Going to town on Saturday was a high point in our week. When we did go to town, we spent the whole day, mostly visiting with people. We would go anywhere to have something to do. We even went on rabbit drives. We had little money to buy stuff with and anyhow, we didn't need much.

Back then, we had something called "All day singings and dinner on the grounds." These events happened in the summer months but folks would sit in a country church all day listening to gospel quartets. The only way we had to halfway cool ourselves was funeral home fans.

The "dinner on the grounds" was the best part. Lord, we had good food brought by the women. I haven't seen a genuine 5 layer chocolate cake since. The kids called it "dinner on the ground" but nobody ate on the ground that I know of. I would have to get that good fried chicken, potato salad, fresh black-eyed peas and chocolate cakes and pies.

Another event we all attended every year was the De Leon Watermelon and Peach Festival. Nobody ever missed that even though most folks got there by traveling several miles in a wagon or buggy.

Tom Brokaw called us "The Greatest Generation" but we didn't know it. It probably would have caused us some embarrassment. We were just a bunch of poor people doing the best we knew how. If we needed something, we invented it. We invented air conditioning to get rid of the funeral home fans. We invented the automobile to give our horses some relief.

We were responsible for the establishment of numerous large corporations which keep our younger generation today from starving to death. They include Dairy Queen, Sonic, Kentucky Fried Chicken, Burger King and Wendy's and a few I can't think of.

We won World War Two because we had more reasons to win it than any other country. We still do.

I have noticed recently that the national news media seems to be trying to elect our president. I guess they have forgotten our existence. We may be getting crippled in the knees and short winded but we are perfectly capable of doing that.

Maybe it is about time to let them know that we are still here and Tom Brokaw was right.

THE KEY TO SUCCESS IS GETTING A GOOD START

One day about a week or so ago, my lady friend called. "I need to borrow your pickup." She said. "I'm going to Wal-Mart to buy a tree and it won't fit in my car."

I wondered why a woman her age would be buying a tree. Then, I gave it some thought. I decided that trees these days are all being planted mostly by middle-aged and elderly people. Young folks have little interest in trees unless they drive into one.

I decided to accompany her to get the tree as she usually gives me some good driving tips. Driving tips are always appreciated and when she drives, I always give her a few. Since it was to be her tree, I allowed her to drive.

"Watch it," I told her as we exited my driveway. "Don't pull out in front of that car. They must be doing eighty and drunk besides."

"Don't tell me how to drive. That driver is not drunk. Everybody in Brownwood drives like that."

After getting the tree loaded, we found that my pickup wouldn't start. A nice fellow from the automotive section brought a battery and jumper cables in a shopping cart. It still wouldn't start. Then another Wal-Mart employee appeared in a pickup to jump it off. The starter refused to budge.

Then I remembered that about 10 years ago, the pickup manufacturers started making starters in direct proportion to the size of the engine. A big engine called for a little starter. By doing this, they could predict, almost to the day, when the starter would fail and stock their warehouses with starters to get ready for the rush.

I remembered the last time it happened to me and I recalled that a sharp lick on the side of the starter would make it work. The nice man from Wal-Mart crawled under the pickup and hit the starter. It worked, allowing us to drive back and unload the tree.

I took the pickup home, thinking I could hit it a lick the next day and start it. It was a no go. I had to call a wrecker to take it to a garage. I found that the price of starters had doubled from around a hundred dollars to two hundred. This, along with the wrecker charge knocked a big hole in my Sociable Security check.

Some twenty years ago, my son Ken was attending school in Waco. He owned an old Mustang. The planned obsolescence of all the parts on that Mustang seemed to be coming due in the same week.

One day, it was the starter. I bought a starter for the bargain price of $40 which was as big as a stovepipe and weighed about 40 pounds. I took off to Waco before dawn on a cold November morning to replace the starter on that Mustang.

About two miles out of Goldthwaite, I located the only highway patrolman in Texas who was awake. It seems that he had been to his ranch to feed his cows. He gave me a $40 ticket, thereby increasing the price of the starter to $80.

I spent most of that cold day putting that starter on with my legs sticking out from under that Mustang where most of the students seemed to want to park. A Mustang, as anybody knows who has ever been under one sits awful close to the ground but I knew my way around, having been under there before.

Nobody was happier on graduation day than me.

Well, maybe he was.

THE LACK OF ONIONS
COULD CAUSE A RECESSION

I don't know if it's global warming or Unidentified Flying Objects but something is definitely messing up my garden growing. I have, without fail, been planting onions in my garden for the past 20 years in January.

Last year, 2007, I couldn't do it. It was too wet and too cold for all of January. This year, it is too dry and too cold. I have not planted even one onion even though my daughter has had the garden tilled and ready for 3 weeks. Last year, I finally got a few onion plants in the ground around the last of February.

Everybody knows, or should, that onions planted in February just don't do right. The weather turns hot before they reach the eating stage.

I have a friend who is a retired doctor now living in Colorado. She moved there so she could fly-fish in the best fishing holes in the West. Every year in January, she sends me a short e-mail that says only, "How are the onions?" All I can say is, what onions?

I have always had a garden if I lived in a place that had a spot big enough for a garden. I guess that's because when I was growing up, a garden fed us in the spring and summer and due to Mama's canning, most of the winter.

Mama canned everything, using Mason jars and cans. Back then, cans were bought along with a can sealer. I haven't seen a can sealer since then. I'm sure they no longer exist. Of course, using a pressure cooker was necessary to the canning process and within a few days if a can swelled up like a toad frog, it was best to throw it away and can another.

This entire garden growing and canning was due to the economics of the times. If anybody wanted to eat, and most people did, it was necessary. Money was not evenly distributed. Some folks had it but most didn't.

The times were so hard at the time our banker wore a fake Timex.

This particular period was known as "The Great Depression." Most families, mine included, were not aware of when it started or when it ended. For us, it was always there. Nobody, as far as I know, ever jumped out a window and the only stock market we worried about was on the ones grazing in our pasture.

Now, it's 2008 and not only do I not have any onions planted but the economist think the country is headed into a recession. The government folks, none of whom have ever suffered from a money shortage plan to dole out a little money to the citizens who will quickly spend it and stop the recession.

Back when I was a kid, Mama called this "robbing Peter to pay Paul."

When I was a kid, nobody knew who to blame for the hard times but in 2008, we can blame Max. Folks have maxed out their credit cards and made an attempt to pay them off at $15 a month which is impossible. They bought houses they couldn't afford along with expensive cars they couldn't pay for. Then, they let their creditors have them back.

This form of economics won't work now and it never has.

One thing about the Depression years, nobody had a credit card to max out and few people bought a $500,000 house. The fact is, nobody bought much of anything. A new Model T Ford cost around $500 and if you couldn't pay for it, you could keep it anyhow.

Nobody wanted the thing back.

THE LITTLE BROWN MULE
THAT WENT ASTRAY

Back when I was a kid, we had no social life at all to speak of. There was little to do and even less to see. There were no SUVs or Japanese cars driving up and down the roads at 80 miles an hour. On rare occasions, somebody in a Model T Ford might pass but mostly it was somebody in a wagon.

We did a little visiting now and then, mostly with our kinfolks who lived close by. I remember one day in particular when I was about five. Mama, my sister Faye and I walked across the field to visit my aunt Annie.

Aunt Annie was getting restless too and decided we should visit Mrs. Butler who lived about a half-mile up the road. My cousin Pauline went along too. Mrs. Butler was a widow with a house full of kids who had married Mr. Butler, a widower who also had a bunch.

Together, they had more kids than Carter had liver pills. Mama said they were as poor as Job's turkey. I didn't know who Job was but if that turkey was anywhere near as poor as we were, it was in pretty bad shape.

Their old house set about fifty yards off the road and like most of the old houses in those days was run down, unpainted and had no window or door screens. Except for the little heads poking out every window and door, it was open from front to back.

Mrs. Butler was glad to see us. Hardly anybody ever came by their place except the Watkins man and he had long ago lost hope of selling his products here. We made our way inside the front room where any company was always received.

Mama and Aunt Annie were given the only two cane-bottom chairs on the place with Faye, Pauline and I left standing. We were surrounded by kids of varying ages.

"How's your family, Mrs. Butler?" Mama asked.

"Well," She said, "We've all been pretty good except my youngest boy. He's been pretty sick lately."

"What's wrong with him, Mrs. Butler?" Aunt Annie asked.

"Well," She said, "He swallered that mule about a week or so ago."

At this point, my sister Faye and cousin Pauline were trying hard to stifle their giggling, with stern looks from Mama and Aunt Annie. I wasn't sure swallering a mule was a laughing matter,

"What kind of a mule, Mrs. Butler?" Mama asked.

"Aw, it was one of them little tin mules off the tobacco my husband chews."

Being familiar with Brown Mule chewing tobacco since my dad chewed a plug now and then, I knew about the little tin mule but I never found any reason to swaller one.

After visiting with Mrs. Butler for about an hour, our problems seemed minor. I didn't even worry about Mr. Job's turkey. Faye and Pauline, however, giggled all the way home about the kid "swallering a mule." I felt sorry for him myself even though I didn't know which one of the brood he was.

I guess the kid eventually recovered and the little mule was turned out in the pasture, the only bathroom they had or ever would have.

THE NIGHT ELVIS LOST HIS COAT

Recently Gene Deason, our editor wrote a column about Elvis. This triggered my memory to the night Elvis came to Brownwood, appearing in the old Memorial Hall, best I remember. I still remember the stage in the Memorial Hall being slanted toward the front. It was a nightmare for bands.

I once played in a band there, fronting for the "Sons of The Pioneers" who was appearing there. My steel guitar was on legs and it kept sliding away from me. The drummer had the worst time. A few good licks and his drums slid past the fiddle player on their way to the footlights.

I don't know who designed the stage but I suspect it was the same fellow who designed the Henry J. automobile. I think it was sold mail order by Sears or Wards and disappeared faster than fried chicken on a preacher's plate.

I don't know if Elvis encountered any trouble with the stage or not. His trouble started after the concert when he went to Chisholm's Chicken Hut to eat. He took his coat off and hung it on a coat rack.

It didn't hang there long. A group of High School boys thought it would be great to take the coat as a souvenir, and they did. I was a member of the Brownwood Police Department at the time and we always got our man, woman or boy, as the case might be.

I'm aware of who actually took the coat off the rack but as a fellow used to say that we often placed in jail, "The stature of imitations" has run out and I won't tell.

For those of you who don't know, the Chicken Hut was on the right side of East Commerce going east, not far from the traffic circle. Our traffic circle was famous for having a big fountain in the middle of it. I still remember too, the night a woman shucked all her clothes and was cooling off in the middle of it.

Due to the subsequent traffic jam caused by drivers continually driving around the circle to get a look at this unusual sight, we had to get her out in the interest of safety. She had a dog with her and we were forced to put both her and the dog in jail. She was, to use a modern expression "Thoroughly hammered." Elvis, as far as I know, missed this show while looking for his coat. Anyway, maybe it happened on a different night.

Our efficient police department quickly rounded up the usual suspects and got the coat back and took it to the police station where Elvis came to get it. At that time, he had not yet attained the fame and fortune he would later have heaped upon him. He was gad to get his coat back. He needed it. No charges were ever filed. After all, it was just a boyhood prank.

I remember him as being a very nice and polite young man who said 'Yes Sir" and "No Sir." In his later years, he couldn't handle his fame and fortune.

One only has to read the papers or watch TV to know what is happening to our current crop of celebrities. They seem to spend as much time in jail as they do performing.

The old Chicken Hut restaurant has been gone now longer than Elvis, the traffic circle is gone, along with the fountain but I still remember it all and the lady who took a bath in it.

I sure won't forget that.

THE ONIONS ARE PLANTED
AND THE CHIPS ARE DOWN

For any of my readers who may be interested, I now have over 300 onion plants set out, fertilized and watered. I give full credit to my daughter Laura, and the work she did. My job, during the entire process was to sit at the end of the rows and make sure they were all perfectly straight.

If you are not an onion raiser, you may not realize how important this job is. Nobody wants onions from a crooked row. Anyway, I had to do something or I wouldn't feel right about eating the onions.

I assume that by reading this column, you have figured out that I had absolutely nothing to write about. I hate it when that happens but it does. A trip to the grocery is a big event for me these days.

Before I got old and stove-up, I was busy doing something, meeting people and going places I hadn't been, which gave me something to write about. Besides, I had an interesting life to write about which in 10 years had been pretty well covered. I have reached a dilemma which has been covered by the Indians who said, long ago, "When the chips are down, the buffalo is empty."

My buffalo is empty.

I have a lot of friends around the country that used to send me interesting stuff by computer but they all discovered the "Forward" key and send me nothing now but junk that somebody else sent them. I predict that e-mail is on its way out like CB radio.

Since the weather has been sunny and warm for the past three days and the onions were planted, I have spent a lot of time sitting on my back porch soaking up the sunshine and watching the birds, I have noticed that the two blackbirds that have nested in the old hollow elm for the past 6 years are back. It seems a little early but they're here. I hope this is an indication that spring is just around the corner.

I have a nice back porch which was built by some kids from Dallas 2 years ago under some type of program to assist the elderly. As for me, I never could build anything. I didn't even understand the Lego kits for ages 2 to 12.

I think the program was called, "Get the old folks on the porch and off the streets." Some folks actually accuse us of being bad drivers. We are not. We seldom drive over 30 even in a 40 zone. We call those drivers that pass us "organ donors." Some will be. Anyway, we spend most of our time looking for a handicapped parking space that is not already occupied. The surprising thing is that the worse the weather, the more handicapped folks are out.

If it's sleeting or snowing, stay at home. Grandma already has your parking place

I have noticed over the years that my readers like my columns better when I write about "the good old days" back in the thirties. I receive a lot of mail about "the good old days." I guess that eventually there will come a time in our lives when our Champagne days will turn into Cold Duck days and our 4-lane paved roads that led us to where we are will again be one-lane dirt roads and we suddenly realize that where we've been is better than where we are now.

Well, maybe. I still like it now and I'm not leaving until they get up a load.

THE REVOLTING DEVELOPERS
MAY GET US ALL YET

When I was a kid, living on a farm near Blanket, it was everybody's ambition to leave the farm and move to town. Things have changed. Now, everybody wants to move to the country. With the help of developers, they are doing it—in large numbers.

The problem is; we're running out of country. In Virginia and Maryland, millions of acres of what was once pristine country is now developed and million dollar homes have taken the place of trees. The country is practically paved over.

About 35 years ago, I spent two days and a night with friends from Baltimore sailing on Chesapeake Bay on their 35 foot sailboat. At that time, the bay was a beautiful body of water. Today, it is polluted and the fish all died. The fish had nothing to do with it. Overpopulation and developers did.

Stopping grass fires in Texas during a drouth is easy, compared to stopping developers. There is no question as to which one does the most damage. The grass will grow back—the land won't.

There are some beautiful and remote places in Texas I thought would be safe from developers. They are not. Just recently, a fellow was all set to buy a part of the Big Bend State Park. We are fortunate that his plan was discovered and stopped.

I think that fellow was like they accused Lyndon Johnson of being. They said, "Lyndon doesn't want all the land in Texas—just what joins his."

And then, there is Lajitas, about as remote as it gets. Several years ago, a millionaire from Houston discovered it, bought all the State land around it and proceeded to build a town which resembled a western movie set He also built a paved landing strip which would accommodate jets.

His plan didn't work out the way he thought so he sold Lajitas to another millionaire who built fancy restaurants, hotels, swimming pools, houses and an 18 hole championship golf course. This, of course, is being done in a country where the most precious commodity is water. Worse still, there are plans to build 1,000 homes.

I first discovered Lajitas some 40 years ago and I fell in love with the place. There was little there but the old Lajitas Trading Post where the Mexicans from across the Rio Grande came on Saturday to buy their supplies. They would sit on the benches around the patio dance floor and drink beer and eat Serrano peppers.

In a pen next door was Clay Henry, the beer-drinking goat that drank every beer the tourists bought for him. He had the ability to hold a bottle of beer in his mouth and guzzle the whole thing in nothing flat. Often, I would find him glassy-eyed and hung over but he never turned down a beer.

One Sunday morning, I noticed the remains of a stand-up bass fiddle scattered all over the dance floor, the strings still attached. "What happened?" I asked the man who ran the place. "Nothing," He said. "Just our usual Saturday night dance."

"Did the bass player survive?" I asked. "I guess so," He said. "He wasn't here this morning."

I watch a lot of cop shows on TV and the usual cause of death of the victim is "struck on the head with a blunt instrument." I wondered if being struck on the head with a large bass fiddle would be regarded as a blunt instrument.

Clay Henry, the beer drinking goat has since died and as far as I'm concerned, Lajitas died too.

THE RICH HAD ICE IN
THE SUMMER AND THE POOR
HAD IT IN THE WINTER

In recent news accounts of the damage done by hurricane Rita, the folks over in East Texas are being referred to as living in "Caveman Days." They have no electricity, running water or gas, and heaven forbid—no ice.

Back in the thirties when I was a kid, we all lived under the same circumstances for years. Cavemen, we were not. The closest I ever remember to being in a cave was when Mama sent us all to a musty old cellar to escape what she called "Cyclones" that never happened.

I am thankful that the only hurricane she ever heard of was in Galveston in 1900. The old cellar wouldn't have helped us in something like that but we would have been stuck in there anyway.

We were pretty well used to most of what the folks in East Texas are suffering from today, because we had never known anything different. Eventually, they will get it all back but we didn't have it to get back.

Nobody ever brought us any food or ice. We raised nearly everything we ate but getting ice required somebody to walk to town and carry it back. That job fell to me. I would walk to the icehouse in Blanket, buy twelve pounds for 12 cents with a piece of binder twine wrapped around it for a handle to carry it with.

Depending on the distance involved, which was never short, the binder twine felt as if it was cutting my fingers off. I could change hands but I couldn't set it down in the dirt under any circumstances. Mama required dirt-free ice.

This ice, regarded as a luxury was not used to preserve food but was strictly for iced tea on Sunday. Iced tea was another luxury we didn't have often. The ice, when I finally got home with it, was wrapped in a quilt and used until there was absolutely nothing left but a damp spot. Then, if we had 12 cents, I had another trip to make and hope for an early winter.

Iced tea on Sunday was very important to us. We didn't have a whole lot to eat but the iced tea made it taste a lot better. It is the little things in life that make it worth living. Some folks today hadn't learned that yet but are learning it now. I, along with a lot of other people, learned it a long time ago.

I sympathize with the victims of the two hurricanes. They are suffering a lot of misery we didn't have but there is a light at the end of their tunnel. Our light was too dim to see.

I still remember when we got electricity. That 40 watt bulb hanging from the ceiling was our ray of hope of better things to come and made our coal oil lamp as extinct as the Prairie Chicken.

Then came the icebox and a man delivered the ice and stopped my trips to get ice and my hands healed. The Great Depression was coming to a close and Dad bought a refrigerator. Things were looking up.

Then came WWII and I was off flying on bombers, dropping bombs on Europe. I saw a lot but I never saw a hurricane. I'm glad I didn't.

I still like ice in my tea.

THE SEVEN DEADLY SINS THAT DOESN'T INCLUDE IRON SKILLETS

Long ago and far away a fellow by the name of Charles Panati, a Greek Monastic Theologian introduced eight deadly sins. They were; Pride, Envy, Gluttony, Anger, Lust, Greed, Sloth, and Avarice.

In the late 6th century, Pope Gregory the 8th cut out Avarice, leaving seven. Hardly anybody knew what it was anyway and they were not too sure about sloth. They thought it might involve dropping gravy on the front of their shirts.

Now, in the 21st century, we are back to eight again. The eighth one, as everybody should know is washing an iron skillet with soap and water. Young housewives today who live within 10 miles of a fast food place don't do much cooking anyway. It is doubtful that they even own an iron skillet. They have little worry about that one.

In my youth, the iron skillet was the principal cooking utensil. It was used for frying chicken, pork chops, eggs, sausage, cabbage, and even making chili. No soap was ever used to clean it for a good reason. From that day on, everything that was cooked in it would stick and required breaking loose with a hammer and chisel.

It didn't take long to find that out. Then, the skillet had to be "seasoned" again, no easy chore. It required burning out the skillet over a hot fire and other steps I won't go into. If you happen to be as old as I am, you already know how.

I do a lot of my cooking in an iron skillet. In fact, I own several of them in case I accidentally put soap in one. Our pioneers would have never made it to California without one. I couldn't fry an egg without one.

Whether or not the Greek Monastic Theologian or Pope Gregory the 8th had one, I have no way of knowing. Maybe soaping one up good was what Avarice was.

Over the years, I learned an easy way to clean one. Dump some salt and hot water in it and it scrubs up slicker than snot on a doorknob. I'm not even bothered with Sloth or Anger. My doctor thinks I'm using too much salt but he doesn't know what I'm doing with it.

I remember a story my old friend George Dolan wrote in the Star-Telegram years ago. A Texan had sent his daughter in New York one so she could cook chicken-fried steaks, a delicacy totally unknown to New Yorkers. It arrived broken in half.

He packaged up another and wrote on the package in large letters; "This package contains an iron skillet. Do Not Bend."

Breaking an iron skillet in half would be quite a chore. It might even be the 9th deadly sin.

Writing a humor column in these trying times is not easy, being fully aware that 500,000 people have lost their homes, their jobs and all they owned in Louisiana, Mississippi and Alabama due to nature's wrath. Many have lost their lives. About all I can do is try to bring a smile to somebody's face and maybe a laugh or two.

I'm sure things eventually will get better. The world will keep turning and life will go on, as it must, and always has.

THE UFOS ARE BACK
BUT MAYBE THEY NEVER LEFT

There was quite a bit of excitement in Stephenville on January 8 when a number of citizens were treated to nice aerial views of UFOs. Investigation of these UFOs is still ongoing.

To properly authenticate a genuine UFO sighting, three people are required. They must be seen by a farmer, a deer hunter and most important, a pilot. This requirement at Stephenville was properly met. Pilots, for some reason or other have become experts in the field of UFO identification.

This may date back to 1947 when a pilot, flying over Washington State encountered a whole flock. People everywhere have regularly sighted these unidentified flying objects since then and can relate their experiences without giggles or folks making circles with their hands over the teller's head.

Back when Jimmy Carter was running for president, he promised if elected, he would tell the American people what UFOs really are. This never happened. Actually, I don't think anybody was ever aware that Jimmy got elected.

I got a close-up look at a UFO while camped in a remote area of the Big Bend. One landed and parked behind my camper. The occupants, which I never saw, showed no interest in me. I think this sighting was in 1989 and they silently left without comment.

This sighting apparently caused no change in my life except a short time later, I was asked to write a column for the Bulletin. Anyway, not being a pilot, when I related my story nobody ever said "Awesome," or "Wow". They just changed the subject and went elsewhere. Had I been a licensed pilot, I might have become famous.

Roswell, New Mexico has made a business of UFOs with a big annual celebration to which folks come from thousands of miles to attend. It seems that a few years back, it was reported that a UFO crashed on a ranch near there. The government came up with some of the wildest and most ridiculous stories anybody ever heard to try to fool the citizens as to what it was.

Then, the story is, the Air Force came to the scene of the crash and removed the bodies of the occupants, flying them to the Wright-Patterson Air Base in Dayton, Ohio where they were placed in "Hangar 13" where, as far as I know, they still remain.

Then, there is the rumor that the government actually captured a UFO intact and keeps it at a secret base in the Nevada desert known as "Area 51." There, they are studying the thing in hope of finding out how it works.

They also are training our pilots to fly it along with three terrorists who somehow got past the FBI. This UFO may possibly be what the folks at Stephenville saw and the one I saw in the Big Bend area.

Erath County in which Stephenville is located is normally a quiet place with rolling hills and more dairy farms than any other county in Texas. Each cow, I'm told, can produce enough milk daily to supply a family of ten and enough methane gas that if converted into electricity to light a town of 39,000 residents and can be smelled for a distance of 6 miles on a clear day.

Maybe this is what attracted the UFOs. The pilot says to the copilot, "Whoooeee, what is that smell?" "Let's zip down there and look." The pilot says.

"It's coming from large 4-legged animals" The co-pilot says. "It might be best if we head for Area 51" The pilot says.

It might be best if we all did.

POKE SALET GREENS, SCRAMBLED EGGS AND ROSE BUSHES

There are certain advantages to writing a newspaper column which sometimes outweigh the disadvantages. During the past 8years, I have occasionally mentioned something that I never had when I needed it and wish I had some now.

Somebody sends it to me.

I have been sent Anasazi beans from Colorado, white doorknobs like we put in our hen's nests when I was a kid to choke the chicken snakes, 10 pounds of pinto beans from San Antonio and a supply of wooden spools to make spool tractors.

I once wrote about a brand of coffee that back during the Depression dad would put in the pot and boil it until it would take the hair of a good-sized hog. A fellow in South Texas sent me a pound of it. It didn't put hair on anybody's chest—it took all off.

In one of my columns recently, I complained that as a kid I was forced to take a dose of a horrible herb called Black Draught when I was trying to get out of going to school. What I wanted was the better tasting Baby Percy, which we couldn't afford.

The company that has been making this medicine in Waco since 1904 sent me three bottles. I didn't know it still existed. They didn't know I still existed either.

This year, I had plans to plant some okra in my garden. I couldn't find any packaged okra seed anywhere. A nice lady in

San Saba who reads my column agreed to look. She couldn't find any either.

Then, she had to go to Houston to consult a doctor who probably doesn't know what okra is. Her daughter who lives there ordered some red velvet okra seed from Washington State and had it sent to me. Then, the lady found some spineless seed in Houston and mailed it to me.

One of my favorite writers is James Lee Burke who resides in New Iberia, Louisiana. His books are hard to find. Having mentioned this to a nice lady who reads my column in Medford, Oregon, She sent me one in the mail I had been searching for.

Having written at times about poke salet we picked on the creeks back during the Great Depression to supplement our meals, a fellow brought me a big mess of the stuff last week. "My wife," He said, "Told me to get this stuff out of her rose bushes".

Out of curiosity, I looked up poke salat on Google, an internet search engine. They showed several recipes and recommended it be mixed with scrambled eggs for the full effect. Don't try this at home, folks. Leave it in the rose bushes. Times have changed since 1930.

Sometimes we wish for stuff which doesn't turn out the way we thought when we get it. An old uncle of mine, confined to a nursing home, had a fondness for a little nip now and then and made his desire known to his son.

His son would slip him a pint of the best brand on the market. One day, he told him, "Son," "Don't bring me any more of that high-priced whiskey. When I drink, I want it to burn all the way down."

Maybe like it did in 1930 when he put poke salat in his scrambled eggs. Maybe not. Some days, we eat the bear and some days, the bear eats us. In 1930, the bear gnawed on us most of the time.

As for the disadvantages of writing a column, I can't think of any except what Tom T. Hall said about guitar playing, "It don't pay much and it may lead to an early grave."

It hasn't yet.

DON'T GET UP A LOAD UNTIL YOU READ MY COLUMN

I just read on the internet that 2000 WWII veterans are dying daily. The last time I checked, it was only a thousand. I plan on being extra careful in the coming days. It sounds to me like they're getting up a load. I have always said I'm not going anywhere until they get up a load.

On the other hand, if you make a trip to the local VA Clinic to see a doctor, you may be forced to sit for as long as 2 hours. That causes me to wonder if their 2000 a day figure is right. I haven't noticed anybody missing. If they are getting up a load, it's not here.

I came in from Wal-Mart rather early one morning where I had been to buy a roll of gauze my lady-friend had ordered to bandage my various injuries I sustained from falling. I found a police car parked in my drive-way. I wondered what I might have done that they were just now finding out about. I also wondered if the statue of limitations may have run out on whatever I did.

The nice policeman asked, "Are you Linda?"

I said, "No, I'm Samantha. Linda lives next door."

"Well, He said, "She reported a large dog on her porch that refused to allow her to go to work."

"The dog lives next door," I told him. "He also plays loud rock music on his car stereo and eats all my high-priced cat food. I really don't like cats, I told him, but I'm trying to catch them so Animal Control can haul them off."

"As for the dog," I said, "You can have him. I don't want to go to work again—ever."

Then, we introduced ourselves. In think he had figured out that I wasn't really Samantha or Linda. I told him that I write a column for the Bulletin and he said, "Wow." Now I know who you are. You're the cat juggler." I said nothing.

Recently a nurse art the VA was taking a sample of my blood. "I read your column every week and I love it." She told me. Then, she busted my bubble. "Do you ever write about anything but fishing?" I'm still wondering whose column she reads and in what paper she reads it in.

One of my readers has expressed an interest in WWII bombing missions. That happens to be something I've had a lot of experience in. Some of the best times I ever had in Italy were on days when I wasn't on one.

Since WWII veterans are reported to be dying like flies and B-17 bomber crews might be included on the list, I'll try to write a column about it sometime before I kick the bucket.

I've had some rather exciting times watching those bombs drop. Actually, I know all the answers but nobody has ever asked me the questions.

I was released from the Army Air Corp in 1945 but nobody showed any interest in what I did until 50 years later. One day, a fellow asked me, "What did you do in the war?" "Well," I said, "Mostly I just chased girls and hung around USO dances."

"Do you still do that?" He asked. "No," I replied. "I can't do that now. There isn't a USO within a hundred miles of here."

THINGS THAT GO BOOM, WHISTLE AND BAWL IN THE NIGHT

Strange noises in the night are a regular occurrence at my house. I should have grown used to them after over 20 years of living here, but I haven't. I doubt that I ever will

There is a huge pecan tree on the northwest side of the house which drops limbs on the roof as big as crossties at regular intervals, sounding as if I were being attacked by rocket-propelled grenades. I dream that I'm somewhere north of Baghdad.

Cows bawling in the fields somewhere north of Vine Street sound as if they are in my back yard. At one time, I considered putting out bales of hay for them. Freight trains regularly rumble through in the middle of the night between my house and my neighbor's, whistling for the crossings that are not there.

There is a two story house on one side which may account in part for the strange reverberations in the night. It is hard to determine where the night sounds are coming from. Pickup trucks pulling trailers hit the large chug hole on Austin Avenue which has been repaired 18 times but is still there and sounds like the wreck of the Hesper.

My house, probably built sometime in the thirties is probably haunted, as most are by something. I have no idea who might have lived here, or who might have died here, scared to death by freight trains, bawling cattle, rocket-propelled grenades and pickup trucks hitting the same chug hole which was here 50 years ago.

I won't even mention the steady firing of heavy artillery guns through the night which I found out was teen-agers passing by with 5000 watt boom boxes in their cars on Austin with the windows down so everybody within a mile radius can hear it

All of whom are totally deaf.

At least, neither the living nor the dead back in the thirties had to listen to it, but unfortunately, I do. Nobody, as far as I can determine should live longer than the house they live in. It is only then that things go bad with strange noises haunting us in the dead of night.

I'm not a believer in ghosts and yet I'm sure I have a few prowling around in the attic at night, occasionally engaged in bowling or touch football. It gets pretty rowdy up there at times

My Chihuahua dog, Bitsy, has only lived here for a year but having far more acute hearing than I do, has the ability to discriminate sounds and know where they're coming from. She, being smarter than I am, ignores them completely. She knows there are no cows in the back yard or freight trains in the driveway.

But when she jumps up in bed with her ears straight up, I turn on all the lights, grab my gun and prepare for an attack by ghosts with rocket-propelled grenades while she crawls back under the cover and goes back to sleep.

I soon join her and listen to the cows bawling in the back yard and the freight trains whistling in the driveway and the bowling in the attic.

A man has to do what a man has to do.

TIME MARCHES ON AND SOMETIMES, IT JOGS

I suddenly realized I was getting old when somebody asked me what year I was born. Up until then, I had given it no serious thought. I had noticed that it takes me longer to get out of bed than it does to get in it.

A doctor once told me, "You'd better take care of yourself. It's getting harder and harder to get 1924 parts."

Then there is the matter of tying my shoes and trimming my toenails, both of which is getting to be harder than getting rid of Ted Kennedy. I assume that at a certain age our body reverts. I had the same trouble when I was four.

Another problem I have noticed is a sudden, almost overnight change in my appearance. With each passing day, I seem to look more like the pictures the police artists draw of serial rapists they can't catch.

Back when I was a kid, a fellow who lived in a rural area near Blanket used to walk to town, having no transportation. It was said that spring flowers wilted and died by the roadside as he passed by and he had to slip up on the water bucket to get a drink. I think I'm getting there. Small children grab their mother's skirts when I walk by.

My Dad always said exactly what he thought and though he bore no resemblance to Tom Cruise himself, he said; "I know that old boy can't help being ugly but he could stay at home." After all of these years, I can now sympathize with the poor fellow.

My friends try to give me some encouragement by saying, "You still look like you always did." If I did, I don't remember it. I can't believe I always looked like I do now. Besides all that, it is now politically correct to lie a little under certain circumstances if it will make somebody feel better.

I am sure that in the general scheme of things we are supposed to age and get ugly. This is to keep us from upsetting the balance of nature and give the young folks a chance. Speaking of balance, I have lost that too.

I am no longer permitted in stores that sell expensive glassware and I can no longer ride my bicycle because the streets are not wide enough.

I don't mean to complain and I'm happy that I have had the opportunity to stay around as long as I have and learn all the good stuff I've learned and meet all the nice people I've met and got shot at in a war on a daily basis. That was a real learning experience.

I figure that in another year I can go dove hunting without a gun and do what a fellow George Dolan once wrote about. I can just "ugly them to death."

My advice to young people who still have their good looks is to spend as much time in front of a mirror that you can. Stay home from work a couple of days if you can and get a good look.

It's all going to change and there's nothing you can do about it. Trust me—I know.

TO CATCH AN IVORY-BILLED WOODPECKER, TAKE A COAL OIL LANTERN AND A TOW SACK

I read recently somewhere that the search for the elusive Ivory-billed Woodpecker up in Arkansas has been called off until the leaves fall. They report spending around a million dollars looking for it and didn't find one yet.

I can sympathize with them on that. I spent a lot of time when I was a kid looking for a bird they called a snipe. It wasn't my idea and the only money we were out was for some coal oil and it cost a dime a gallon.

The older boys in Blanket, being cruel like they all were, would take the younger boys out and send them deep into the woods in the dark of night to catch snipes. Snipes apparently were hard to catch. We were furnished with a coal oil lantern and a tow sack and told not to come back until we caught a sack full. We didn't know how to get back anyhow.

Snipes, they said, were attracted to the light of a coal oil lantern. What we were supposed to do with them, I don't know but we never saw hair or hide of one, or feather either. This was usually done in the winter and we got cold and miserable out there with that lantern and tow sack.

Finally, when I got older and smarter, I found out there was no such bird in existence and never had been. It didn't even have the honor of being extinct like the Ivory-billed woodpecker.

By then, it was my time to join a group and send gullible kids off in the woods with a coal oil lantern and a tow sack to catch snipes. I had spent my time and I deserved to send somebody else.

Today, with TV, computers, video games, cell phones that take pictures and Lord knows what else, it would be nearly impossible to find any kids dumb enough to go snipe hunting. Anyhow, a coal oil lantern would be as hard to find as a snipe.

Still, there are a lot of smart grownups out hunting that woodpecker but they must be well paid. We didn't get a dime.

Anyway, we all learned what a scam was at an early age and the scammers today stay strictly away from us—what few of us there are left. There may be a few women around that can be scammed as girls were not allowed to go snipe hunting.

Just think what kind of story a girl would have told her mama, coming in a two in the morning carrying an empty tow sack and a coal oil lantern.

There are times when I think I would like to go back to the glorious days of my youth when we went possum and coon hunting at night with our old dog Ring and could cross any fence and hunt on anybody's land and they didn't care. I even might like to go out and try to catch a few snipes.

But, it won't happen and can't happen and I'd miss a lot of good things I have now like fresh vegetables the year round, no building fires in old wood stoves in the winter, a computer to write stuff like this on, and good people to read it.

If I just had a coal oil lantern, things would be fine.

MY WISH IS TO GATHER AGAIN FOR SOME ORGANIC FOOD AND A POT OF STEW

In today's hectic world, it can sometimes be a struggle for families to keep their togetherness. When I was growing up, we had no such problem. We were all "hunters and gatherers." We were always hunting something to gather. If it wasn't something to eat, we were gathering the crops Dad raised.

We gathered corn, maize and cotton in the fields. If we somehow got a Saturday off, we gathered in Blanket with other hunters and gatherers to check out who was doing what and see the latest fashions in overalls.

Back then, there was a song, often sung at funerals called "Shall We Gather at the River." From where we lived, it was too far to even consider. Blanket Creek was the best we could do.

Sometimes on Easter Sunday, my family would all gather there and cook a wash pot full of stew. It didn't cost much to make stew. Somebody always gathered up a bunch of stuff from somewhere. There was nothing better than a family gathering and a pot of stew.

Sometime later in our lives, Buck Owens, a country star recorded a song, maybe in our honor. It was called "To Gather Again." I once owned a 45 rpm record of it but I lost it somewhere. I'm bad about losing things.

So far, I've lost part of my hearing, some of my eyesight, my ability to jog and my checkbook. I spend a lot of time hunting my checkbook. I know a lady who is in constant search for her car keys. Finding them does no good. She immediately loses them again.

I have been reading a lot recently about the organic and whole food craze. I'm not too sure what whole food is unless it is organic food that hasn't been chopped up. I realized after reading about all this stuff that I was raised on it and didn't know it

We didn't have any pesticides or commercial fertilizer on the place. We also had no bugs. Bugs were introduced after the invention of pesticides. The motto of the firms that made the stuff was, "Spray it and they will come."

The organic food seems to be rather expensive. We didn't know that either. Folks are raving about "range-free chickens" these days. Our chickens were all "range-free." So were the kids, dogs, pigs and cows. We all ranged anywhere we wanted to go. I guess we even had "range-free" eggs.

As for whole foods, we had both whole chickens and whole hogs. In those days, nobody would settle for anything less than the whole hog. It was "whole hog, or nothing."

Our milk was from the "range-free cows," that were never given hormones or steroids. As far as I know, Ernest Allen's drug store didn't sell steroids. We had enough trouble keeping them fenced in as it was. As far as I know, there is nothing worse than a mad bull on steroids.

I'm glad to have grown up in an era where I was privileged to eat all that good organic food. I wish I had known it at the time. As for whole food, I did eat a bit of raw cabbage now and then and lots of raw turnips.

I have been thinking for all these years that we were behind the times back then. Now, I find out we were at least 80 years ahead of everybody today.

Some things are just plain good to know.

TOMATO PLANTS, SNOWSTORMS AND BOMBERS

My daughter managed to set out 17 tomato plants and 5 pepper plants before the snow storm hit. That takes some planning and frequent consulting with the weather bureau. I failed to do it last year, but then a hail storm wiped out my whole crop. I have discovered that when you get old, nothing works out right anyhow.

Don Graves of Arlington, a master gardener states in the Fort Worth Star-Telegram in an article by Amanda Roger, "If people knew how much trouble tomatoes are they'd never plant them." I agree but I just can't stop doing it.

Around the same time of the tomato planting, I had a problem with my computer. I consulted my son Ken who is a computer engineer in Phoenix. He fixed the problem by remote control but without my knowledge, put a password on it. The next morning, I couldn't get on it. It took awhile to find him to get the password. I was frantic. It was the day to e-mail my column.

I just read that the Collings Foundation is sending some WWII planes on a citywide tour as a part of the Collings Foundation's Wings of Freedom tour. The bombers consist of a B-24 Liberator, a B-17 Flying Fortress and a B-25. The B-24 is the last of its breed still in flying condition.

The planes were on display in Austin and Abilene. A fellow called me and inquired if I was interested in going to Abilene and taking one last ride in a B-17 for only $425 for a 30 minute ride. I had to decline. It seemed to me, to use an old boyhood expression that is "too much sugar for a dime."

If I had been paid that for every time I got in a B-17 during WWII, I would be richer than halfway across a cow lot. I just about lived in one for 2 years and sometimes slept in one.

I understand the reason for the $425 ride. These planes are expensive to maintain and it takes 40 gallons of gas to warm up the engines. In addition to this, food and lodgings for the crew is another expense. If you think our gas prices are high, try aviation gas.

Of course, if I had a choice of a ride in one, I'd take the B-17 every time. There were several B-24 groups in Italy within rock-throwing distance of our group and we had some good argument about which was the best plane. Maybe we even threw a few rocks. The B-17 crews called the B-24s flying goat sheds. Actually, they did look a lot like a goat shed with engines.

The B-17 is a beautiful plane and 28 of them in our group flying in formation against a blue sky would bring tears to a glass eye. I will always remember that sight. Another sight I will always remember is the big puffs of black smoke when the .88 millimeter shells exploded around our plane and the sound of the scrap iron in them hitting the plane. I was scared then and sometimes I'm scared even now, 60 years later.

My friend Hondo Crouch, the guru of Luckenbach used to say, "Don't forget memories." I don't think I'm likely to.

I think it's great that various organizations are keeping those old WWII planes flying to remind us that we won that war and a big part of what we won it with.

If we have won another since, I don't remember it.

TOO SLOW ON THE DRAW TO BE A GUNSLINGER AND TOO HONEST TO RUSTLE COWS

When I was about 8 or 10 years old, we lived on a farm about 3 miles east of Blanket. On every Saturday, Mama would give me a dozen eggs in a paper sack to take to town and sell. It was my spending money for the day.

I took them to Charley Baker's grocery where Charley's son Claude would take them to the back of the store where he had an apple crate with a hundred watt light bulb inside and an egg-size hole in the top. He would examine each egg carefully. If no spots showed up in the yolk, I was paid twelve cents.

Twelve cents in those days was all I needed for a big day on the town. I could have two ice cream cones at Macon Richmond's Drug store or one Baby Ruth candy bar. Then, I would have 2 cents left to ride Billy Chenault's bicycle to the Methodist church and back. What more would I want?

I never took the road directly to town. I meandered a lot. I would cut through the pastures where my imagination came into play. Imagination can furnish far more entertainment than anything in the world. I used mine a lot back then and still do.

I would imagine that I was a Comanche warrior sneaking through the brush, maybe on my way to attack a homestead somewhere. I might even kidnap a girl and take her to Monument Valley, wherever that was.

Just how I was going to accomplish this while carrying a dozen eggs in a paper sack, I didn't know. I had already been instructed by Mama not to break a single one or my goose would have been cooked.

I gave up that idea and decided I was the Marshall of Dodge City, on my way to clean up a mean town somewhere. There again, I would have trouble with that sack of eggs. I wasn't about to lose those eggs so I put my imagination to work again.

I was on a great adventure to deliver a dozen eggs to Blanket where Claude Baker was anxiously awaiting my arrival. After fighting off dozens of marauding Indians and possibly vicious mountain lions lurking in the brush, I finally made it with only a few scratches from dangerous mesquite trees.

I don't know how I would have ever grown up without my imagination, or how I could face adulthood without it. Our dreams come from our imagination. My brother Ray and I would sometimes play a game when our folks were gone, all from my imagination.

He would mix up a glass of water and syrup and have it ready on the kitchen counter. I would swagger in with a toy pistol on each hip; just like the movies we saw, slap a nickel on the counter and say, "Whiskey." I would quickly down the syrup and water and then ask, "Bartender is there any work around here?"

He would follow our script and say, "You might try the bar-nothing south of town. I hear somebody has been rustling their cattle."

"Cattle rustlers are my specialty." I would say. "I believe I'll just mosey on out there."

Child psychologist today may have more imagination than we did. They may say that our childhood behavior may plant a seed as to how we act in adulthood. I doubt that. My brother never was a bartender and I never was a gunslinger.

I was far too slow on the draw.

TRAFFIC CONTROL, SELF-CONTROL AND THE WORST DRIVERS ON EARTH

People do weird and unusual things all over the world on a daily basis. One only has to read a newspaper to see that. Brownwood, however, is unique. Our weirdness seems to be confined to our driving habits. Brownwood people are probably the worst drivers on the planet. There is a reason for this. We have no traffic control.

I can drive from my house on Austin Avenue to town and see from 5 to 10 traffic violations. Nobody cares. It seems to be par for the course. Drivers making left hand turns from the right lane seems to be acceptable. Driving 25 miles an hour in a 40 mile zone doesn't bother some drivers a bit. They even stop in the crosswalks, I guess to get a head start on the other slow drivers.

It does, however, bother most people, especially if they are driving in both lanes as they usually are, and nobody can pass. At the downhill side of the overpass approaching Fisk with the traffic light green, they slow even more causing everybody to have to stop.

Well, not quite—they don't. They go through that red light, to use an old country expression, like a dose of salts through a widow woman." Nobody cares. The sign that says "No Right Turn on Red" is completely ignored all over town. Nobody cares.

Drivers traveling east on 183-84 turn right at the traffic T and make a beeline across four lanes of traffic on Main heading for Fisk, even though the sign prohibits it. Nobody cares. The four-way stop sign at Parkway and Vincent might as well not be there. Few drivers stop. Few even slow down. Nobody cares.

Speed limits everywhere in town are completely ignored. I live in a 35 mile an hour zone and yet it sometimes takes me 10 minutes to emerge from my driveway without getting rear-ended or hit head-on by a driver doing 60. Nobody cares.

Parking on the street heading the wrong way is the way drivers do it in Brownwood. Parking large utility trailers with one wheel sticking out in the traffic lane is also apparently acceptable. Nobody cares. Stop signs cost the city thousands of dollars, yet in most cases drivers only slow a little. Nobody cares.

Traffic in our city has probably tripled within the past two years. The Chief of police wants more patrol cars. Where are the ones we already have? When I was a cop back in the fifties, we had two patrol cars—one for the north side of town and one for the south side

I will admit, our traffic was minimal back then. Each morning, the Chief would put a cigar box on the counter and inform one and all, "Boys, I want this cigar box full of tickets by noon. They are out there, you go catch them." Today, they are still out there but nobody is catching them.

We do have a lot of senior citizens in town who are in no hurry to get anywhere like the young folks are. They know from past experience that whatever place they may be going will still be there when they get there, if they get there without a traffic violator running over them.

They care and being one of them, I care too

TRAILER PARKS, USED CARS
AND THE STUDY OF BUGS

I might have been an entomologist when I grew up. By the time I was 6 years old, I knew a lot about bugs. I studied bugs, mostly because there wasn't much else to do. Due to the times I grew up in we didn't often get to choose our occupation. It chose us.

By the time I entered the military at age 18, I had worked at so many different jobs the military folks at the reception center were unable to classify me. They put me down as a "labor foreman," something I had never been. Of course, they knew nothing of my childhood study of bugs. Bug specialist would have been more appropriate and I might have made second lieutenant on the spot. They were always bugging somebody.

Maybe it was best I didn't become an entomologist. One of my nephews attended TCU on a football scholarship and graduated with a degree in entomology. He immediately started selling used cars and stuck with it until he made enough money to buy a trailer park. Maybe there was some connection between the study of insects and operating a trailer park and selling used cars.

When I was about five, I would ride my tricycle which my brother had built from parts found in a junk yard, right in the middle of an ant bed. I watched the ants while they watched me. I'm sure that this undersized giant on a machine which none of the wheels were the same sizes, smack in their middle of their home, created a panic.

Ants, it seemed to me, were in a state of panic most of the time anyway. They also got lost a lot. I have noticed ants carrying a load 8 times their size going around in circles trying to find the den which was only about two feet away. There is no doubt in my mind now that these were elderly ants.

I also became a tumblebug specialist at an early age. I was always curious of what they were going to do with the ball of manure they rolled over insurmountable objects for hours, going somewhere. I followed them until I found out.

They rolled the ball until they reached a haystack where the soil was soft and rich, laid their eggs on it, and buried it. When the eggs hatched, the baby tumblebugs had a supply of food for the winter. Maybe they then rolled up one of their own.

I also knew all about wasps, including red wasps, black wasps and the smaller variety we called yellow jackets. All were mean when disturbed. My buddies and I disturbed them at every opportunity, knowing full well we were going to get stung. It was all a part of our education in entomology though we hadn't a clue it was called that.

We made paddles from wood shingles and fought bumble bees. If we managed to win the battle, we dug up their nest in the ground and sampled their honey. It tasted awful. We decided they made their honey from blossoms on broom weeds, the same thing that made a cow's milk taste so bad.

We also studied doodle bugs. A doodle bug digs a hole in the soft dirt leaving a funnel-shaped depression. This was for the purpose of catching lunch. A stray bug of some variety would come by, fall in the hole and the doodle bugs ate it.

We would take a stick, poke it in the hole and the unsuspecting doodle bug would rush out to see what was for lunch. It was pure entertainment for us.

Like I said, we didn't have much else to do until we grew up and sold used cars.

WHEN OLD PETE PLAYED
THE TRUMPET

My dad, a fiddle player of sorts, contributed to our support back in the thirties by playing at country dances. Often, in the middle of the night, somebody would come to fetch him when their regular fiddler had fiddled the hair out of his bow, or got an overdose of the contents of somebody's quart fruit jar.

Although he disliked playing for dances, it could mean earning enough money from the contributions of the dancers to buy enough groceries to last us for a week. Country dances, in those days often went on until dawn. The "Great Depression" had a good hold on the country and its people, and a Saturday night dance provided both an emotional and physical relief from the hard times.

Dad would put on his clothes, tune his fiddle, and go, often not returning until the sun was well up. He never complained. In fact, I never heard him complain about anything. Few people did. They accepted life for what it was, the same way they accepted death. It was the way it was, and there was little they could do to change it.

The hair in dad's fiddle bow often became fiddled out too, even with a generous application of rosin, and had to be changed. He had the ways and means to do it, though his system is not used today. He took the hair from one of our horses tails, fitted it into the bow, tightened it up, rosined it good, tried a few licks of

"Wednesday Night Waltz," and he was ready for another Saturday night dance.

It was somewhat of a mystery to me how this was possible, as none of our horses seemed to be musically inclined. Obviously, they weren't aware of it either, but they seemed glad to make their contribution.

We had an old mule named Pete who may have had some musical ability. On more than one night, I heard him playing a trumpet, or perhaps a French horn, somewhere in the back of the pasture. At least, that's what it sounded like. Old Pete though, never played for dances. He never got the hang of "Wednesday Night Waltz."

I guess country dances ended when the Depression ended, along with the hard times we knew then. World War II came along, scattering folks to the four winds, ending the closeness they shared then and maybe the good times, along with the bad.

Farmers moved to town, neighbors became further apart, both in distance and in spirit. In the small towns air conditioning stopped neighbors from visiting on the front porches in the late summer evenings, plastic replaced horse hair in fiddle bows, and tractors replaced horses, pickup trucks replaced wagons, television replaced our old radios, and old Pete no longer played the trumpet in the back of the pasture.

Things are better now, they say, and perhaps they are, but the future is even more uncertain now than it was back then. We knew then that things couldn't get much worse, and could only get better. We no longer know that. The cycle always goes up, then back down.

Maybe it all started when we took the horses tails out of fiddle bows and started electing them to Congress.

TWELVE CENT GAS, NICKEL BREAD AND OUTRAGED LAWMAKERS

In reading the news on the internet, I noticed a headline proclaiming "Lawmakers Outraged." I didn't read what they were outraged about. Possibly being confined in a room with Ted Kennedy all day might do it. It would for me.

I try never to become outraged. It might possibly raise my blood pressure which is already getting close to the price of milk. I won't even mention the price of gasoline. It is best not to look at the pump when you fill up. The credit card company will let you know the total cost.

This permits you to pass out in the privacy of your own home instead of a service station driveway. You might get oil on your pants there.

I came pretty close to being outraged when I paid $1.78 for a loaf of bread. Mostly, I guess because I still remember when it was a nickel. This is progress? Of course, this was in a time when a nickel was hard to come by. Along about this same time, gas was 12 cents a gallon and everybody bought a gallon at a time.

The Legislature is going to put an additional dollar tax on a pack of cigarettes to educate our kids. Most likely, it will also prevent them from ever smoking. Believe it or not, I went to school too, and during the whole time, cigarettes were 15 cents a pack. I don't know where the school money came from. Cigarette money was pretty hard to scrape up even at that price and there wasn't a horse race track in Texas.

We tried various substitutes including grape vines, cotton leaves and cedar bark. There wasn't a fence post on our place that had any bark left on it. Dad never did figure out where all that bark was going. To tell the truth, their bite was worse than their bark.

Smoking anything was strictly prohibited by our parents. This probably contributed to our burning desire to do it. Any prohibitive substance attracts kids to it like deer to a peanut patch. Mama told me lots of times, "You stay away from Blanket Creek until you learn how to swim." I learned to swim there but Mama didn't know it.

When the price of oil goes up, so does everything else. All the stuff we buy in the grocery is hauled there by trucks and they use a lot of it. Then, the trucking companies have to pay their drivers more to buy that expensive bread and milk. It's a vicious circle and it doesn't take a rocket scientist to figure it out. As you all know, I'm not one.

I heard somebody say just the other day, "We have plenty of oil in Texas and plenty in Alaska but all the dipsticks are all in Washington." Sounds right to me. The Congressmen don't worry about gas because they don't buy any. A limo picks them up every morning.

I am sure that things will eventually get better. They always have with a few exceptions. When General George Custer rode over that hill and was confronted with 5000 Sioux, he said, "Maybe things will get better."

They didn't.

WAITING FOR A TRAIN
OR A SALESMAN TO LIVEN
UP OUR LIVES

When I was a kid, growing up in Blanket, Texas, things were generally pretty dull. We seldom ever got into what Mama called meanness. Actually, there wasn't much meanness to get into except what our fertile minds could think up. Somehow, we thought up some pretty good stuff.

Every day at approximately the same time, a Frisco freight train made its way through Blanket, headed for Brownwood and points west, or east. We had no idea where it was going and didn't care. It was there and we were there.

About three miles west of town, there was a railroad trestle which passed over the gravel road to Brownwood. Beyond the trestle, there was a hill which the railroad followed for about a half mile.

Today's diesel locomotives, sometimes five to a train would scarcely notice a difference in the grade.

Back then, the steam locomotives used by the Frisco, pulling a string of boxcars did. They huffed and puffed and often got down to a speed of five or ten miles an hour. It was this hill that our meanness centered on.

Back then, axle grease was quite common. Farmers used it to grease the axles on their wagons, or anything on the place that needed greasing. It was as slick, they said, as snot on a doorknob.

In a pinch, it was used to treat burns or cuts and bruises. Farmers are addicted to cuts and bruises.

My friends and I managed to get a whole can of the stuff somewhere, and riding our bicycles to the hill and stashing them in the brush, we greased the rails of that Frisco track with the stuff from the trestle to the top of the hill.

Then, we retreated to the brush by the track to wait for the train. When that steam locomotive hit that axle grease, the drive wheels spun and with steam and smoke belching from the smokestack, it made a sound that would warm the hearts of steam locomotive lovers from Peoria to the Mexican border.

We couldn't hear what the engineer was saying but we had a good idea. He would hit the sand lever to blow sand under the drive wheels and they would catch momentarily, then spin some more.

Finally, the train would top the hill and we made a beeline away from there. I assume that had we been caught, we could have been charged with numerous state offenses and a federal offense of interfering with national transportation. If the engineer had caught us, it would have been worse.

We had little entertainment but we took advantage of what we had. We would sit on a bench in front of Charley Baker's grocery watching what would happen when Charley lowered a canvas curtain down about three in the afternoon to shade the store. On the bottom was a heavy wooden roller.

Invariably, a salesman would alight from his car, misjudge the height of the roller, jump to the sidewalk from the street and the roller would catch him about the middle of his forehead. He would fall back in the street, knocked out cold as a cucumber.

Our three doctors, sitting on the bench in front of Ernest Allen's drug store across the street watched this too, being as interested as we were. After all, concussions were rare in Blanket and they needed the business.

A cold dipper of water usually brought the salesman back to life and all of us waited patiently for the next salesman to arrive, or the next train, to liven up our otherwise dull lives. We sort of liked it that way.

SOME MEMORIES OF WALKING DOWN DIRT ROADS

I was born within rock-throwing distance of a dirt road. I loved dirt roads then and I still have a fondness for them now. I loved to walk down a dirt road when I was a kid, barefoot as usual and feel the warm dirt between my toes. I loved to smell the spring flowers growing by the road and in the adjoining pastures as I walked by.

Today, dirt roads are fast disappearing and will never return. Folks who live on dirt roads today call their County Commissioner and tell him, "You've got to pave this road by our farm. The dust from the traffic is stirring up Grandma's asthma."

When I was a kid, Grandma didn't have asthma and there was no traffic. Wagons passing by didn't attain a speed of 70 miles an hour, or put out clouds of dust and invisible carbon monoxide. The carbon monoxide is most likely the cause of Grandma's asthma in the first place.

"From dust thou art and dust unto thou shall return" Where will we go without it?

Grandma didn't breathe the stuff in the air we all do today. Our environment has changed and dust is the least of our worries. We breathe industrial pollution 24 hours a day. It helps the economy but is hard on Grandma's asthma.

When I was a kid, I admit the economy was in a terrible shape but the air was clean. We traded the good things for the bad in order to exist in our present world. Grandma was known to go through about two bottles of Garrett's Snuff a week and in doing so, she may have breathed a tad of it.

Anyway, it didn't bother the rest of us or foul up the ozone layer above our planet and we could still walk down a dirt road if we wanted to and smell the flowers.

Sometimes I drive around searching for a nice dirt road but they are getting harder and harder to find. Due to my age, I can no longer walk as I once did. I can no longer go barefoot as the hot dirt burns my feet and stepping on one sharp rock might disable me for life. It's the price I have to pay for hanging around too long.

The Big Bend National Park, where the Rio Grand bends around the tip of Texas has miles of dirt roads. I have driven every one of them. They also have a pollution problem. At Park Headquarters at the base of the Chisos Mountains, there are days when the Sierra Del Carmen Mountains, thirty miles away are no longer visible. It is blamed on pollution blowing in from the East Coast, thousands of miles away.

Fifty years ago, it wasn't there. I know this because I was there. I'm sure back then I breathed air that nobody else had ever breathed. No dust to stir up Grandma's asthma if she had any, which is doubtful.

I will always have a love for dirt roads and keep trying to find one I can drive down in the quiet of the evening and smell the flowers and remember when the world seemed to be a better place.

I'm glad I was there.

I WOULD HAVE WASHED MY
HANDS IN THE BAYOU TECHE

One of my favorite writers, James Lee Burke, either lives in New Iberia, Louisiana, or has lived there over a period of years. Successful writers are hard to keep up with. He may live somewhere else now for all I know but he still writes about it.

Anyway, for years, he has written about the characters in that small town and I feel I should know them all. This is entirely acceptable and I'm guilty of doing the same thing. I like New Iberia and I like their hot sauce and Burke's characters.

However, I have never met or even seen on the street any of the characters he writes about. A few, I might not want to meet. I have never even been able to find his main character, Dave Robicheuax's bait shop where he rents boats, sells barbecued chicken, boudin sausage, fish bait and cold beer. It must be there somewhere on the Bayou Teche but I never found it.

By the same token, If James Lee spent a week in Blanket driving all over the place; he wouldn't find any of the characters I wrote about. They are all gone now except me. Some moved away, some died and some I don't know what happened to.

In spite of being older than rope, I still remember most of them. I remember our neighbor and his family that lived just up the road from our little farm when I was about five, or six. Some days, I would walk up there to play with their son Roy, who was my age.

If I happened to be there around noon, I was always invited to stay and eat dinner. I seldom ever did for what I thought was a good reason. Roy's dad was a stickler for hand-washing before dinner. Other than Roy, he had two daughters. He insisted that the whole bunch wash their hands before eating and that included me. I didn't see much use in it myself.

I couldn't think of a single thing I might have had ahold of all morning that would get my hands too dirty to eat with. I would just walk back down the road and go home. By the time I got there, anything we might have had for dinner was all gone.

Anyway, back in those days, we never had enough to require hand washing. I figured as long as I used a fork or a spoon, washing my hands was totally unnecessary. Even today, I have never noticed the owners of restaurants making everybody wash their hands.

Nobody then had a nice sink to wash their hands in like they do today. Hand washing required going to the windmill and catching a wash pan full to wash in. It was far too much trouble any way you looked at it for a five or six year old to do.

I never was invited to eat with any of our other neighbors because they had no kids my size to play with. As far as I know, the whole bunch may have washed their hands before dinner. I never heard any of them say if they did or not.

I don't know if my favorite writer, James Lee Burke, made his kids wash their hands or not. He has never mentioned it but I still wonder if he did. I guess if he did, they washed them in the Bayou Teche which was right behind their house.

I wouldn't have objected to that.

STICKING AROUND TO
WATCH THE BUZZARDS

Around March 15th for the last 50 years, a small town in Ohio welcomes the return of the buzzards. The name of the town is Hinckley, located about 20 miles south of Cleveland. As far as I have been able to determine, everything in Ohio is about 20 miles south of Cleveland. The map I consulted shows most of the state being "unoccupied territory."

Of course, I probably was looking at a map of Afghanistan. I do make mistakes now and then since my last birthday.

Anyway, the citizens of the town of Hinckley, according to an article written by Thomas Sheerhan of the Associated Press who actually found the place, are happy to see the return of the buzzards. Apparently not much else happens there. On the day of the buzzards return, about 3000 people attend a pancake breakfast to celebrate and watch the buzzards arrive. It is a festive occasion and T-shirts are available that say, "I saw the return of the buzzards."

It seems to me, under the circumstances, a covered dish breakfast might be more appropriate. Here in Texas, we are familiar with the habits of buzzards and we know what they do best.

In contrast to Hinckley's celebration, we have some folks in our own town who are not celebrating the flocks of buzzards that have taken up residence in trees around their palatial homes. No breakfast is being served or T-shirts sold in their neighborhoods.

The fact is they want them gone. They have called on various government organizations to do something about the situation. If worst comes to worst, they may even hire some lobbyists. As anybody knows, lobbyists can accomplish nearly anything and regularly deal with buzzards of various kinds.

Buzzards, from what I can learn from reading about them are migratory birds and are protected. Obviously, as far as their migratory status, they migrate from one neighborhood to another. I have never seen them all leave at one time and I have been here about as long as they have.

When I was a kid living on a farm northwest of Blanket, there was a large buzzard roost located on the Heptinstall place. This buzzard's roost afforded hours of entertainment to folks on Sunday who would walk over there and watch the buzzards.

In the spring there were hundreds of just-hatched snow-white baby buzzards in the nests. Seeing all these baby buzzards was better than staying at home doing nothing. Other than buzzard watching, our only other entertainment was climbing Salt Mountain.

There was no television and radio was in its infancy. If you possessed a radio, you might hear somebody blowing in a microphone and asking, "Can you hear me now?"

This all took place during what they called the "Great Depression." Much has been written about the Depression but as far as I know, nobody has ever written about how really dull it was. It was bad enough being poor but when things were so dull we had to watch buzzards that was really too much.

It is funny how certain things stick in your mind forever. I remember once my brother Ray had bought a really slick '41 Ford. He was demonstrating his driving skills to me on a country road when we drove through a flock of buzzards at about 70 that were having a dead sheep for breakfast

One of the buzzards was reluctant to turn loose of his breakfast and dropped a rather ripe leg of sheep in the middle of the windshield.

Yep, there are some things that stick to your windshield forever too.

ROADRUNNERS, VARMINTS AND A JUDGE WITH A HEART

I'm not a board-certified bird watcher. I don't drive all over Texas with a Peterson's bird book and a pair of binoculars. I can watch all the birds I want to while sitting on my back porch. Mostly, the reason I watch birds these days is that my neighbors all work and I can't watch them.

Even when I was a kid, I had an interest in birds and in the spring, I soon located every nest around our farm. I would watch their progress from the time the eggs were laid until the young birds hatched. I learned never to touch the nest, or the eggs or the nest would be abandoned.

Back in the sixties, George Dolan was writing a column for the Star-Telegram. He received a letter from a reader who stated he had never seen a baby roadrunner. I hadn't either and I decided to make a movie about these birds.

I put the word out and a fellow down on the Colorado River found a nest with eggs in it on an adjoining ranch. I would take my camera to the nest every Saturday, filming the progress of the hatching.

One day the fellow who owned the land caught me. I explained what I was doing. He wasn't interested. He told me in no uncertain terms to stay off his land.

Since I already had a lot of time invested and some expensive film, I wasn't about to quit. I found a different way into the place, hid my car and continued. One day, I found the nest totally destroyed. I don't know if the landowner did it, or some other varmint.

Then, a friend located a nest on his place with several young roadrunners in it, about to leave the nest. I rescued one, took it home, built a cage and raised it to maturity. I could now shoot all the film I needed.

I took the bird with me to the Big Bend area where I could film it in more picturesque surroundings. The bird would often ride on the steering wheel of my VW, frequently disrupting traffic when I stopped for a traffic light in San Angelo.

George Dolan wrote about my adventures with the roadrunner and my fame apparently spread to far off places. Since the roadrunner is a member of the Cuckoo family, George often mentioned the word Cuckoo when writing about me.

On one trip, I allowed my 14 year old daughter, Laura, to drive in a rather remote area. She had just finished Drivers Ed but had no license. Unfortunately, there was a remote highway patrolman in the area who gave me a ticket.

I was told that the judge I was to see in Fort Stockton was really rough on all law violators and I dreaded to present myself before him. The day came when I had to. I left the roadrunner at home.

He looked at the ticket as I stood before him, visibly trembling and said, "Are you that fellow that George Dolan writes about that chases roadrunners?" I admitted that I was.

"Son," He said, "If you will write me a letter explaining why you were letting your daughter drive and it suits me, I'll dismiss the ticket." I did and he did.

I later turned the roadrunner loose when the "call of the wild" started bothering him and he started making noises like somebody dragging a stick along a picket fence.

I missed him and I'm sure he missed the ground chuck I fed him for two years.

WATERMELONS, SWEET POTATOES, AND FREEDOM

Sometime, between Hoover and Roosevelt, my family starved out on one farm and moved to another. We were somewhat nomadic in those days, always seeking a place where the grass was greener and the crops grew better. To use an old country expression, we peed on the fire, called the dogs, loaded the wagon, and moved to a place called Gap.

Gap, once a thriving community before we moved there, was located in what folks called "the sandy land." It was well named. A good supply of sand was about all there was but grass burrs and bull nettles. The sand was hot to my bare feet in the summer, and even running as fast as I could through the grass burrs to escape their vicious stickers did little good.

The bull nettles seemed to have the ability to jump four feet and sting me as I passed by. Their only redeeming feature was that in the fall, they were loaded with nut-like seeds which were good to eat. These seed were impossible to pick without being stung. Considering the hard times we faced, we picked them anyhow.

The land produced three crops—watermelons, sweet potatoes, and peanuts. The watermelons thrived in the sandy land. Three Tom Watson's or Black Diamonds would fill a wagon bed. Our sweet potato crop would fill our cellar to overflowing.

The peanuts were harder to grow. They seemed to grow best among the bull nettles and grass burrs. They were tended, I always thought, by the devil himself. At maturity, unlike James

Bond's martinis, they were shaken, not stirred. It was necessary to pull up every plant and shake the sand off before the thresher came to remove the nuts from the vines.

We found it difficult to survive on watermelons and sweet potatoes. The watermelons played out in the late summer, and we were stuck with the sweet potatoes. We had fried sweet potatoes, baked sweet potatoes and sweet potato pie. Due to the high content of gas, we called them "music roots."

After a supper of these things, our living room often sounded like the Boston Philharmonic Orchestra was in the middle of a practice session. The only thing missing was the kettle drums. We also noticed that after a steady diet of sweet potatoes, our complexion was starting to turn a pale yellow.

I longed to be back where the black jack oaks grew and the squirrels barked from the tall pecan trees, and the dogs could chase something besides their tails.

Finally, dad decided that sandy land farming was worse than picking cotton, and we again peed on the fire, loaded the wagon, and moved back to our familiar haunts. Our diet was changed back to pinto beans and turnip greens and the Boston Pops went back to Boston.

We moved a time or two after that, always seeking something we never seemed to find, a better house, better land, and a better life It wasn't a good life, but it wasn't a bad life either. We had one important thing—freedom. It was the best thing we had. It still is.

WE HAD MOSTLY NOTHING
WHEN I WAS A KID,
BUT WE GOT 100% OF IT

Since I live alone, during the hot summer months, in order not to heat up my kitchen by cooking something, I eat a lot of ham and cheese sandwiches. Now, I have a problem. All of the sliced ham I can find has 98% of the fat removed.

A slice of ham with 98% of the fat removed tastes like cardboard. Cardboard doesn't go with cheese very well. I have even tried frying the stuff but it sort of curls up and goes away. Putting a lot of mustard on my sandwich helps a little but actually, the taste comes from the mustard, not the ham.

There was a time, some 2 or 3 years ago when I would buy a ham butt that weighed around 7 pounds, smoke it on my smoker and I had a good supply of ham that hadn't been messed with. Of course, they always injected it with water to make me think I was getting more ham than I actually got.

The producers of ham and bacon found out years ago that the general public was easy to fool. Give them 12 ounces for a pound instead of 16 and they'll never notice. Being an old country boy, I noticed it right away.

Another thing I noticed was that the butts I was buying kept getting smaller. As a matter of fact, so did mine. The human body has to have a little fat to survive. If it doesn't get it from the usual source, it starts taking it from some other place.

You may first notice it after watching TV for 2 hours in your favorite chair and find you can't get up to get another beer, or the beverage of your choice. You have lost 98% of your fat, along with about 50% of your muscle tone. Depending on your choice of beverage, these figures may not apply.

I have read that Eskimos eat a lot of whale blubber. I assume that is fat. No mention was made of their cholesterol levels. Maybe they keep it down with exercise. After all, catching whales isn't easy. I do admit though that I know practically nothing about Eskimos or catching whales or eating blubber.

I have found no blubber in our stores. Even if they had it, I'll bet 98% of the fat has been taken out. I wonder what might be left. Probably about the same as in a slice of the ham they sell.

I grew up in an era that when "hog killing time" came around in the fall on the first cold day, we ate everything but the squeal and it was sold to General motors to put in their Chevrolet brakes. Nobody ever heard of cholesterol, either high or low.

Nobody ever pumped water into the hams or took the fat out of the sausage. Our ham butts remained the same size as when they came off the hogs. Ours, best I remember, did too.

Like the Eskimos, we got plenty of exercise picking cotton, gathering corn and heading maize, not to mention plowing and planting. What little we had to eat was 100% all there.

We are referred to today as "The Greatest Generation." If we were, it was because we had to be to survive.

Nobody, I guarantee, would have taken 98% of the fat out of our ham.

WEAVING A WEB
WE CAN'T GET OUT OF

We are all living in the computer age. There is nothing we can do about it. We can't beat them, so we might as well join them. Join them, I did, some seven years ago. During this period, my computer has been replaced once, and been updated more times than Alan Greenspan has updated the interest rates.

From what I read in the papers, I'm still running about as far behind as a Senior Citizen in a 20K race. There is no way we can keep up with modern technology. Such advances are mostly for the purpose of making more money for the software and computer manufacturers to enable them to pay Alan Greenspan's higher interest rates.

Computers are fun. I'm totally hooked. I can search for any subject I want to know about, and some, I don't. News is available from several sources and it's possible to learn that Victoria no longer has a secret. Without my computer, I would be back to writing with an old Underwood typewriter that went through ribbons like a dose of salts through a widow woman, to use an old country expression.

E-mail is great too. It has been responsible for bringing back old jokes that I haven't heard since we used to gather behind the outhouse at Blanket High School when I was about ten. It has its downside too. People have lost the ability to write letters, and possibly their ability to think, or pay scarcely any attention to what is happening in our world.

Hardly a day goes by that I don't receive stuff of no consequence which has been "forwarded" from hundreds of people I don't know who obviously have the brain cells of lemmings, those little rodents that annually commit suicide by jumping in the ocean.

Home computers are time stealers. They steal time that we might be using to wash the dishes, make the beds, mop the floors, or spend with our families. Psychologist say they are turning us all into social outcasts. We might as well be living in a cave somewhere as far as our visiting friends or taking part in community activities. We are hooked, but we hooked ourselves.

I learned long ago to never be actively engaged in cooking while on the internet. Whatever we might be cooking is going to be burned blacker than midnight in Moscow. Actually, the house could catch fire and we might not notice it until the roof caves in. What we are afflicted with is the "Internet syndrome." There is no known cure.

I'm thankful, in a way, that I grew up in a world without these infernal machines. I learned things I would never have learned staring at a monitor. I learned to appreciate nature, and to take the time, as they say, "to stop and smell the roses." I learned to appreciate the companionship of friends and good neighbors. I learned of the healing qualities of walking down a country road, or skipping rocks on a creek, or simply lying on my back on a creek bank watching the white clouds move across a blue sky. Sure, I can I can still do these things, but heck, I might miss something on the web.

Well, I agree the war is over. We finally got them fighting amongst (I love that word) themselves and our help is no longer needed. Halliburton won the Toyota dealership to replace hundreds of junkyards full of those that were blown up.

We are currently looking for a new enemy to invade and right now, Iran looks good. We may give them their very own nuclear bomb on the city of their choice, dropped from 30,000 feet.

IT TAKES A LOT OF SPACE
TO BE A GENUINE TEXAN

I have a good friend who lives out in West Texas. Actually, he lives in what might be termed one of the worst parts of West Texas. Sandstorms in the spring and fall block out the sun for days. When the sand is not blowing, there's nothing to look at anyhow but last spring's tumbleweeds.

He recently told me that his sister was coming for a visit from California, bringing another lady with her who is a native Californian who wanted to "see Texas." "If a sandstorm is blowing, I told him, the first thing she will say is, Lord, I always thought "The Grapes of Wrath" was fiction"

When Lyndon Johnson was president, the first lady whose name happened to be Lady Bird was trying to get rid of billboards which littered the highways blocking out the tourist's views of Texas. It was rumored that she made an exception to that area so the folks out there would have something to look at.

Being born and reared in East Texas where the tall pines reach to the sky and the grass grows green and then being a long-time resident of the Hill Country where the bluebonnets grow so tall they hide the beer cans in bar ditches, Lady Bird was perhaps a bit prejudiced wanting to take down those billboards. I did agree with her though.

We have all viewed some unlovely parts of West Texas while on our way to somewhere else. Most have never considered actually living there. The folks who do live there are victims of circumstance. They either went there to drill for oil or to furnish the folks who drilled for oil the necessities of life which consisted mostly of beer and a place to fight.

Some had homesteaded their land long before oil was discovered and found a place in their hearts for this rugged country and chose to stay for a lifetime.

Then, the oil booms played out and the roughnecks moved on, leaving a lot of nice and friendly people who live there today. They weather the sandstorms and the tumbleweeds and turned the honky-tonks into churches. They are a close-knit people who look out for each other and welcome anybody into their fold.

Still, West Texas, compared to a lot of other places is pretty raunchy looking country. Most likely if your car broke down anywhere near Big Spring, you'd stay just long enough to get it fixed and drive on to where the grass is greener and the bluebonnets grow tall.

You might be passing up something really good that won't be found anywhere else in Texas. Where else would a friendly neighbor come over and help you shovel the sand out of your garage or pull the tumbleweeds out of your fence?

Drive-by shootings, car-jackings and muggings are rare and people out there just borrow stuff in the daytime instead of stealing it at night. They bring it back too.

In West Texas though, the hearts of the people are as big as their blue skies and when the sand is not blowing, one can see almost into tomorrow, which, if you happen to live there, looks better than yesterday.

Having once lived in the area until the Korean War broke out and the army reserve yanked me away and took me to far off places, there will always be a place in my heart for the people and the wide open spaces of West Texas, dust storms and all.

After all, it takes a big state and a lot of variety to make a genuine Texan.

WHEN MODEL T. FORDS BOUNCED AT FIVE DOLLARS A DAY

I guess 1924 was a good year since it was the year I was born. There were a lot of Model T Fords around then and they were almost indestructible. I'm still here but most of them are gone and we all thought Henry built them to last forever.

I remember once when I was a kid, I caught a ride with somebody in a Model T. As we were going down the hill from the school where we had attended a basketball game, the Model T in front of us suddenly stopped. We hit it in the rear at about 20 miles an hour and all we did was bounce.

The Model T's had no bumpers but they did have the front wheels extending from the fenders. Those high pressure tires hit that car and nothing happened. I guess they were sort of early air bags. No insurance claims were involved because nobody had any insurance in those days and no damage was done.

Now, progress seems to be going backwards. Cars these days have no bumpers either and some of the more expensive models have gone back to 30 inch tires and wheels exactly as old Henry's Model T's had. They do have air bags though to protect the driver and passengers as some of these cars disintegrate when hitting a brick wall at 5 miles an hour.

Mr. Ford's cars were all built in Detroit from heavy steel and he paid his employees the unheard of wage of $5.00 a day. Not once, as far as I know, did he consider moving his factory to China. Even with the high wages he paid, he made money, selling the cars for $600 or less. Besides, nobody knew for sure where China was.

When I was a kid, green as a gourd and living on a farm, I was told more than once if somebody dug a well a little too deep, they hit China. I have listened with my head in a well numerous times to see if I could hear anybody speaking a strange language.

The only strange language I ever heard was while hanging around the garages in Blanket. If a wrench slipped off a nut and the mechanic took the top off his knuckles on a hot engine, he said words I was not familiar with. I tried to learn them all in case I grew up to be a mechanic. I found out later they came in handy in several different occupations I later had.

I never got far enough along to ever be Vice-President but from what I recently read, I'm convinced that ours hung around garages a lot. No education is complete without at least spending one day in a garage.

Still, I guess the times we live in today are somewhat better. No longer is anybody paid $5.00 a day or $5.00 an hour either for an honest day's work. We now have the minimum wage law. Still, some folks won't work for any price. With the help of our generous government, they no longer have to.

For some reason, I missed out on all of the good deals during my working years but I don't mind. I'm still here and the Model T's are gone. 1924 was a good year.

WHEN THE LAW WORE A COLT .45 AND THE CRIMINALS HAD NO RIGHTS

I have always been proud of Blanket, my old home town. When I lived there, crime was unheard of and all the good folks I knew hadn't yet died. I have written books and columns about it. Now, I find frequent news stories of various goings-on that nobody then would have approved of.

Occasionally somebody takes a shot at somebody else over some type of family argument, sometimes resulting in a fatality. Nothing like that happened 50 years ago. Nobody ever got arrested for running a meth lab or otherwise doing something illegal within the confines of Blanket. Now, they do

It is my fervent hope that a stray shot doesn't hit a mule. Mules have far more character than some of the folks living there now. There are still some good people living in Blanket but being good doesn't make headlines these days.

My dad was City Marshall and later Constable there for a number of years. No way would he have put up with law breaking. He wore an old Colt .45 thumb buster on his hip and folks didn't mess with old "Matt" Marlin.

W.A. Middleton who was then Chief of Police in Brownwood gave dad a siren which he mounted on his 1950 Chevy and now and then, he would turn it on and drive the streets of Blanket so folks would know he was still there.

When he passed by, young children grabbed their mother's skirts and hound dogs ran under the porches and cows hiked their tails and headed for the barn. This was long before law officers had to read criminals their rights and indicate they could keep their mouths shut and promise them a lawyer if they didn't have one.

Back then, criminals had no rights and if they needed a lawyer, it was up to them to get one. The tax-payers sure didn't hire them one. It was a good system and it worked, only to be changed by a Federal Judge over in East Texas.

Today, we have more criminals than we do Federal Judges and we have a lot of those. Mostly, they make laws instead of interpreting the laws, causing criminals to have more rights than the law officers. The law, today, is difficult to enforce with too many restrictions on the enforcers.

I'm glad Dad didn't have to worry about things like that back then but knowing him, I'm sure he would have ignored it all. He was a rather stubborn fellow from the "old school."

He once arrested the engineer and the conductor on a freight train for blocking the crossing in Blanket over five minutes in violation of the law. A Justice of The Peace in Brownwood dismissed the charges, for whatever reason I don't know, but the train crew got the message. They didn't do it again.

He lived for 92 years in and around Blanket and the most distant point he had ever been was Littlefield when I took him to his sister's funeral. He liked Blanket and he stayed there. He warned everybody that the bank was about to be closed and nobody believed him. "That banker," He said," Is spending all your money" He was right.

In his declining years, he drove to Brownwood every week to visit his friends in the courthouse. Sometimes, he got confused and entered the wrong side of the four-lane divided highway. In the interest of safety, somebody would call the highway patrol.

They would locate him, pull him over and say, "Jesse," You're driving on the wrong side of the road again" His standard answer was always the same, "Well," I pay taxes on both sides."

He was right about that as he was about nearly everything else. His last words to me at the Brownwood hospital were, "Harry," My string is running out." He was right again.

Where Is Everybody Going?

I would love to do a survey on the traffic that passes my house on Austin Avenue to find out where everybody is going in such a hurry. I'm led to believe that I'm missing something important somewhere. I don't go anywhere much except to the grocery store and when I get there, they're not all there.

I thought for awhile some were late to work, or just getting off but it goes on all day. I'm aware that we have firms here that work different shifts but do they work on 15 minute shifts? The police department seems to have regular shifts and don't drive up and down Austin all day at 65 to 70 miles an hour.

The fact is I seldom see a police car pass by. From reading the police reports in the paper, I assume they are all congregated in a particular area where the domestic fights occur and the drug business is located. Somehow, these two offenses seem to be connected. Obviously, they take a hit on a big doobie and beat their wives.

When I was a cop, back in the dark ages before crime was introduced by TV showing "Law and Order" and "Forensic Files." and "48 Hours", there wasn't much crime. "48 Hours" is the show where when somebody gets murdered; the police are required to solve the crime within 48 hours. This seldom ever happens except in Memphis and Miami.

Our police department in the fifties wrote a lot of speeding tickets, not having much else to do. Every morning the Chief would place a cigar box on a desk and indicate in no uncertain terms that he wanted the box full by noon.

Today, with a couple of trips down Austin Avenue, it could be filled by nine. He would say, "They're out there—go get 'em." They're still out there but nobody seems to be getting them. Maybe they're outrunning the police cars.

WHO KNOWS? CHICKEN LITTLE MAY HAVE BEEN RIGHT

Back when I was a kid growing up in the thirties when folks said "times was hard," we always had a lot of chickens. They probably saved our lives. We always had fresh eggs and when kinfolks arrived unexpectedly as they always did, we had fried chicken for dinner.

Mama would take a long piece of wire with a hook on the end and quickly catch an unlucky fryer. She would just as quickly wring its unlucky neck, scald the feathers off and before the chicken even knew he was among the missing, he would be frying in an iron skillet.

To complete the meal, she would cook up a big batch of biscuits, open a can of corn, slice up a big onion, make a skillet of gravy and she could feed the National Guard. Depending on the number of kinfolks who had arrived unexpectedly, she might do two chickens, make two skillets of gravy, and slice up two big onions.

As usual, the grownup kinfolks got the pulley bones and the breasts and the kids got what we called in the military service, "Air Corp Chicken"—all wings and tails and stripped for action." In my entire youth, I don't recall ever getting a pulley bone when company was present. As far as I knew, our chickens were totally devoid of breasts.

When I started to school in the first grade, which was as low as one could start back then, we all heard the story of Chicken

Little. I'm not sure if Chicken Little was a little chicken, or a full-grown chicken suffering from mental incapacity.

Anyway, the story was that Chicken Little was standing under an oak tree one day when an acorn fell on his head. He immediately ran through the chicken yard yelling, "The sky is falling." The other chickens, being somewhat smarter, totally ignored him.

Being born and raised on a farm, I ignored the story too. Still, it was apparently an important part of our education, not to be taken lightly, along with Goldilocks and the three bears.

I heard a story once which involved Chicken Little, a kindergarten teacher and a little girl about three. The teacher was telling her class the story of Chicken Little. "—and when Chicken Little told the farmer that the sky was falling, do you know what the farmer said?" She asked the little girl.

"Holy shit, a talking chicken "she replied.

Makes sense to me. I didn't believe it either, which proves to me that kids are getting smarter these days. I'll bet she didn't believe that about Goldilocks and the three bears, or Little Red Riding Hood and the Big Bad Wolf either.

These days, our politicians regularly tell us bigger stories than that and it seems to me that a good part of our population believe them. The sky is falling? It just might be.

GREASING THE WINDMILL
AND USING UP THE WIND

Back when I was growing up in the middle of the "Depression," any kind of job was hard to find. My family was lucky. We lived on a farm and I learned at an early age, jobs never end on a farm. I also learned that nobody, as far as I know, ever starved to death on a farm.

Another good job, if you didn't live on a farm, was "windmill fixing" Every farm in Brown County had a windmill. Having a reputation as a windmill fixer guaranteed steady work to any man who could do it.

Windmills require greasing at least once a month. Somebody had to climb that tower, stand on that little platform and take a handful of axle grease and grease the gears. Hardly anybody wanted to do that because heights made some folks dizzy and the grease made the rungs on the ladder slick. The trip down was worse than the trip up.

There was one person on the place who actually wanted to climb that windmill and that person was me. On more than one occasion, my folks would go to Blanket on Saturday and I'd find some excuse to stay at home. As soon as they got out of sight, I would head for the windmill. As the wagon drove away, Mama gave me a final warning; "Stay off that windmill."

A couple of times I managed to reach the platform but getting on it seemed beyond my expertise. And then one day—I made it.

I could see for miles. It was like being on top of the world. I knew I had accomplished something worth telling everybody about but I couldn't say a word.

I felt like Columbus when he returned from his voyage. "Where did you go, Columbus?" Somebody would ask. "I don't know," Columbus would answer, "But it sure was pretty."

Windmills had other problems besides needing greasing. The leathers would wear out on the pump, located on the bottom of the well, or a sucker rod would break. It took a good man knowing what he was doing to fix it. To be known as a "damn good windmill man" was among the highest compliments a man could get back then.

I like the sounds windmills make and they never seem to be totally silent. They can lull us to sleep at night and wake us in the morning. Nobody who has ever lived on a farm will forget the sound.

Although our water-pumping windmills are disappearing, we now have hundreds of those huge electricity generating windmills marching in rows across our horizons. Their capability for furnishing electricity is unbelievable according to their brochures. Nobody in the areas where these things are operating seems to have any idea where the electricity is going. One source said it was all going to Florida, or maybe North Dakota.

I heard a story that I don't know is true or not but I like it. It seems that residents in one small Texas town sued one of those large windmill corporations "For using up our wind." The corporation, after conducting various tests concluded that used wind worked as good as the unused kind for any purpose wind might be used. The case was dismissed by a judge as being "frivolous." "Texas," the judge said "probably has more used wind than any place on earth."

Regardless of that and who gets the electricity generated by these things, the employment possibilities are practically unlimited to any half-way good windmill man.

One thing we know; every one of those things has to be greased every month.

WHEN THE COTTON BLOOMS, WORRY ABOUT THE PEACHES

I have a friend who lives out in West Texas who spends a lot of time from January to September worrying about the cotton crop. Every drop of rain that falls is carefully tabulated against what will be needed to get those cotton plants up.

Not only does he worry about droughts but he worries about getting too much rain which might in some way have an effect on the tender cotton plants. I really don't think he gets a good night's sleep until the cotton is blooming.

What is puzzling about this is the fact that he is retired and doesn't raise cotton and never did. If the entire West Texas cotton crop was wiped out by some act of nature, including cyclones, it wouldn't affect his income or his lifestyle one bit.

Still, he has many sleepless nights worrying about that cotton crop until it is harvested, ginned, and sold to China, or whoever they sell it to.

Since he and I were born in the same era and lived through the Great Depression, I understand his feelings perfectly. As for worrying, I'm booked up until around September myself. Every year, among other things, I worry about whether the peach crop at Fredericksburg will be successful.

I don't really know why. I have never bought a Fredericksburg peach in my life. I don't even like peaches. They are far too acidic for my taste. Still, I would be devastated if they all froze out. Occasionally, it does happen and I feel bad about it for days.

I have noticed that when I happen to be in the area during pcach season, the tourists are buying every peach in sight. Any enterprising soul could buy a load of peaches anywhere in the state, back his pickup in the bar ditch near Fredericksburg and sell the whole load in 10 minutes at a premium price. I'm sure it has probably been done.

Tourists, I have noticed, will buy anything if they are at least 50 miles from home. I once saw a fellow in Fredericksburg pay $200 for Grandma's old rocker that she threw away in 1924.

I really don't know why but neither I nor my friend has ever worried about the cantaloupe crop at Pecos. I guess we really should. I know we both like cantaloupe. Maybe next year, we'll save a little time for the folks at Pecos. We can do that after the cotton blooms and the peaches are past freezing at Fredericksburg.

Back during WWII, the Air Corp had a bombardier training school at Pecos. As a result of this, every bombardier I ever met hated Texas. All they ever saw of Texas was Pecos. I never heard any of them say one word about cantaloupes.

It seems that after we all age a little we start worrying more. We go to the doctor for a checkup and worry about what he tells us. Actually, it's what he doesn't tell us that cause us to lay awake at might. We know, beyond a doubt, that he's withholding something.

There is one thing in regard to my health that I no longer worry about. Some 4 or 5 years I ago, I was sitting on a bench in the mall listening to two old men discussing something. I'm not sure what it was but one told the other, "If you're past 70 and you ain't got it yet, you ain't gonna get it."

I'm past 70 and whatever it was "I ain't gonna get" makes me feel a lot better.

Now, I can worry about the cantaloupe crop.

WRITING A COLUMN
AND MILKING COWS
ON THE OVERPASS

Writing a column for a newspaper is like milking cows on a dairy. About the time you think you're through, you have to do it all over again. It can be a pretty hard row to hoe, maybe even worse than milking but somebody has to do it.

To make matters worse, a few folks around here don't believe what I write. A doctor I know here refers to me as "The biggest liar in Brown County."

He may be right but he's not old enough to prove it. I have reached what is known as "The age of incontestability." I no longer have to prove what I write. I can lie all I want to as long as I don't steal it from somebody else. That, I think, is called promiscuity.

Having reached the age that I am, I have a lot of respect for anybody older than me, whether they lie or not. I just read in the Bulletin where a fellow 86 years old was driving home from feeding his cows when a fellow being chased by the police ran a stop sign and hit him.

I have a lot of respect for that man for two reasons. He is contributing something to us all by raising cows. At age 86, he is still able to drive his pickup and go out to feed them. He and men like him are what made Texas the great State it is today.

I have never won a Pulitzer Prize for column writing, or anything else. I'm still hunting for the prize in the bottom of a box of Crackerjacks I bought when I was about eight. About all I have accomplished is getting old and a lot of people do that.

Several years ago when I first started writing a column, Gene Deason, the editor, told me; "one thing you have to avoid is repetition." Gene was a lot younger at the time and wasn't aware that with age comes repetition. We can't avoid it.

Otherwise, we wouldn't start every conversation with, "Did I ever tell you about the time I—?" This is known as one of the best ways to break up a mob or send your guests home early. Only last week, a friend told me six times about how the transmission went out on his truck on the Bill Monroe overpass.

I have an advantage over the regular columnists at the paper. They have other duties which include writing news stories, feature articles and taking pictures. The editor, of course, has to supervise the whole bunch and warn them about repetition.

I don't have to do any of that. I just sit in the comfort of my own home and try to think of something to write before the deadline. Actually, that's what I'm trying to do now while thinking of a dairy I might be able to find employment with.

Sooner or later, maybe I'll think of something to write, but up to now, I haven't. I've still got a few days to think of something before I have to send it in. In the meantime, my transmission might go out on the overpass or I might get a job on a dairy.

Somebody in a week or so is going to tell me, "I tried to read your column last week but it didn't make any sense."

It didn't to me either.

SEPARATED RIBS AND WRITING
ONE SENTENCE PARAGRAPHS

Writing a column every week can sometimes become a chore. My present condition makes it a lot worse. Two weeks ago, I fell on my laurels while trying to get to the phone before it stopped ringing. I didn't have to do that. The answering machine would have kicked in giving me the message on how I could obtain a nice medical insurance policy for practically nothing.

I could use one since, according to my Doctor; I "separated" my ribs when I fell. He didn't say how many I separated but I'm of the opinion it was all of them. I have been in constant pain since it happened and nothing seems to help. If I take the pain pills I received, I suddenly don't know if I'm washing or hanging out. I can only hope that sometime soon the ribs make up and go back together. My entire social life has been ruined, what there was of it.

Other than running to answer a telephone, there is another thing one should not do. Never chase your hat on a parking lot when one of our gentle breezes blows it off. Somebody will always chase it for you. Texans love to chase hats. I have seen at least three people chasing one hat. They bring it back with a triumphant look on their faces like they just made the winning touchdown in the last thirty seconds of the game.

Just writing a column every week, as I said, can be a chore. A fellow down in Houston who is currently 83 years, old writes three columns a week. He has been doing this since who laid the chunk.

I read his columns, and I have noticed that he writes a lot of one sentence paragraphs, making it appear that he is writing a lot more than he actually is. Another columnist I know, out in West Texas writes his whole column in one sentence paragraphs.

I have tried that with the Bulletin and somebody down there lumps it all together and I don't wind up with much. I don't know a whole lot about grammar. The day they studied grammar at the Blanket school, I had to finish up picking the cotton on the lower forty.

I have though, received a lot of advice about it over the years from various folks all over the country. I have noticed that people in the Northwest who read my columns on the internet don't know what I'm talking about most of the time. They don't understand "Texan."

Other than Larry L. King who lives in Washington D.C. and was born and raised at Putnam, I don't think I have a single reader east of the Mississippi. That suits me fine. Larry, a distinguished writer in his own right is enough for me. By that, I don't claim to be either distinguished, or a writer. I can't even write one sentence paragraphs and get by with it.

Larry was recently presented with a Lifetime Achievement Award in Austin at the Texas Book Festival. He refers to it as the "One Foot in the Grave Award." My advice to him is to never separate his ribs or he will get a lot closer. He invited me to the festivities but I didn't go. There are no parking places in Austin.

A newspaper columnist can't afford to get sick. The newspaper is not going to leave your spot vacant. They're going to put some other dude's stuff in there. Once that camel gets his head in the tent, you're gone.

You will be lucky to find a job writing one sentence paragraphs for a little paper in West Texas.

YOU AND ME AND US AND THEM AND BOBBY MCGEE

I was around during the "hippie" days in the sixties and early seventies. In fact, I was around long before talk radio and TV. Actually, it was rather nice then. Sometimes, you could hear real music.

The young folks were prowling the Southwest in old VW vans in the sixties and seventies and had an aversion to work. I wasn't crazy about it myself but I liked to eat.

I too, had an old VW van and done a little prowling of my own. I was often mistaken for a hippie and I did like their idea of freedom but I couldn't pay the price they were paying for it.

I guess I was too much of a redneck to be a hippie and too much of a hippie to be a redneck. I tried to stay out of the way of both.

Then, in 1971, Kris Kristofferson, somewhat of a hippie himself, wrote a song called "Me and Bobby McGee." The song became the hippie's theme song. Anybody who knew three chords on a guitar and could carry a tune in a sack was singing the song around campfires from Luckenbach to Santa Fe.

Everybody who was anybody in the music scene recorded it, even Janis Joplin. It had a haunting melody and was really a sad song about a fellow who was "busted flat" in Baton Rouge where he met the girl, Bobby McGee and "feeling good was easy when Bobby sang the blues and buddy, that was good enough for me."

They went all the way to Salinas before "he let her slip away, looking for the home she'd never find."

Bobby McGee became a myth throughout the Southwest and maybe she really did exist somewhere. Maybe Kris Kristofferson really knew her when he wrote the song.

Somebody said she slept in the old cotton gin at Luckenbach one night and I saw her once on Interstate-10 east of Fort Stockton. It was a cold day and I was going in the opposite direction but I stopped and made her a sandwich.

On another occasion, I was camped in the basin at the Big Bend National Park and she came to my camp and asked me to take her to El Paso. I thought about it but had I done so, I might not be here today. Like the fellow in the song, I most likely would have gone all the way to Salinas.

If Bobby is still around today, like the rest of us, I guess she's getting a little old. That doesn't matter to me and Bobby McGee as long as we're both still here.

A week or so ago, I think I saw her sitting on a bench in front of a grocery, smoking a cigarette and drinking a Coke. Of course, I could be mistaken as I was the time I swore I saw her cutting hair in a little barber shop in the Texas Hill Country.

I am pretty sure that Bobby is still around somewhere and I'll watch for her as I always did, and not one of us who prowled the country in old VW vans, living on next to nothing will forget her and the freedom she stood for.

We'll see you around a campfire somewhere, me and Bobby McGee.

THERE ARE 700 NEW LAWS ON THE BOOKS NOW, SO WATCH YOUR STEP

The Texas Legislature after a regular session and two special sessions failed to do what they went to Austin to do. They were supposed to cut property taxes and raise every other tax to the hilt to fund the schools. This included raising the sales tax and putting a dollar a pack tax on cigarettes.

I guess they decided that old duck wouldn't quack so they went home. Before they did however, they passed 700 new laws to go with the thousands we already have. It seems they are dead-set on making criminals out of all of us.

One law they passed makes sense. It gives every citizen the right to carry a concealed weapon in their vehicle if they are "traveling." It is the assumption of the law that anybody who leaves their driveway is about to travel somewhere. They are not going to just sit there.

This is nothing new. Most Texans have been carrying guns in their cars since who laid the chunk. It's just an old Texas custom. Now, they can't charge you with anything unless you are engaged in criminal activity, prohibited by any other law from possessing a firearm and not a member of a street gang.

Prosecutors don't like this law. Some say they will prosecute anyway. Our only hope if we get caught in a county where one of these prosecutors resides is to get a jury that all 12 members have a gun under the seat of their car.

Gun laws in Texas have always been rather vague. At one time, it was permissible to carry one in your saddlebags. Since cars these days don't have saddlebags that law wouldn't apply.

Back when I was a law enforcement officer, we seldom ever charged anybody with carrying a gun in the car unless they were known criminals. We left the good citizens alone unless they happened to be dragging somebody behind their car and had a gun in their lap.

There are a lot of laws we don't know about. I just read recently where a McClennon County deputy arrested a man at Crawford for "shoving" a protestor. Shoving is a law I never heard about. We have to watch that from now on when anywhere near Waco or Crawford.

When I was a kid, fighting was a form of recreation. Now, it's illegal. It is aggravated assault to hit somebody and can carry a jail term and a fine. It was just good clean fun then, except for the dirt and grass stains on your clothes.

In the late forties, I played in a country band for Saturday night dances at the American Legion Hall over Earl Tate's pharmacy. One old boy never missed a dance. By ten O'clock, he was usually engaged in a fight out on Brown Street with anybody he could find to fight with. Nobody ever got arrested. I see him around town now and then but now, he is fighting old age like we all are.

With the 700 new laws going into effect on September 1, there will be a crime of some kind happening every ten seconds. It might be best to just stay at home and put your gun in the dresser drawer. If you must go to the store though, by all means, take it with you.

Anyway, schools all over Texas started on time as usual. The Governor found the money somewhere. He probably violated a law of some kind by doing it.

HARRY MARLIN DISCONTINUES COLUMN—AUG 5TH, 2008

Harry Marlin will no longer be writing his column. See today's editorial for further information.

The date was Tuesday August 5th, 2008 when in the place of my father's column the Bulletin posted the following notice. It was the end of a long run and one that had kept my dad busy as he was always looking forward to writing his next article. He had written a weekly article for 12 years with only a small vacation. At times he would write 3 or 4 articles so that he always had a spare just in case his health took a turn for the worse.

I always thought how stressful that must be on him to have a weekly deadline and always having to come up with something to write about each week. But it never fazed him. He loved to write his articles and he always turned to his memories of growing up or to the internet to find inspiration.

The overwhelming response and support from Bulletin readers was incredible. Harry received so many emails and letters thanking him for his stories. The Brownwood Bulletin even received many threats from people saying they would cancel their subscriptions if they couldn't read Harry's articles. For many it was the only reason they subscribed to the paper and many looked forward each week to his stories.

For my Dad he struggled with the decision but he knew his time had come and it was time to move on to greener pastures.

My Dad didn't like saying good bye and he honestly didn't want to write his last article. He was such a humble man that for him he honestly thought nobody would notice and that life would just continue on with a new columnist in his place.

He occasionally got to have his articles reprinted to fill in for columnists out on vacation and the typical response was always please bring Harry back but Dad was done and had moved on.

Many thanks to the people at the Brownwood Bulletin for supporting my Dad all those years and for allowing him to bring laughter to so many and keep our history in perspective.

HARRY DECIDES TO HANG'EM UP—AUG 5TH, 2008

In the place of Harry's Column, Brownwood Bulletin ran this column

It would be improper to allow what has become an institution in the pages of the Brownwood Bulletin to end without formal notice. And since Harry Marlin is not going to do so in his own words, this must suffice.

It's official: Harry won't be writing any more columns.

As best as we can determine, Harry began writing his weekly column for the Bulletin on Sept. 15, 1997. It was introduced as part of a redesign of the daily viewpoint page that began the previous Sunday with the announcement of several new columnists, including those by two Bulletin staff members. Harry may have offered some articles prior to this, but memories fail. What is certain, though, is that the September 1997 date is when Harry's observations and recollections became a weekly feature.

Harry was no stranger to those of us who had been at the Bulletin for a period of years. Usually, we saw him at various public functions—most often staged by the Brownwood Mafia—where he was the "official" photographer while Bulletin staff members shot film for newspaper use. Harry always had some dry observation about the world condition or some such, and the day was much brighter for us as a result.

Harry put such thoughts and his remembrances of times long past to good use in his columns. He gathered many of his works together and published a series of books. In addition to the Bulletin, Harry's articles were also carried in a few limited-circulation magazines, such as the "Goat Gap Gazette" and "Old Sorehead Gazette." In 2001, noted Texas-based reporter and author Mike Cochran wrote a major feature about him for the Fort Worth Star-Telegram.

Harry's experiences during World War II as a gunner on a bomber were well documented in his columns, and his military service was honored just last Sunday by the Dyess Air Force Base chapter of the Non-Commissioned Officers Association. In true form, the biography he submitted for reading at the ceremony drew the biggest—maybe it was the only—laugh of an event that recognized seven other World War II veterans. Harry pointed out the irony of his earning a Good Conduct Medal from the military, comparing that achievement to the odds against Al Gore winning the Nobel Prize.

Harry has tried to step away from his weekly assignment several times before, saying that the well had simply gone dry. But he always managed to produce another gem to offer within a few days, so we didn't immediately believe it when he sent an e-mail last month saying that he was going to have to quit. We found a timeless classic from the files, something first published several years ago, and waited until the next week. This time, though, he was serious.

Harry explained that he simply didn't have any more recollections to share, or if he did he couldn't remember them. His fans might say that point alone would be an interesting column in Harry's hands, but he could not be convinced.

At Sunday's ceremony where he and other World War II veterans were honored, Harry confirmed the verdict to us—although he has warned that he may start writing letters to the editor periodically. We hope he was serious about that, because even during a short conversation, it's obvious that Harry hasn't lost his flair or his wit.

Harry told the audience Sunday he had been having a little trouble lately with his equilibrium. While we certainly hope it's temporary, that seems somehow appropriate. Harry has been keeping his faithful Bulletin readers happily off-balance for almost 11 years.

We have column to put in its place, but no one can ever replace Harry. Tuesday mornings just won't be the same anymore.

Brownwood Bulletin

THE END OF AN AMAZING JOURNEY

By Ken Marlin

The morning of May 18th, 2010 was just like any other morning. The Sun rose, the wind blew and the birds sang, but the world would never be the same. My Father had passed away earlier that morning.

24 hours earlier I had received the phone call that we all dread as our parents grow older.

I had received the news that my Dad had suffered a serious stroke and he was not in good condition at all. I was instructed to get to Brownwood as quickly as I could. I made the decision to drive instead of flying because I wasn't sure how long I would be staying. At the same time I felt really strongly that my Dad would be fine. He was after all the strongest man I knew and nothing took this man down. We all believe our parents are indestructible.

We loaded up the car and headed to Brownwood, TX from Phoenix, AZ. The drive would take us just over 12 hours to reach the hospital.

We arrived around 1:45AM in the morning and it was a very calm and quiet night. The hospital appeared to be a ghost town and the emergency room was dimly lit with no one there.

We made our way to the elevators and up to the floor of his room. It is all very vague in my memory as it seemed to happen in slow motion.

As I entered his room and saw him in the hospital bed it was then that I quickly realized just how bad his condition was and that his breathing was really difficult and loud. The stroke had done damage to his controls and he could not speak nor could he even blink his eyes. His body was pale white and he seemed smaller than I had remembered him being from the last time I had seen him.

At first I wasn't even sure that he could tell I was in the room but as I got closer, I could see in his eyes that he knew I was there. In fact I would find out sooner than I realized that he had actually been hanging on for all those hours just to see me one last time.

I sat on the bed and held his hand while my wife did the same on his other side. I couldn't even speak as I was in shock. For some reason I felt as though I was 10 years old and I was seeing my Dad for the last time.

Time seemed to stand still at this point; I don't recall any of the conversations in the room. I just remember moving to the head of his bed and drawing in close. I hugged him one last time and kissed his forehead. I told him I loved him and that everything would be ok.

Having been in the car for hours and extremely tired and thirsty, I stepped outside and left his side for only a moment. As I stepped back into the room it was then that I saw my father's spirit leave his body. My wife was still at his bed side, holding the same hand that earlier had no movement, was surprised when he grasped her hand will full force and lifted his body upwards and then he sank back into the bed.

He was gone.

I should have been there by his side I thought to myself. I shouldn't have left his side I kept thinking. But then it hit me, he didn't want me to see him go. He had held on all those hours so that he made sure he got to see me one last time. His body had simply given out and he had waited till I left the room on purpose.

I'm convinced my Dad had talked the angels into giving him those last hours so he could say goodbye. He always had a ton of stories handy and I'm sure he simply told the angel's stories to buy him time until I could get there.

His memories quickly flooded my mind. 86 years of a man's life where he had grown up during the depression, went to War in the 40's and lived through some the greatest times in our history.

Just like that, it was over.

The world continued and life went on just as my Dad had always told me it would.

From there I woke up the next morning to see my Father's Obituary. The love and support of so many of Brownwood and the surrounding towns began to pour in on our family.

> *Funeral services for Harry Marlin, 86, of Brownwood will be held 10 a.m. Friday, May 21, at the Heartland Funeral Home Chapel. Burial will follow in Rock Church Cemetery near Blanket. Visitation will be from 6-8 p.m Thursday at the funeral home.*

> *He died Tuesday, May 18, 2010, at Brownwood Regional Medical Center.*

On Thursday morning, I went down to the lobby of our hotel to check the newspaper for any more updates about my Father. I was completely surprised as his face and story covered the entire front page of the Brownwood Bulletin. I've included the story published on that morning on the next page as well as a few other stories that followed.

He truly was my hero.

I hope everyone enjoys my Father's stories for generations to come. It was very important for me to get them published one last time and into electronic format so they can exist for years and years.

I love you Dad—your son—Ken.

FAREWELL HARRY: 'PRAIRIE PHILOSOPHER,' CHARACTER, PATRIOT

Thursday, May 20, 2010
By Candace Cooksey Fulton-Brownwood Bulletin

As word spread Tuesday that long-time Bulletin columnist Harry Marlin had died, friends and fans would pause for a moment respectfully, then smile slightly and share a funny story they remembered of the man sometimes referred to as "the Will Rogers of Central Texas."

And there are some stories.

"Harry was a unique character," Bulletin editor Gene Deason said. "And a character is what he really was. He had a unique way of looking at things, particularly historical events."

Marlin was born 86 years ago in Brown County, Texas. Or as he explained once, "I was here when the earth was still cooling and Sam Walton was buying groceries at the Piggly-Wiggly."

Though surely the most popular and widely-read columnist in the paper's history, writing a column or anything for pay was something Marlin took up in retirement or in his spare time. Marlin wrote his books and some of his columns he confessed to

Fort Worth Star-Telegram writer Mike Cochran in a July 2001 interview, "to let his children know what it was like to have lived during the Great Depression."

And, in true Marlin grit and wit, Marlin had panned, "They weren't impressed."

As Bulletin readers who anticipated his Tuesday columns were well aware, Marlin grew up in Blanket in the '30s, in a family "so poor we had no dirt in our yards and our rainbows were in black-and-white." In World War II, he was a ball-turret gunner on a B-17 bomber, and flew 50 missions over Germany. Or as Marlin also explained, he "managed to get involved in a couple of wars which I didn't start."

In his book, "Last Train to Blanket," Marlin wrote, "The trains came through Blanket and carried us all off to war, and took our youth away. Forever."

It was similar "true grit and wit" observations that led Cochran to describe Marlin as a "prairie philosopher."

Those who came to know Marlin only through his 15 years of weekly columns in the Bulletin, may not have known he was a steel guitar player in a local band; a fine photographer; but were probably at least aware he had been a policeman in Brownwood for five years "a long time ago" and surely knew of his love and frequent trips to Big Bend National Park and Luckenbach, Texas, and great friendship with Hondo Crouch, the "Clown Prince" of Luckenbach.

"Those who remember those things about Harry or shared in those adventures are all gone too," said Marlin's long-time companion Bernell Dewees.

Marlin's official weekly Tuesday columns began running in the Bulletin Sept. 15, 1997.

Bulletin Publisher Bob Brincefield remembers, when he arrived at the newspaper a month or so later, "What a genuine pleasure it was for me when I arrived to find Harry Marlin as a columnist for the newspaper.

"Harry's keen observations of everyday life and his witty style of sharing them with readers made Tuesday a day to look forward to each week. Whether he was providing his explanation of the "five-second rule," describing life growing up in Blanket during the Depression, or his experiences in WWII, his columns were insightful and extremely humorous. I am glad I had the chance to know him and publish his work."

Chronically self-depreciating, Marlin told Cochran, in the 2001 interview, "I never really amounted to much, and don't care if I didn't. I never sued anybody, got sued, stole anything of any value, or got in jail.

"What more could anybody ask for?"

When it became apparent that Marlin's resignation from column writing in August of 2008 was "for real," Deason wrote in a Bulletin editorial that though there would be a replacement columnist in the space that for 15 years had been Marlin's, "no one can ever replace Harry."

The observation will forever hold true.

MARLIN LAID TO REST IN THE COUNTRYSIDE HE LOVED

Saturday, May 22, 2010
By Steve Nash-Brownwood Bulletin

Traveling through the verdant and bucolic countryside he loved, friends and family members in a lengthy procession of vehicles escorted Harry Marlin to his final resting place Friday morning.

Marlin, who died Tuesday at age 86—leaving a sweeping legacy that includes author, prairie philosopher, humorist and

World War II veteran—was buried in Rock Church Cemetery near Blanket.

Before the trip to the cemetery, about 150 people attended a funeral service at Heartland Funeral Home in Early, where Marlin's body lay in an open casket draped with an American flag. Before the service began, dozens of photos from Marlin's life were projected in a slide show on a large screen.

The photos depicted a handsome, vibrant and grinning Marlin in a variety of settings and at different ages—usually either surrounded by family members or friends, or standing alone before a mountain vista.

Richard Hetzel, who officiated at Marlin's funeral, referred to a group of Bible verses which, he said, are "the Gospel in a nutshell."

"Unfortunately we can't put Harry's life in a nutshell," Hetzel said.

Remarks from Hetzel and Marlin's daughter, Laura Marlin of Brownwood, portrayed a man who was loved by his family and admired by those who knew him well or knew him little—or knew him through his witty but pointed columns that used to run Tuesdays in the Brownwood Bulletin and other literary musings.

"He was a guy who might have marched to a little bit of a different drummer," Hetzel said. "But he was a man who loved life and who loved people. And oh my goodness, he could put words together . . ."

Referencing Marlin's own writings, Hetzel described the seminal events that helped shape Marlin including the Great Depression, which Marlin experienced as a boy growing up on a farm near Blanket, and, of course, World War II. Marlin, as most folks know, was a ball turret gunner in a B-17 bomber. He survived German flak and German fighters to make it home in one piece.

"He went through lots of good times, but he also went through lots of troubles," Hetzel said.

On the way to the cemetery, Hetzel said. "we'll pass some scenery that he loved . . . . I know how much he loved the God of all creation."

Marlin, Hetzel said, "might not have followed all of churches but he could never get away from the love of God."

Hetzel referred to an Old Testament scripture that proclaims "a merry heart doeth good like a medicine."

Marlin, he said, "made many hearts merry on so many occasions."

'FRIEND' GIVES LITTLE GIFTS OF TIME AND PLACE

Sunday, May 23, 2010
By Candace Cooksey Fulton

Eight years ago, when Harry Marlin came into the Bulletin newsroom to meet me, he had one thing to ask and one thing to say.

First the question. Which one of the Cooksey's did I belong to? "Well," I answered honestly, "My dad was Bill Cooksey."

"Used to be a Highway Patrolman, then became sheriff out in Terrell County?"

"Yes sir."

"Bill Cooksey was my friend," Harry told me.

I've learned in my life, you can generally trust, and will probably like, the kind of man who would claim my dad as a friend. I know now the same could be said for a friend of Harry's.

The thing Harry had to tell me was that he wrote the columns on Tuesday. If I decided they would need to be edited very much, he would stop writing them. If we could have tricked him into doing it, the better plan might have been for Harry to edit the stuff we wrote. Not everything would have been the God's honest truth, but the high points and important stuff would have gotten covered, and we'd have all been a lot happier—laughed ourselves silly probably through the process.

Now there was this one time, and I've forgotten a lot of the particulars. But Harry used a metaphor in his column for some big mess, comparing the mess to a famous shipwreck, and I thought he'd misspelled the ship's name. I thought he was writing about "The Wreck of the Hesperus," as in the narrative poem by Henry Wadsworth Longfellow.

He wasn't, and boy did he let me know about it. I groveled, apologized and never admitted that of all the ways to get scolded for something, an e-mail from Harry, was the most fun.

More than a few times since I've been at the Bulletin, I've gotten compliments from Harry. Those really meant something when they came, and they were funny too.

Once, I wrote a column about watching a sunrise, and Harry really liked that one. He said he supposed he'd seen a lot more sunsets than sunrises, but either seem to give the comfort and assurance and put things in perspective.

The memories Harry shared in his columns weren't too different from the kinds of stories my parents told, with that same "might as well laugh and make it funny" reflection. Sometimes a certain phrase in Harry's Tuesday column would make me think of my dad, and for just a moment, I wouldn't miss him as much. Harry in Tuesday's Bulletin made everything better. For somewhere, in each one, was a nugget of humor and a spark of real Texas wisdom. Little gifts for us, I think they were.

At Harry's funeral Friday, the program had something Harry wrote in 1990. "Jesus said, 'In my Father's house are many mansions, and I go to prepare a place for you.'

"But I don't want a mansion," Harry wrote. "Just make a place for me where I can see the beauty of wildflowers, the green of the grass, the blue of the sky and the majesty of the mountains, and all the glory of Heaven will be mine."

A long line of cars made the procession to Rock Church Cemetery and those of us who went, I think, paid extra special attention to the wildflowers blooming along the roadside, the very pretty spring blue sky. Then as we made our way to the grave site and watched the pallbearers bring Harry's flag-draped coffin to the pyre, we could hear the birds chirping and singing.

Normally on a Friday morning, we'd have been out doing important work—not thinking of taking the time to see and enjoy God's creation. For a long time now, when I remember Harry, I'm going to remember this last little gift he gave us.

Harry Marlin was a friend of mine. May he rest in peace.

THE END